# Minong—The Good Place

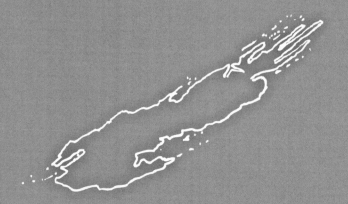

# Minong—The

# Good Place

## OJIBWE AND ISLE ROYALE

*Timothy Cochrane*

Michigan State University Press • East Lansing

Michigan State University Press
East Lansing, Michigan 48823-5245

Printed and bound in the United States of America.

15 14 13 12 11 10 09   1 2 3 4 5 6 7 8 9 10

LIBRARY OF CONGRESS CATALOGING-IN-PUBLICATION DATA
Cochrane, Timothy.
Minong—The Good Place: Ojibwe and Isle Royale / Timothy Cochrane.
p. cm.
Includes bibliographical references and index.
ISBN 978-0-87013-849-2 (pbk. : alk. paper) 1. Ojibwa Indians—Michigan—Isle Royale National Park—History. 2. Ojibwa Indians—Michigan—Isle Royale National Park—Antiquities. 3. Isle Royale National Park (Mich.)—History. 4. Isle Royale National Park (Mich.)—Antiquities. I. Title.
E99.C6C63 2009
977.4'99700497333—dc22
2008038138

Book design by Sharp Des!gns, Inc., Lansing, Michigan

Cover art is "Crossing to Minong," a watercolor by visual artist Carl Gawboy. Raised in Ely, Minnesota, Gawboy is an enrolled member of the Bois Forte Band of the Minnesota Chippewa Tribe. He is well known for his realistic historical portrayals of Ojibwe life and has focused on bringing to life scenes of Ojibwe life that have never been documented by a painter or photographer. Through his art and lectures, he often challenges popular and academic paradigms about American Indian cultures. He has participated in more than 75 exhibits and recently has painted large murals for Ojibwe Heritage Centers, universities, historical societies, and libraries. He is retired from teaching Art and Indian Studies at the College of St. Scholastica and the University of Minnesota–Duluth.

**g** green press INITIATIVE Michigan State University Press is a member of the Green Press Initiative and is committed to developing and encouraging ecologically responsible publishing practices. For more information about the Green Press Initiative and the use of recycled paper in book publishing, please visit www.greenpressinitiative.org.

Visit Michigan State University Press on the World Wide Web at www.msupress.msu.edu

# CONTENTS

# FOREWORD

·······························································

M any Grand Portage families have ties to Isle Royale. The Corcorans, my wife's family, are one of them. Jim Corcoran, my father-in-law, worked at Todd Harbor picking up pulp lumber washed up on the rocky beaches. Jim's brother and cousins—Scott Family members—worked with him. Jim's dad, William Corcoran, ran a successful logging company. And William's father-in-law, Andrew Jackson Scott, spent many years on the Island. Andrew Scott raised his family there for a while, fished sturgeons, and was elected justice of the peace at the McCargoe Cove mining settlement.

Jim and others told me about this pulpwood operation. It was during World War II, and many of the younger Grand Portage men were overseas fighting. But Jim and the others collected the pulp sticks that had gotten away from busted log booms and washed ashore on the north side of Isle Royale. Todd Harbor had piles of logs six- and eight-feet deep. They would push the jumbled logs back into the water and collect them in small booms anchored at the sheltered ends of the harbor. When the boom was full enough, a tug would come and pull the raft of logs to Ashland, Wisconsin.

These were hungry times here, and jobs were scarce. Being on the Island away from stores and their families made it harder yet. There weren't many rangers there then. Jim told me that one time they shot a moose, put the meat in gunny sacks, and sunk it in the harbor. Todd Harbor is pretty deep, and the deep water preserved the meat. The deep water lacks much oxygen, and its cold helped preserve the meat a long time. It was good food for men working hard.

Much of this book is written about a very different time than today. Only a few years ago, people walked long distances that sometimes seem long to us even when driving in a car. My dad walked to Saganaga Lake to learn about old medicines. At one time Portage Ojibwe paddled to Montreal, Hudson Bay, and Chicago. Old-time Ojibwe were great travelers. They were also part of the lake; they ate from it, and they learned from it. Today we live beside it, and we haven't turned our backs to it, but it is different now. We never tried to conquer it, but live with and respect it.

I often wondered what would it have been like to live when groups of Portage Ojibwe traveled by canoes to Minong. What it would have been like to live off the land then? Your mind wouldn't be cluttered with stuff like it is now. What would they be talking about? It would be a different mindset. And their sense of time would be different. Today, people go to the Island and they have to "be back by three." Years ago, it would be flat water, and knowing the lake, that would trump time.

One thing that has stayed the same is the Grand Portage people's economic interest in the Island. We are interested in how we might work there and make a living. Years ago, it was the economics of living and finding your food there—fish, caribou, and maple sugar—or maybe a job. Food from the Island was traded or bartered. We were part of the economic system then and remain interested today. But it is different now, because other people make up the rules of being there. Some rules are good, but they remain other peoples' rules.

It is important that this book is written, because it captures much of our relationship with Minong. Isle Royale is part of our territory, part of our history, and part of our families. We continue to fish there. Grand Portage Ojibwe lived, died, and were born there. My dad fought a forest fire at the Island a few years before I was born. That history does not fade in a few generations. We remember. This book helps us be more aware of that history and helps us tell that story to others.

NORMAN DESCHAMPE
*Chairman, Grand Portage Band, and President, Minnesota Chippewa Tribe*

# ACKNOWLEDGMENTS

This book was written while I was an employee of the National Park Service—first as a back-country ranger, and then as a historian at Isle Royale National Park. It was completed after independent research and while I worked nearby at Grand Portage National Monument. Despite my employment, this book was largely researched and written at home when "off-duty." Hence, it does not represent the views of the National Park Service, but only my own. I needed to be on my own to ensure greater objectivity in this accounting of events. But it is also true that my "day job" managing a park that is historically connected to Isle Royale put me in a privileged position of frequently conversing with Grand Portage Ojibwe. Indeed, those many conversations started friendships with a number of residents and members of the Grand Portage tribal council. But these conversations were more often about sharing historical information and good stories, rather than official interviews. Because of these peculiar circumstances, the book does not represent an official National Park Service perspective. The core of the discussion is also about a time long before Isle Royale National Park was dedicated in 1946. Still, implicit in some of the discussion is some criticism of the National Park Service, an agency that is showing increased maturity in accepting such views.

Many people have assisted me in the long production of this work. A handful of colleagues and friends have rattled around some of the ideas contained herein, including Caven Clark, Bud Sivertson, Dave Cooper, Bruce White, Rick Anderson, Carl Gawboy, and Liz Valencia. Grand Portage residents have been wonderfully helpful and include Norman Deschampe, Gilbert Caribou, Ellen Olson, Rosie Novitsky, Ken Sherer, Lorraine Wipson and Kalvin Ottertail—now at Lac La Croix. *Meegwitch!* Fortunately, three Grand Portage people were particularly instrumental in enhancing this book: Norman Deschampe willingly read the manuscript, Gilbert Caribou answered (and tolerated) many of my inexpert Ojibwe language questions, and Ellen Olson candidly shared her family history use about Minong and encouraged this work. Dick and Lou Anderson became early and fast friends spurring my interest in Grand Portage. I apologize in advance for any poor translation of Ojibwe names, which unfortunately exist in a bewildering number of variants. For convenience sake, I have standardized names to provide consistency to readers. Celebrated artists Carl Gawboy and Howard Sivertson freely offered the use of any of their art. Generous help also came "from across the border," from the now late Father William Maurice, Shawn Allaire, Liam Kilmurray, Brian Walmark, and Tory Tronrude. In Duluth, I was helped by the very capable staff at the Duluth Public Library, particularly Mary Anne Norton and Kristin Aho. The Grand Marais, Minnesota, Public Library staff have cheerfully worked to find my many atypical interlibrary loan requests. A number of scholars and archivists have graciously answered my cold-call email questions: John Nichols, David Pentland, Charles Bronte, Rolf Peterson, Warner Wirta, Valerie-Ann Lutz, Theresa S. Spence, Mark Romanski, Chel Anderson, David Grinstead, and Sheree Peterson. I owe a great deal to archivists and librarians in Winnipeg, Toronto, Ottawa, Princeton, Philadelphia, Washington, D.C., and at the Minnesota Historical Society. Others have been indirectly helpful in encouraging me to complete this work, including Curt Roy, Tom Theissen, Alan Woolworth, Theresa Schenk, Ted Karamanski, Dave Miller, and John and Regina Bendix. Barbara Cobb adeptly edited this manuscript and Ralph

Latham patiently read this text and quietly helped me improve it. Thank you to the fellowship from the American Association for State and Local History that made this research quest legitimate in my and others' eyes. Long ago, Dr. Robert Bieder introduced me to ethnohistory, the primary disciplinary thread in this work. Others have encouraged me by example, such as Dr. Joseph Epes Brown, Dr. Ted Birkedal, and Dr. Ernest Birch. And thank you to those who kept me from writing: Meg, Cassie, Jeff Peterson, and the 2005 undefeated Two Harbors girls soccer team.

My family, especially my wife Jeannie, has provided support, time, and a sympathetic ear for many of the ups and downs of what she dubbed "this elucubration." She too knows the Island well. By listening, she unwittingly helped me compose much of the manuscript. My mother cheered on any endeavor of mine that might be construed as a success. My father gave me a love of the outdoors that eventually would be married with my interest in Isle Royale from which this book springs. The "three wonders"—Cory, Andy, and Maddy—have heard for too long that I was going to finish "this thing." It apparently is one of many one-sentence sermons they have endured.

# Minong—The Good Place

# INTRODUCTION

E nthralled to be on Isle Royale the first time, and better yet have a job there, I was chastened to learn that it was a park without a recent Native American history. I listened to fellow ranger talks, plowed into the headquarters library on Mott Island, only to discover that there were, at best, few records of Ojibwe on the Island. Within that first week, while entranced by the archipelago, I wondered openly what its history of aboriginal use was. Later, as a new park historian, I was asked to review a park-commissioned history that did not include a chapter on historic Native American use. Reflecting on this lack of knowledge and portrayal of Ojibwe on Isle Royale, I realized it made even less sense. How could the park with such a distinguished prehistoric past, and with Ojibwe living all around it on the mainland shores, not have much use? The ancients came to the Island to mine copper, and Lake Superior copper was traded widely throughout North America. Why would usage stop? I wondered. This work is a response to my hunch that Isle Royale may have had regular Ojibwe visitors, or residents. I set

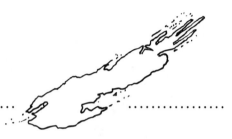

out to document the nature and extent of Ojibwe use of the Island, whatever that might or might not be.

Within that first summer of 1976, I began collecting stray bits of evidence that definitely placed Ojibwe on Isle Royale. More than thirty years and countless diversions later, this book is the result. Along the way, there were related or corollary myths encountered that I hope I dispel here. Isle Royale's legal connection with Michigan, rather than Minnesota or Ontario, overemphasized real or imagined historic links with the Upper Peninsula of Michigan—never mind that it is a very long paddle from the Keweenaw to Chippewa Harbor on the Island: over forty-five miles.[1] Paddling from the Minnesota or Ontario side was closer—thus safer, and more practical.

Implicit in some of the history written about Isle Royale was another myth—namely, that Isle Royale was separated from the mainland enough to have its own history.[2] Instead, it would be more true to think of Isle Royale as modifying regional patterns, much like it modifies, but does not change,

# Lake Superior and the Border Lakes Area

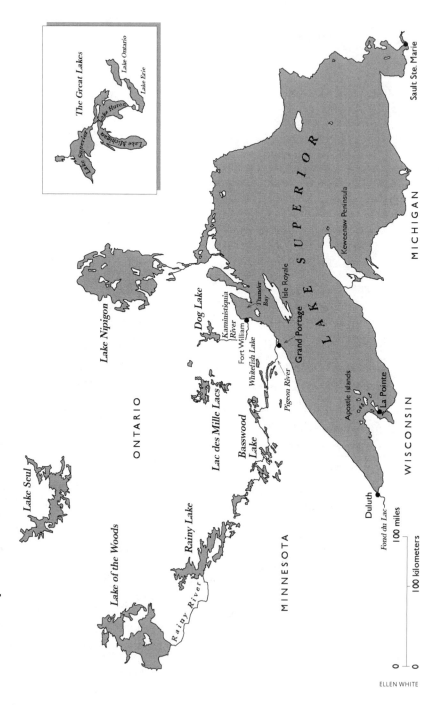

The Great Lakes

Lake Ontario
Lake Erie
Lake Huron
Lake Michigan
Lake Superior

Lake Seul

Lake of the Woods

Lake Nipigon

ONTARIO

Rainy Lake

Rainy River

Lac des Mille Lacs

Basswood Lake

Dog Lake

Kaministiquia River

Fort William

Whitefish Lake

Pigeon River

Thunder Bay

Isle Royale

Grand Portage

L A K E   S U P E R I O R

Keweenaw Peninsula

MICHIGAN

Sault Ste. Marie

Apostle Islands

La Pointe

WISCONSIN

Duluth

Fond du Lac

MINNESOTA

0        100 miles

0        100 kilometers

ELLEN WHITE

regional weather patterns. Essentially some have thought that the Island is both large and separate enough to be endowed with its own history. But from the first string of islands along the southern border of Thunder Bay, the Island is only twelve to fourteen miles away. It is close enough that on a calm summer day, the clerk at the Hudson's Bay Post at Fort William heard a cannon shot from the American Fur Company vessel at Fish Island—now Belle Island—Isle Royale.[3]

Research for this book picked up speed as I spent more time on Isle Royale as the park historian. A fellowship allowed me to unearth a few new important sources and gave me hints of more. Moving to Grand Portage and enjoying a privileged situation with many Portage Ojibwe greatly encouraged me, and I learned what was supposedly lost: oral history accounts of Portage Ojibwe use of Minong—the Ojibwe name for Isle Royale. The trust extended to me by a number of Portage Ojibwe made me quicken my writing. For a few elders it was less of a godsend, as I would occasionally pester them with odd questions, such as the meaning of the word Minong. I tried to be restrained, and I tried to separate this endeavor from my position as a park manager. But I remember one day visiting with the Grand Portage tribal council and being struck by the fact that all five council members had family histories that connected them to Minong.

A number of new sources literally made this portrait of North Shore Ojibwe use of Minong possible. Until we rediscovered the Jesuit records from the Mission of Immaculate Conception—first located at Pigeon River and then at Fort William—we had little detail about that use. The mission diary and letters, written in French, contained rich information about where Ojibwe were on the Island, what they were doing—fishing and mining in particular— and so on.[4] Using these and other Catholic records, Father William Maurice assembled single-handedly a nineteen-volume genealogical masterpiece for area Catholics. Included in this magnum opus are death, birth, marriage, and baptismal records that name Ojibwe on Minong living, dying, and making do. Suddenly, with Father Bill's help, we learned of twelve-year-old Josephte Aiakodjiwang's death at Todd Harbor in the depth of winter.[5] We learned of her family pulling their daughter's body across thirteen miles of wind-swept and frozen Lake Superior so she could be buried in consecrated ground at the mission. Clearly, Ojibwe were not just mentioned as being on the Island; the records allow us to repopulate stories with images of specific use, times, and circumstances.

Other, newer sources compounded what we could learn of Ojibwe on Minong. Oral history information from elders humanized what I was piecing together. What was sometimes an abstract pursuit for me was brought to life as I learned that a person's grandfather was born on the Island, fished there because he thought the fish were purer, and made maple sugar in the highlands—even likely leaving his maple-sugar kettle, sugar molds, and wooden utensils behind. Transcribing the records from the Hudson's Bay Company post at Fort William provided information about Indian hunts and fishing on Minong not to be found anywhere else. Few Americans interested in Isle Royale have deeply plumbed Canadian sources. Important records are to be found in numerous Canadian and U.S. cities, such as Thunder Bay, Ottawa, Toronto, New York, Washington, Ann Arbor, Sault Ste. Marie, St. Paul, and Duluth. Newspapers from all along Lake Superior shores—Thunder Bay, Sault Ste. Marie, Houghton, Duluth, Grand Marais, and Grand Portage—also yielded unexpected gems of information. The new sources of information allow us to reach new conclusions about Ojibwe use, and the waning of Ojibwe use, of Minong, particularly in the latter third of the nineteenth century.

A number of primary sources were used to piece together this ethnohistory. Each has its own type of biases that must be constrained. I have tried, at minimum, to confirm one type of source with that of a very different kind. For example, I was able to compare Indian agent with Jesuit accounts, whose unfortunately too-sparse Ojibwe testimony made it difficult to make sense of the three treaties that engulfed the North Shore Ojibwe and dislodged them from Minong. In some cases I was able to triangulate three sources and raise the level of certainty of my claims. It is difficult to neatly compare the biases of an archeologist with those of a Jesuit father. Mostly, I have felt more comfortable when I am using an archeological source for its descriptive value, just as I am more comfortable using the Jesuit diaries for their records of nonreligious events. At other times, without any other source to confirm or deny it, I have had to conservatively use what the source says. For example, the Hudson's Bay Company clerk's journal entry cannot be accurately used to map everywhere a prominent Ojibwe hunter went. But it will tell us, on occasion, that the Ojibwe hunter Bete used to paddle to Minong and hunt caribou.[6] In fact, one of the clerk's biases—namely, to record Indians' travels into the United States—works to our advantage in providing more records than of travels inland into Upper Canada.

This is primarily an ethnohistorical work. It reflects my interest in blending history and the particulars of one cultural group. It is not meant to be a full-blown description of Ojibwe culture. Nor is it meant to be a definitive history of the North Shore Ojibwe. Instead, historical, geographic, cultural, and economic conditions are added to help us understand Ojibwe use of Minong. It is opportunistic in using history, geography, folklore, place-names, biology, and anthropology to tell the most complete story I can. And whenever possible, I try to give an Ojibwe perspective—particularly through narratives—about Minong. And when the historical trail really gets hot, we are able to arrive at unintended conclusions, such as using an overwhelming number of historical sources to dispute accepted biological wisdom. My goal is to provide as detailed a discussion of Ojibwe use and understanding of Island places and conditions as is possible. An eclectic use of sources and subject matter is used to detail the ingenuity, courage, and traditions of Ojibwe use of the archipelago.

An additional thread of this work, albeit a lesser one, is a focus on the public discourse on what non-Indians thought about Indian use of Minong, and some of their early notions about Minong. In both a symbolic and legal sense, we are interested in how non-Indians appropriated Isle Royale for their own. Following this inquiry, as well as being dependent upon available sources, much of this work focuses on a seminal time period between the 1820s and 1855. This is the bulls-eye of our interest, but we also examine the historic periods that pre- and postdate this block of time.

This work falls within a small but growing genre of studies detailing park and Native American relationships. Many of these books detail big, western natural-area parks—Yellowstone, Yosemite, Glacier—and little comment is made about midwestern or eastern parks. Common themes are the removal of Indians from these parks, underrecognition of their presence within parks, and taking possession of tribal lands for parks. Removal of Indians from these lands permits the manufacturing of wilderness and also leads to misconceptions of Indian use.[7] In my work history, I have noted a pattern of proclaimed "uninhabited landscapes" at Isle Royale, Glacier Bay, and Katmai, despite each park unit having a distinguished prehistoric past, let alone a misunderstood historic use. Or, if the public record admits historic Native American use of park lands, the overall impression is that it was in the distant past, long before the park was created, and the use was marginal, ecologically invisible, or—even more subjectively asserted—"natural."

While sharing some of these other books' concerns, this work is also quite different. Much of our story begins earlier than the other studies, and in the case of Isle Royale, there is much intervening time between the effective Ojibwe removal and the creation of the park. In other words, Ojibwe removal is only faintly linked to the creation of the park. Unlike most big western national parks, whose lands were often initially considered to be less valuable than more fertile lands nearby, Isle Royale was deemed extremely valuable for its copper deposits. Thus, its copper created an early commercial interest—some called it a fever—not seen in many other park histories. Our story, too, takes us frequently into the province of Ontario and international affairs, adding another layer of cross-cultural concerns. Our story also tends to linger more on resource use, such as fishing, than other studies. As a marine park—difficult to get to—Minong is different from those crisscrossed with aboriginal trails leading to other homelands. This work is also distinctive, as it is written by a National Park Service (NPS) employee in a privileged position to watch contemporary relationships flourish. And indeed, to help those relationships flourish.[8]

Peter Nabokov and Lawrence Loendorb's *Restoring a Presence: American Indians and Yellowstone National Park* is closest to this work in a number of ways. Like this, it is a book-length monograph about one park, rather than a series of case studies. It also considers Yellowstone myths—such as Indians being scared of the geysers—which eerily echo statements made about Ojibwe being scared of copper and of Lake Superior.[9] Thus, it considers Indians relations with Yellowstone and how whites characterized that relationship. Like this manuscript, it reflects on how Native American religious lifeways are integrated into that peculiar landscape. We conclude, like *Restoring a Presence*, with some hopeful signs of growing interest and even collaboration between the Grand Portage Band and the National Park Service.

Since crossing the lake to Isle Royale is inherently risky—in summer or winter—any users of the archipelago were most likely to come from points nearby. The Native American groups living closest to the Island are the Ojibwe of Grand Portage and Fort William. Further, this book will repeatedly demonstrate that they were the principal Island users. The core area of the North Shore Ojibwe included Arrow and Whitefish lakes on the west, the Kaministiquia River basin to the north, and the Pigeon River and Grand Portage to the south. The periphery of this area is marked by Lac des Mille Lacs to the northwest, Basswood Lakes to the west, and almost to what is now Duluth (Knife River) to the southwest. Two dominant resources defined this area: Lake Superior and the transcontinental portage located at Grand Portage, or the more northerly route up the Kaministiquia River. Either route linked rivers, Great Lakes, and strings of inland lakes, providing a watery road from the Atlantic to the Pacific, and north to the Arctic or southward to the Mississippi River and the Gulf of Mexico.

In relative terms, the natural resource base to draw upon was not as rich as their kinsmen to the east and west—Ojibwe along the Nipigon River and Rainy Lake. The Lake Superior highlands forming the lake basin were considered by Ojibwe to be barrens in terms of producing food.[10] In contrast, the Rainy Lake Ojibwe had a large sturgeon run, numerous wild rice beds, and a climate warm enough for corn, beans, and other crops. Not so for the North Shore Ojibwe, where rock prevails over soil, and a cooler and shorter growing season predominates. Much of their traditional territory was within the Lake Superior watershed.

The obvious dominant resource for the North Shore Ojibwe was Kitchi Gami—Lake Superior. Most of their fishing was done on the lake, as was a major portion of their travel. In the nineteenth century, fish were a much more important part of North Shore Ojibwe diet than big game. The predominantly northwesterly winds and the outer islands on Lake Superior, from Grand

Portage to Black Bay, made for relatively sheltered and calmer waters. Lake conditions defined most movement. The calm, but sometimes foggy late spring and early summer months were excellent for traveling on the Big Lake. The more predictably rougher seas in September and October made canoe or small-boat travel on Lake Superior very dangerous. Water as much as land contributed to their food base, provided for travel, and was a part of daily and ceremonial life.

North Shore Ojibwe moved throughout the year. During the winter months, they lived inland in widely dispersed family groups. By March and April, they had moved to their traditional sugar bush to collect sap and boil down maple sugar. This belt of trees parallels the lake only a few miles inland (where conditions are slightly warmer). By early summer, they were fishing the streams and near-shore waters for spring spawning fish such as suckers and sturgeon. Their attentiveness to natural phenomena hastened their knowledge of special, or atypical, natural phenomena, such as the small whitefish that would come to the Kaministiquia River mouth in late June.[11] Ojibwe then would move to areas with abundant plants to harvest, particularly berries—raspberries, blueberries, thimbleberries, and currants. For most of the seasons, they were dispersed throughout their territory—an exception being the multifamily gatherings harvesting wild rice at Whitefish Lake and other lakes.[12] Occasionally passenger pigeons were snared in aerial nets. Fall fishing was largely on Lake Superior for trout, including *siscowet* or fat trout, and whitefish. Ojibwe harvested an unusual upriver fall run of whitefish at the "little falls" on the Kaministiquia River. If a Lake Superior fishing ground was rich enough, a few families might camp together. More often, Ojibwe families dispersed along the lake shore from as far as Beaver Bay to the southwest to the Shangoina Island off the Sibley Peninsula—more than a 140-mile sweep from one end of the territory to the other. By the late fall and early winter, they took their trading credits—of cloth, ammunition, and trapping gear—and went inland to trap furs. They would time their travel to go inland before or after ice-up on lakes, often by early November, and on the rivers by late November. In the depth of winter, when rabbits were numerous, many were snared and were an important food source. In the late winter or spring, the Ojibwe would return to the fur post and trade their furs for their debts, fishing gear, and cloth. Again their travel would be before or after the "fast ice" gave way in the rivers in mid-April, and in the lakes a few weeks later. Ice on Lake Superior was less predictable, as high winds—and thus surges or rolling seas—could break up the thickest ice, including during cold weather in January.

The entire North Shore Ojibwe population would gather in large groups when holding Midewiwin rites. They appear to have held Midewiwin ceremonies at different times in the summer, sometimes in June and sometimes as late as October.[13] North Shore Ojibwe and others from adjacent bands might travel great distances to attend a Midewiwin ceremony. Many Ojibwe gathered in early June for the ceremonial meeting and gift-giving with the arrival of Hudson's Bay Company governor George Simpson and other dignitaries. Also the New Years' fur trade custom of "gifting" employees and Indians with free food and drink brought many Ojibwe to posts.

For the North Shore Ojibwe, the fur trade was an additional economic resource to rely upon. And the post had jobs to be done in exchange for reliable stores of food and goods. The advantages of the post lured some Ojibwe to live nearby permanently, while others would only resort to it for trade and special occasions. The fur trade was built upon aboriginal knowledge, routes, and important places. Aboriginal trade that flowed east or west through this vicinity would be carried up or down the two portage routes—either the Grand Portage or the Kaministiquia River. The two routes would merge together many miles westward. One route might predominate for a time, then another, but they functioned similarly. They were a portal, or even a geographic bottleneck, that connected east with west. From the North Shore Ojibwe perspective, this geographic portal ensured additional economic opportunities and supplies in an otherwise relatively hardscrabble environment.

When the fur trade opened posts in the area, the North Shore Ojibwe opportunistically shifted their trade, and sometimes their seasonal residence, from nearby one post to the other. And when two fur trade companies competed, it shifted some advantage to Ojibwe traders who could seek other alternate trading partners. North Shore Ojibwe could potentially act as guides, traffic in information with others, and gain trading advantage—such as exacting tolls from those crossing Saganaga Lake in 1775.[14] Through time, a succession of trading posts oscillated between the Kaministiquia River and Grand Portage. First the Ojibwe traded with the French at the Kaministiquia River mouth area, then the North West Company at Grand Portage, then back to Kaministiquia, the Hudson's Bay Company at Fort William, and the American Fur Company back at Grand Portage and even Grand Marais. The North Shore Ojibwe had to contend with a large, powerful fur trade entrepôt in their midst, as well as more than a thousand company men streaming through their territory in the summertime.

The "North Shore Ojibwe," relatively small in numbers, lived between two very large Ojibwe bands: the Nipigon Ojibwe and the Rainy Lake Ojibwe. For example, the Nipigon Band population was three times larger than the North Shore Ojibwe in the early 1800s. The number of Rainy Lake Ojibwe was more than twice that of the Portage Ojibwe at roughly the same time. Occasionally, a leader of one of these groups would try to assert dominance over their kinsmen. Most often this was expressed as one dominant clan leader expressing his status and leadership when traveling through the area. Once, the North Shore Ojibwe leader Peau de Chat unsuccessfully tried to extend his sovereignty over the Nipigon Ojibwe during the 1849 British-Ojibwe treaty negotiations.[15]

For the first half of the historic period, from roughly 1670 to 1840, clans were a primary way in which Ojibwe society was ordered. Also, during this clan period, Ojibwe were highly dispersed throughout the area, with encampments at Grand Marais, Grand Portage, Red Sucker Bay on Saganaga Lake, Rove Lake, Gunflint Narrows, Moose Lake, Arrow Lake, Whitefish Lake, Kaministiquia River, Squaw Bay, at the upper end of Thunder Bay, and at Isle Royale. Clan leaders, such as the overall *ogimaa* (leader), led more by example and because of respect than by blind allegiance.[16] There were approximately forty to seventy people in each clan. Bloodlines were protected through the custom of marrying outside your clan. Your clan membership was determined through your father. Many North Shore Ojibwe would marry outside their clan by marrying spouses from Nipigon or Rainy Lake. For example, in an 1850 treaty census at Nipigon, 40 out of 107 households had Grand Portage roots.[17]

If you were an Ojibwe woman, it was customary that you would eventually move to your husband's home. North Shore Ojibwe were related to kinsmen at the Sault Ste. Marie, Michipicoten, Pic, Nipigon—and westward at Lac La Croix, Nett Lake, and Rainy Lake.

The relative makeup of clans on the North Shore was different than along the South Shore and Michigan and Wisconsin. Some clans, like the Bear and Crane, were present throughout. Dominant clans at Grand Portage were the *Awa si wag* or Bullhead, *Uda ja ta gamig* or Caribou, *udci ja Kwag* or Crane, and *No Ka ag* (or more commonly today *Makwa*) or Bear. However, other clans were present, such as Moose, Marten, Wildcat or Lynx, Loon, Sucker, Eagle, Kingfisher.[18] Some clans, such as the Bear clan, had subclans—such as the Bear-grease, a name still recognized today because of the renowned sled-dog race. Because small family groups traveled to Minong—Isle Royale—these family groups were likely clan-based. Further, we know that Caribou and Bullhead clan members and their families traveled to Minong.[19]

Complicating our overall story is the imposition of the international border. The present-day international border segmented what was once a single group.[20] As a result of treaties on both sides of the border (1850 and 1854), the British and American Indian agents demanded that North Shore Ojibwe declare whether they were British or American Indians. Both the Brits and the Americans wanted consistency in who received treaty payments. The problem was that the North Shore Ojibwe frequented and used lands and waters on both sides of the now very real border. Families had freely crossed the border, and one group might tap maple sugar in the Grand Portage sugar bush, fish in what are now Canadian waters, harvest birch bark throughout, fish at Isle Royale or Pigeon River, harvest wild rice in Canada or in the border lakes, and winter at Arrow Lake (in what is now Canada) or near the Grand Portage or even Grand Marais. Peau de Chat, the principal chief among the North Shore Ojibwe, unabashedly stated during the institutionalizing of the border that his band was the owner of lands on both sides of the border, and thus he should be able to receive payment from both.[21]

Finding an agreed-upon and distinctive name for the Ojibwe who now live in Grand Portage and Fort William is not easy. A common name for the Ojibwe

# Pre-Treaty North Shore Ojibwe
# Traditional Use Area, Circa 1835

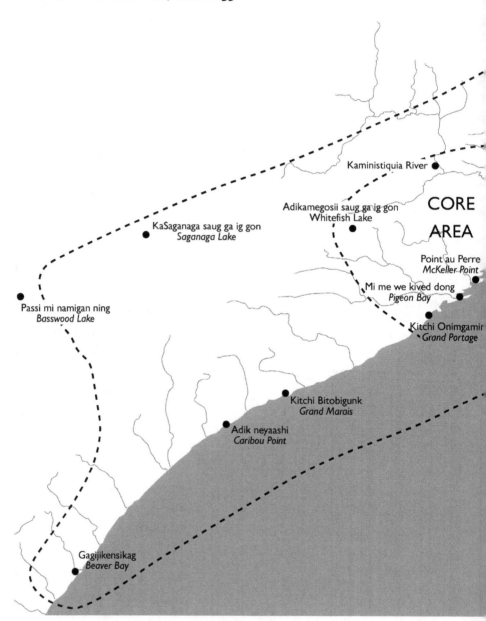

Kaministiquia River

CORE
AREA

Adikamegosii saug ga ig gon
Whitefish Lake

KaSaganaga saug ga ig gon
*Saganaga Lake*

Point au Perre
*McKeller Point*

Mi me we kived dong
*Pigeon Bay*

Passi mi namigan ning
*Basswood Lake*

Kitchi Onimgamir
*Grand Portage*

Kitchi Bitobigunk
*Grand Marais*

Adik neyaashi
*Caribou Point*

Gagijikensikag
*Beaver Bay*

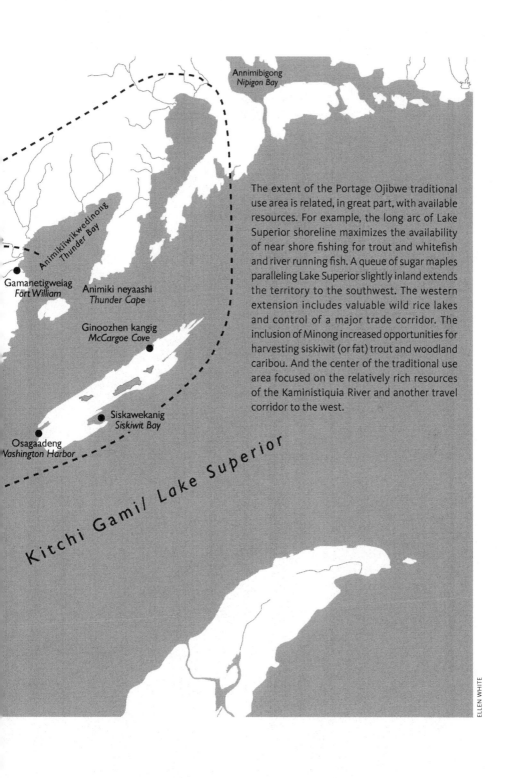

The extent of the Portage Ojibwe traditional use area is related, in great part, with available resources. For example, the long arc of Lake Superior shoreline maximizes the availability of near shore fishing for trout and whitefish and river running fish. A queue of sugar maples paralleling Lake Superior slightly inland extends the territory to the southwest. The western extension includes valuable wild rice lakes and control of a major trade corridor. The inclusion of Minong increased opportunities for harvesting siskiwit (or fat) trout and woodland caribou. And the center of the traditional use area focused on the relatively rich resources of the Kaministiquia River and another travel corridor to the west.

Annimibigong
Nipigon Bay

Animikiiwikwedinong
Thunder Bay

Gamanetigweiag
Fort William

Animiki neyaashi
Thunder Cape

Ginoozhen kangig
McCargoe Cove

Siskawekanig
Siskiwit Bay

Osagaadeng
Washington Harbor

Kitchi Gami/ Lake Superior

people living along the shores of Lake Superior was *Ke-che-gum-me-win-in-e-wug*, or "men of the Great Water." Those who live in the neighborhood of Lake Superior were occasionally called *Pi-to-na-king Ka-ma-bi-tcig*. To the west of Superior were their close kinsmen the *Sug-wun-dug-ah-win-in-e-wug*, or "men who live amongst the thick fir woods." But for the French period and up until the 1820s, it would be more accurate to speak of Ojibwe clans living in this territory.[22] Once, in a petition to the U.S. Commissioner of Indian Affairs, the Grand Portage Ojibwe identified themselves as "North Shore Indians." I have adopted this name, slightly changed to North Shore Ojibwe, knowing that it is a reasonable option, if not one that was frequently used historically.[23]

Whites had alternate names for this band. The name would shift from Grand Portage to Kaministiquia or Fort William Ojibwe depending upon where the author was writing. Thus when the North West Company made an agreement to justify their move from Grand Portage to the Kaministiquia River, they wrote "Grand Portage chiefs." However, the Ojibwe themselves signed by their clan. Essentially, the Euro-Americans called this group Grand Portage Ojibwe when they were in Grand Portage. But when in Fort William, they called them Fort William Ojibwe.

After the death of the Rainy Lake leader "Premier," who held some limited power in a vast area and was held in high regard by the fur traders, the North Shore Ojibwe recognized their own leaders.[24] By 1824, many North Shore Ojibwe recognized "Espagnol," or the Spaniard, as their overall leader.[25] This fact suggests that the importance of clans was starting to shift towards a new social structure, with a more hierarchical leader. There was a slow decline in the role of clans as a social institution as Ojibwe women married Euro-American men (with their children thus not having access to established clans) and as the demands for a more centralized leadership grew.[26] However, leadership remained more a matter of leading by example and consensus than by sheer authority. But from Espagnol on, there was one principal leader— even more reinforced when Western-style elections and governments were established. After Espagnol it is proper to speak of a single Ojibwe Band, still shaped to some degree by clans, in Northwestern Lake Superior. However, only a couple of decades later, after the international border had real ramifications, the one band became, for legal purposes, divided into the Grand Portage and Fort William bands. Thus, for purposes of this work, the North Shore Ojibwe clans became the Grand Portage Band and the Fort William Band. With the establishment of the reservation and reserve, the geographic divorce became more extreme.

Isle Royale fell into the traditional use area of the North Shore Ojibwe. However, other Ojibwe also used it. Occasionally some Nipigon and Rainy Lake Ojibwe would voyage to and use Minong. On a few occasions, Ojibwe from the Sault Ste. Marie traveled to Minong. This probably was more a consequence of strong ties between North Shore Ojibwe and those from the "Soo" than a distinct event. Indeed, a number of Grand Portage families trace back to the Soo. Unfortunately, we do not know if these other Ojibwe sought permission to use Minong, or to what degree it was recognized as the territory of their North Shore kinsmen. Nipigon, Rainy, and Portage Ojibwe continued to travel great distances during the early 1800s, including shorter, but still unpredictable, trips to Minong.

The east–west orientation of travel, trade, and kinship manifested itself in another way: Ojibwe from Nipigon in the east through Fort William and Grand Portage all the way west to Rainy Lake spoke a single Anishinaabemowin dialect. To the north and south of this string of Ojibwe groups, other Minnesota and Ontario Ojibwe spoke different dialects.[27] The sweep of this dialect mirrors the unique makeup of North Shore clans and Ojibwe oral tradition of a group migrating westward along the North Shore.[28]

This book examines the rough-and-tumble meshing of North Shore Ojibwe heritage and history with the presence of the Euro-American newcomers at Isle Royale and along nearby shores. Ironically, during the height of the international fur trade, Isle Royale was a backwater. Grand Portage, the summer headquarters of the powerful North West Company, was known by name in London, Vienna, and Paris. The first documentary record of someone being on Isle Royale is that of the Indian captive John Tanner, circa 1794. Tanner accompanied an Indian, helping his struggling family, and had a successful hunt on the Island. The record of use of the Island largely goes silent until the 1820s, when Hudson's Bay Company clerks and U.S. border surveyors made occasional notations

# Map of Isle Royale or Minong

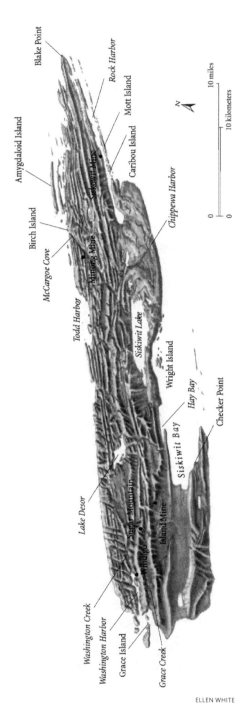

Blake Point
Rock Harbor
Amygdaloid Island
Mott Island
Caribou Island
Siskowit Mine
Birch Island
Chippewa Harbor
McCargoe Cove
Minong Mine
Todd Harbor
Siskiwit Lake
Wright Island
Hay Bay
Siskiwit Bay
Checker Point
Lake Desor
Sugar Mountain
Island Mine
Windigo
Washington Creek
Washington Harbor
Grace Island
Grace Creek

N

10 miles
10 kilometers
0
0

ELLEN WHITE

about it—but these were not widely available or known. The American Fur Company's fishing experiment on Lake Superior, which included a number of stations on Isle Royale in the late 1830s, throws some documentary light on Ojibwe knowledge of Minong. By the time of the Copper Treaty of 1842 and the first "copper rush" on Isle Royale in the late 1840s, Ojibwe presence on the Island was much debated, and conclusions were made which were not to the benefit of North Shore Ojibwe. The highpoint of Ojibwe presence on Isle Royale was during the 1850s with a large-scale commercial fishing operation. Hundreds of Ojibwe fished for entrepreneur Hugh H. McCullough, but the fishing went bust with a nationwide economic panic.

After the majority of North Shore Ojibwe sold salted fish in barrels to McCullough, they were economically marginalized on the Island. A second mining period began in the 1870s, but by this time, mining companies on Isle Royale hired few Ojibwe. A third mining era in the 1890s, and the rise of Scandinavian immigration in the area in 1880–1900 dramatically changed Isle Royale use. Scandinavian fishermen established fisheries throughout the archipelago, and some overwintered there. Resident game wardens— *gizhaadigewininwag*—and then rangers populated the Island in the twentieth century. Early in the century, recreational visitors also became common on the Island, and well-to-do midwesterners purchased islands and prime lands. An era of park recreation began, culminating in the creation of the Isle Royale National Park—in concept in 1931, and in reality in 1946. A succession of events on the Island and on the mainland impacted the Grand Portage and Fort William Ojibwe. We will track the waxing and waning story of Ojibwe use of Minong in the chapters that follow.

# **1** KNOWING MINONG

Ojibwe lived in a landscape made distinctive by islands, which marry their geography of lands and waters. Ojibwe frequently made camps on islands, and while there, collected bird eggs and harvested berries. Islands were places of safety when paddling in hard winds and growing seas. Certain islands were particularly important as Ojibwe homelands—and perhaps even Ojibwe capitals such as Manitoulin in Lake Huron and Madeline as part of the Apostle Islands. More locally, the Ojibwe of the North Shore paddled in the sheltered lee of islands strung along the coast from Grand Portage to Thunder Bay. Kinsmen lived on Saganaga Lake, speckled with islands, making navigation a feat of geographic virtuosity. From the highlands and cliffs of Thunder Cape or Wauswaugoning Bay, Isle Royale is visible, and its size hinted at by its silhouetted ridges. Ojibwe have used these vantage points to search the horizon for paddlers and gauge traveling conditions.[1] Viewed from the mainland, Isle Royale is an extended, ribbon-like mass surrounded by water. Most often it appears as a lumpy, dusty gray, but in the sunshine the dark greens of its many evergreen trees are visible. On bright

spring days, looking out from the mainland, a thick ring of shore-fast ice on Isle Royale radiates light back. Like other major island archipelagoes, such as Manitoulin and the Apostles, surely Ojibwe made use of it.

Islands such as Minong are potent geographic entities.[2] They are preeminently imaginable as a geographic unit. They have distinctive borders, unlike mainland places. And they are recognized and talked about with wholeness—a place the mind's eye can envision. There are many ways of knowing a distinctive place. We will follow up on three essential ways of knowing Minong—getting there, naming it, and mapping it.

### Getting to the Island

A number of historic observers asserted that the Ojibwe were too scared to cross the lake to Minong.[3] But this assertion does not hold up under scrutiny. Crossing the lake to Minong was possible, but was not a feat to take lightly. Both Ojibwe and voyageurs made lake traverses of ten to twelve to fifteen miles. Father Baraga and his Ojibwe paddlers made one astonishing (and nearly deadly) seventy-mile crossing from the Apostle Islands to the Minnesota shoreline. The twelve-mile "la Grande Traverse" across Black Bay to Thunder Cape was traditionally made by voyageurs, but still could be difficult. A fifteen-mile traverse from cape to headland or island was the customary upper limit for Ojibwe and voyageurs.[4] From a Jesuit's biography, a crossing is described:

> The distance of Isle Royale from the Canadian main land, on the northwest is from twelve to nineteen miles, according to the point you start from. This distance in those days had to be crossed generally in bark canoes, which offered no small risks. . . .
>
> We were five leagues from the island; and in that stretch there is not the smallest islet, where one could flee for shelter in case of surprise. Consequently, the crossing is always looked upon with dread by the 'voyageurs'; and before undertaking the Christian does not forget to say his prayers, nor the pagan to throw to his manitous the traditional plug of tobacco.
>
> I had yet to visit the people of another mine, which they call Siskawit Mine. I started in company with a young man of our mission at Fort William who arrived there shortly before me. His canoe was very small; however I managed to cramp into it the things absolutely necessary for our camping on the way, and the exercises of the mission. After having paddled for about nine miles, we steered north-east, entering into a bay called by the Indians Pike Bay, and by the Americans McCagos [*sic*] Bay, or Cove.[5]

To cross to Minong, North Shore Ojibwe had to carefully plan their trip to bring needed supplies and goods such as kettles, rolled birch bark for the wigwam walls, guns, ammunition, gill nets for fishing, and staples. The crossing would take many hours of hard paddling.[6] Even when taking advantage of flat (calm) lake conditions, the many hours taken to pass over the inky-colored water meant that the weather could change during the voyage. Getting across as swiftly as possible was a prudent safety measure. Ojibwe travelers knew the lake was more likely to be calm in early morning hours and roughest during the afternoon.

On a good day—calm and clear—paddling would begin before sunrise. In the early morning hours, the paddlers would watch the sun rise out of the lake to the east between mainland and the Island. The sun's arc in the sky would accompany their crossing and give increasing color and definition to Minong. While not preferable, some traverses to Minong were made at night if there was enough moonlight to guide the paddlers. Or, if leaving during the night, Ojibwe would use birch-bark torches, made of a twisted spiral of bark, to cast firelight so they could pack up their gear. The same torch might be used to melt the pitch or gum used to seal any leaks in the canoe. To find any small leaks, Ojibwe sucked the location where the water seemed to come in. After finding the leaky spot, they would then melt pitch into the hole or leaky seam between birch-bark panels of the hull.[7] When the lake was calm and the weather conditions appeared to be steady, the paddlers would set out. Often the traverse was made in small groups, providing some security in numbers.

There was not one absolute jumping-off spot for paddling across to Minong. Instead, paddlers making the traverse might depart from Pie Island at the end of Thunder Bay, or from the island chain stringing southwest from Pie Island. Leaving from this location made for the shortest and safest crossing to Todd Harbor and McCargoe Cove, a traditional portal to Isle Royale for Native Americans. Crossing from the off-shore islands off Thunder Bay would be advantageous for other reasons: Isle Royale itself becomes a block to wind and waves from the south and southeast. Crossing on this water route also means you are paddling towards the whole length of Minong versus its narrower ends. A Thunder Bay to McCargoe Cove crossing would minimize the potentially disastrous effect of prevailing lake currents pushing paddlers away from the Island. Those foolish enough to contemplate a South Shore crossing would have to struggle with the Keeweenaw Current— the strongest current in Lake Superior—which would push paddlers away from Isle Royale.[8]

Ojibwe leaving from Grand Portage Bay would more often paddle by Hat and Pigeon Points and canoe northeast until behind the string of Victoria, Spar, and Thompson Islands. From there, closer to Minong and behind the breadth of it, they would paddle when the seas seemed safe.[9] We have found only one account of a traverse leaving from Pigeon Point, made by a Jesuit father with Ojibwe guides. Explorer David Thompson knew North Shore Ojibwe paddled to Isle Royale. Thinking this over, he concluded that the best traverse to Isle Royale was from Little Pipe Island, one of the chain of islands southwest of Pie Island. The main worry about this long traverse is that weather conditions can change from the time the party starts to the time it arrives. Still, paddlers crossing to or from Minong might encounter surprising events besides changing weather conditions. In one instance, a Grand Portage woman gave birth to a boy in a canoe as the family made landfall near the Little Spirit Cedar Tree en route back from Minong.[10]

Contradicting the opinion that North Shore Ojibwe were scared to cross the lake to Minong is a more sophisticated view that they were maritime peoples who lived from and on the lake. They traveled frequently on the water and knew it well. The village of Grand Portage faced the lake to provide easy access for residents. Known as *Ke-che-gum-me-win-in-e-wug*, or Great Lake Men, they were at home on the water.[11] Their dietary mainstay was fish, including whitefish and siscowets caught in great numbers during the fall spawning season, as well as sturgeon and suckers. Fish were a comparatively reliable resource, which prompted one Isle Royale mine financier to exaggerate that "They [Indians] lived almost entirely on fish, & so do their large dogs." Evidence also points to their employment on some of the early vessels to ply Lake Superior and to travel to Isle Royale.[12] Further, one Indian commissioner reports: "They rely chiefly upon fishing for subsistence, and the supply of fish in the great lake is apparently inexhaustible. They are expert sailors and display a high degree of skill both in the construction and management of their sailing craft."[13] As with lake crossings today, there was a special feeling of exhilaration and mystery that overcame Ojibwe making the traverse. Grand Portage elder Dick Anderson explained the feeling:

> It's a very awesome thing. . . . You get a peculiar feeling when you leave the land mass, and of course, Lake Superior is very clear. And you can see into it a pretty good depth. And you leave Hat Point and you see. . . . The [Grand

Portage] bay is shallow and you are seeing bottom and all of a sudden everything just goes into blackness. You are talking five, six, and seven hundred feet of water out there. You kind of remember that [*chuckling*].[14]

Belief in the lake as a living entity heightened the Ojibwe paddlers' sense of being and vulnerability. Further, the spirits that might affect their crossing must be addressed and placated for a safe crossing. Those Ojibwe departing Grand Portage for Minong passed the *Manido Gee-zhi-gance*, or Spirit Little Cedar Tree, on Hat Point. The ancient and gnarled cedar standing alone on a basalt ledge overlooking the lake is a place of reverence for the life and powers of Lake Superior. The Spirit Little Cedar Tree is the traditional place to bring prayers and offerings for a safe crossing and fishing success. Offerings of reverence, of tobacco and ribbon—and earlier, vermilion—were left at the foot of the tree. Paddlers must be careful and behave appropriately, as the *Mishipizheu*, the Underwater Lynx, was thought to have an aquatic lair in the depths nearby. Offerings and ritual attention were prudent for lake-traveling people. Offerings made at the Manido Gee-zhi-gance that reached and appeased Mishipizheu were of utmost importance.[15]

Before returning to Grand Portage from Minong in 1794, John Tanner described a ceremony he had witnessed.

> We were ten canoes in all, and we started, as we had done in coming, at the earliest dawn of the morning. The night had been calm, and the water, when we left the island, was perfectly smooth. We had proceeded about two hundred yards into the lake, when the canoes all stopped together, and the chief, in a very loud voice, addressed a prayer to the Great Spirit, entreating him to give us a good look to cross the lake. "You," said he, "have made this lake, and you have made us, your children; you can now cause that the water shall remain smooth, while we pass over in safety." In this manner, he continued praying for five or ten minutes; he then threw into the lake a small quantity of tobacco, in which each of the canoes followed his example. They then all started together, and the old chief commenced his song, which was a religious one.[16]

A hundred years later, John Linklater's grandfather and his Ojibwe wife Tchi-ki-wis's grandmother made a similar crossing. Retelling what his grandfather had said, Linklater recounted that a ceremonial dance was held and offerings were given to appeal to the underwater spirits.[17] It is also likely that those who had dreamed of smooth water and thus had a spiritual link to water spirits were also asked to make prayers for a safe passage.[18]

Crossing the ice to or from Minong was a precarious business. It was, however, done repeatedly, with or without dog teams and "cariole," or sled. While not made as often as summer crossings, they were made in order to bring mail, or for other compelling reasons. To do it safely required much knowledge about ice and weather conditions. Heavy winds and lake swells in open stretches of water can break up thick ice in minutes. Lake currents can rip away ice or eat away at its thickness. Ice cover is not uniform throughout Lake Superior, and in many years much open water remains. The ice crossing from Thunder Bay was comparatively the most reliable, given its relatively long life span, or duration, and thickness.[19]

Optimism about the prospects of copper mines in the 1870s and 1890s led to a number of wintertime crossings. Indeed, crossings were so common that a mail contract was open for bid from Pigeon River to Island Mine that scheduled a nine-hour crossing time, summer or winter.[20] Two Ojibwe miners crossed from Isle Royale to Fort William in February, 1854, and reported that the ice was one and a half feet thick the whole crossing. During the cold winter of 1875, the ice was thick enough that teams of horses were driven from Silver Islet off the tip of Thunder Cape to McCargoe Cove. During a northern gale, a desperate miner attempting the crossing was badly frostbit in his hands, feet, and face. A year later, two non-Ojibwe mail carriers crossed ten miles on ice and were within three miles of Jarvis Island when a gale blew up, broke up the ice, and they drowned. An Ojibwe saw the men struggling, but could not help them. In December of the same year, two other non-Ojibwe mail carriers drowned. Some of these records are of desperate people trying to get off the Island. But in March 1849, six Ojibwe crossed over to Minong to hunt caribou. They returned eight days later.[21] Ojibwe led Jesuit priests across the winter ice to Minong and down the shore from Fort William to Grand

Portage on a regular basis. Ojibwe knowledge of ice conditions was such that one week after twelve-year-old Josephte Aiakodjiwang died in February 1857, family members pulled a sledge over the ice from Todd Harbor bearing her body back to the Mission of Immaculate Conception.[22]

Once across the lake and on the Island, Ojibwe guides' geographic knowledge remained essential to moving throughout Minong. While entering McCargoe Cove during a summer proselytizing trip, Jesuit father Du Ranquet wrote:

> There we were obliged to leave our canoe and reach the opposite side of the island by a portage of eight miles. We entered a small stream which discharges into the bay at this point, hauled our canoe out of the water and taking with us our tea-kettle and our blankets, went to look for a shelter for the night on the skirts of the bush. There was lots of grass on the spot, and the weather was clear.
>
> After tea and night prayers we lay down to rest in the open air. On awaking at daybreak next morning, we found our blankets covered with dew, so we waited for the first rays of the sun to dry them. After having folded and put them beneath our canoe, my companion shouldered my sack and started off through the bush, I following behind.
>
> The first travellers that had gone over the portage since winter, could with the greatest difficulty distinguish the trail, a terrible storm having thrown down many trees which now encumbered it in its entire length. Even before the storm the path was already almost imperceptible. We had to make frequent use of our hatchet; and had it not been for my guide I would in many places, never have so much as suspected even the existence of a trail. After walked thus for several miles we reached a little lake which I took to be about a mile wide, but which could not be seen in its entire length. We had to follow its shores, which proved to be the most difficult part of the road, because it was the most obstructed.
>
> At last we saw the lake (Superior) on the other side of the island, and by coming down a long declivity we reached the bay on the shore which is Rock Harbor mine.[23]

"Getting to the Island" illustrates just a small part of the vast geographic knowledge of North Shore Ojibwe. They made trips on their own to the Island and guided others there. Early visitors were particularly dependent upon aboriginal travel routes, knowledge of local conditions, technology such as canoes, snowshoes, dog teams, and tumplines for packs, and traditional foods. Records of this dependence on, and tradition of, guiding began with the arrival of the first whites. For example, in 1731 the guide Auchagah showed Frenchman La Verendrye the Grand Portage route that opened up canoe routes to the Canadian West.[24] Roughly a hundred years later, during efforts to establish fisheries at Isle Royale, American Fur Company officials directed that company fishermen "avail yourself of Indian information . . . on the Island."[25] Even in the 1920s, in midwinter, a Grand Portage Ojibwe was called upon to search the Island for a missing man. Willie Droulliard was left off at the Island by a Coast Guard cutter and snowshoed along the entire Island checking fish camps for the missing man.[26] Droulliard's intimate knowledge of the Island came from his work as a lumberjack and fisherman, but his woodsman's skills made him the ideal solo searcher.

### Naming It

Place-names such as Minong can be revealing. They can provide us with hints as to what the namers thought of the place. Many commentators have noted how Isle Royale is aptly named, yet its first name, Minong, has very different connotations.

The word "Minong" does not readily give up its meaning. Only a few know much about it. Minong has been much misunderstood, celebrated, and almost forgotten, only to be revived and enjoy renewed popularity. It has long been understood as the Native American name for the island archipelago in Northwestern Lake Superior now known as Isle Royale.[27] The name Minong has enjoyed some popularity within the region. It has been applied to a variety of Isle Royale features, such as a major ridge running the length of the Island, a post office, a settlement, a copper mine, a mining company, a resort, cabins, and various boats. One novel celebrating regional history mentions a sailing schooner named *Minong*.[28] The Minong Ridge Trail is widely acclaimed as the toughest hiking trail on the Island and features prominent views of Pie Island, Thunder Cape, and Thunder Bay. The sweeping view from Minong Ridge encompasses the canoe route to the Island and much of the traditional territory of North Shore Ojibwe.

Scientists, too, have appropriated the name Minong. A pioneering geologist on the Island named a group of common rocks on Isle Royale "Minong trap." He also sought to name an individual type of rock "Minong porphyrite."[29] "Minong" is now a recognized scientific term for an early lake level—the "Minong Lake Level"—occurring 10,000 years ago. Ironically, the Minong Lake Level was three hundred feet higher than today, so that much of what we know now as Isle Royale would have been underwater.[30] Lake Minong was the first lake to appear after the glaciers retreated, suggesting a primal nature. There is also an officially recognized archeological site on Isle Royale called "Minong." The name has the special appeal of a word whose meaning is just shy of a secret. Only those who are truly interested know of its meaning, or so they have been led to believe.

Few have written about Minong and fewer yet knew of it. Most of the major explorers in the Lake Superior basin did not mention it, beginning with the first Euro-American, Pierre Radisson. He did not mention Minong despite having likely established a trading post in what is now Thunder Bay. Yet an intendant of New France in distant Quebec used the word "Minoncq" as the formal name in a 1710 letter. Two decades later, the French explorer who opened up trade to the Northwest, La Verendrye, did not mention Minong. Clearly La Verendrye lingered in the area with Native guides, and Isle Royale is drawn on his map—but it remained unnamed. Because Grand Portage was both a destination and portal to the great Northwest, hundreds of voyageurs and traders would paddle parallel to the length of Isle Royale to reach Kitchi Onimgaming. In 1767 Jonathan Carver's expedition paddled along the North Shore and met with the prominent Grand Portage Chippewa leader, and he still only referred to the archipelago as Isle Royale. John Tanner (quoted earlier), who was adopted into an Ottawa family, trapped and fished on Minong circa 1794 with Muskego Indians. He, too, did not report its Native name.[31] Other non-Indians who came into the area—such as the Northwesters at Grand Portage, and Hudson's Bay Company clerks and factors at Fort William—rarely mentioned Minong. Nor did the American Fur Company personnel when they established their fishing stations at Isle Royale in the 1830s.[32] Even Ojibwe author Henry Schoolcraft, who lived at Sault Ste. Marie much of his adult life, never mentioned it by name. The second wave of Jesuit fathers from the newly established Mission of Immaculate Conception in the late 1840s and 1850s voyaged repeatedly to Minong with Ojibwe paddlers, but did not report its Ojibwe name. The celebrated Ojibwe historian William Warren, whose relatives migrated westward along the South Shore of Lake Superior, did not mention it.[33] What was more common than naming it, or knowing its relatively obscure meaning, was ignoring it if known. The disdain many nineteenth-century Americans had for Indian people and culture may explain their desire to affix their own name—Isle Royale—to the archipelago.

Even when voiced, its meaning eluded most people. Minong is the Ojibwe or Anishinabe place-name for Isle Royale. But its beginning root word, "mino," is shared among Cree and Ojibwe. Its ending, -ong or -ing, is a marker of Ojibwe language. It is not, for example, a Cree or Menomini, Potwatomi, or even a Dakota suffix.[34] In composite it has an odd word structure for Ojibwe, which likely has led to multiple interpretations. Pronounced one way, "Mee-nong," it could be interpreted as meaning something like "to give to" or "give a gift to."[35] Only a handful of authentic records of Ojibwe verbal tradition of Minong have been recorded. And "Minung" has been traditionally rendered Minong in those few accounts that bother to mention it at all. First noted in 1672 in the *Jesuit Relations*, a result of communications between Jesuit fathers and Ojibwe, it was neglected in verbal tradition for hundreds of years.

For many Ojibwe speakers and linguists, the word is an enigma. Posed with the question of making sense of the word, Gilbert Caribou, a Grand Portage tribal councilman, and Kalvin Ottertail hazarded the idea that it could have been slang, an archaic word form, a loan word, or a corruption.[36] They were unsure which. The "mino" stem can lead to words that are built around the concept of good/beauty or berries/blueberries. *Miniss* is Ojibwe for island, leading to another branch of interpretation.[37] What is clear is that Ojibwe speakers who have used the word have been consistent about what Minong means, namely, the good or beautiful place. Grand Portage Ojibwe elders such as Ellen Olson, Alexis Memashkawash (Alex Posey), and John Flatte interpreted Minong as "the good place," or "the beautiful place," or "the place of abundance."[38] Learning from his grandmother, Kalvin Ottertail mentioned that the meaning might extend to "good sheltered place." Other Ojibwe speakers, such as Billy Blackwell and Roger Roulette in Manitoba, confirm Minong as meaning "a good place." Ironically, the first detailed government report about Isle Royale got the translation right—"the good place"—but this had little subsequent effect on others. The geologists who recorded this name spent much of the summer on Isle Royale, noted Ojibwe trails, and likely conversed with the North Shore Ojibwe who were on Minong at that time.[39] In addition, many of these recent Ojibwe speakers reject other possible interpretations, such as a "place of blueberries" or "great island."[40] An enthusiastic newspaper reporter, Arthur Juntunen, built upon the reputation of Minong to come up with "a good place to get copper."[41]

Non-Indian interpretations of the meaning of Minong have been varied, creative, and persistent. One major interpretive tradition is that Minong means "a place of blueberries." Appearing in two credible works, *Wolves of Minong* and "Indian Names in Michigan," this interpretation remains.[42] Even a recent National Park Service website professes this interpretation. A second interpretive tradition renders Minong as meaning "a good high place." Again, credible sources, including one early source in 1892, engendered a different interpretive tradition. This tradition is not yet dead, as it too is being used on a website.[43] Other possible meanings of Minong include "floating island," "the safe place," "great island," and "the place between." Interpreting Minong to mean floating island is mistaking one element of a traditional Ojibwe story, often about Minong, as its meaning.[44] What is clear is that for most of its life in documents, Minong has been misunderstood. The power of the written word, even when wrong, eclipsed the few scattered references to Minong by Ojibwe speakers. The good place has not been a place of good interpretation. Misunderstandings professed by non-Indians have clouded widespread knowledge of the positive referent about Minong in the Anishinabe language.

The historical use of "Minong" blossomed in three different eras. The Jesuits first reported "Minong" in 1672. Father Claude Dablon and Jean Claude Allouez recorded it on their seminal map of Lake Superior and in their report about the lake and its inhabitants.[45] It then played out in a long tradition of maps, which are all heavily derived from the 1672 Jesuit map. Ultimately, though, the first wave of use died out in great part because the original *Jesuit Relations* was not widely available, nor translated into English. A second spurt in the use of Minong came with the republication of the Jesuit map and excerpts about Minong in a government document in 1849.[46] The notable historian Francis Parkman's 1869 publication on *La Salle and the Discovery of the Great West* kept the name in the forefront among elites. A more locally published book, Swineford's 1876 booster work *History and Review of the Mineral Resources of Lake Superior*, again pushed the word forward by quoting the *Jesuit Relations*.[47] Suddenly, during the days of copper fever in the region, Minong became fashionable as a favorite place-name. Finally, the third period of resurgence in the use and pondering of the name occurred with the efforts to establish the national park in the late 1920s and '30s. Radio broadcasts, travelogues, and even reports on the efforts to establish the park bantered about the relatively exotic word "Minong." Many of these reports sought to introduce readers to Isle Royale and its worthiness as a national park, pointedly introducing "Minong" and one of its many meanings. It lingers in use today, though dependent upon published sources and place-names, especially the rugged Minong Ridge Trail.

### Minong on Maps

Most Ojibwe maps were ephemeral, made of charcoal on birch bark and used to guide or reunite traveling parties. They were often based on distances traveled in a day's march.[48] And, a map might reflect two different routes and speed of travel to the same destination: a riverine canoe route and an upland winter road, such as up to Dog Lake west of Thunder Bay.[49] Unfortunately, however, no Ojibwe maps of Minong have survived. Instead, for its mapping history, we must turn to its mapping by non-Indians.

The confusion about what Minong meant to non-Indians was paralleled in the mapping tradition that underscored geographic uncertainty about Lake Superior and Isle Royale. The shape and location of "Minong" in Lake Superior maps is mercurial and takes some interesting turns through time. For many years it existed on maps more as a blob than a geographic certainty. Using an early map to travel there would be cold comfort. Other maps would leave Isle Royale out, not bothering to chart the archipelago. Only a segment of it shows in many other maps, or it appears only on the seams. In many contemporary maps it is made to fit into the map of the Upper Peninsula of Michigan, oftentimes greatly reduced in scale, and cut and pasted to fit into an "unused" section of Lake Superior. Two hundred years ago, the location of Isle Royale was also up for grabs, and it would frequently be sketched in closer to Thunder Bay and the North Shore in particular. Just as there is an Ojibwe storytelling motif of floating islands, Euro-American mapmakers did, in effect, the same; they had the Island move in the lake and shape-shift. The shape of Lake Superior was also dynamic and not agreed upon for hundreds of years. Its outline was rounded in some maps, angular in others, and approaching a rectangular shape in another.

Three factors contributed to the sometimes fanciful representations of Minong and Lake Superior in historic maps. First, few if any mapmakers had been there. Instead, the few interested souls paddling or sailing closer to the mainland shore observed the Island from afar, typically over ten miles away. Second, for much of the historic period, maps were drawn and printed long distances from Lake Superior and Minong. European mapmakers dominated the ranks of early map producers, most of whom had never been to the Great Lakes, let alone Isle Royale. And, third, early maps were printed from engraved copper plates. It was technically difficult to correct what was already there, so mistakes persisted.[50]

Amidst this geographic muddle, four documents stand out as instrumental in mapping Isle Royale and Lake Superior. Three of these were influential in accurately mapping the lake and Isle Royale, while the other one caused geographical confusion and puzzlement among international border surveyors and government agents. The first influential document is the Jesuit Map of

1672, which uses the Ojibwe name Minong for Isle Royale.[51] The map began a tradition of the French monopolizing information about the Great Lakes up until 1760—or the end of their regime.[52]

Jesuits Dablon and Allouez likely coasted along the North Shore, viewing Minong from fifteen to twenty miles away. They were exacting enough to draw its elongated outline, its northeast–southwest orientation, and the few islands that are off the southwestern point of the main Island. They apparently did not circumnavigate Minong, as major geographic features such as Siskiwit Bay and Rock Harbor and even Washington Harbor are not present on their map. Their rendition of Minong is likely the product of sketching from a headland or two on the North Shore. The southwestern islands as rendered live on in other subsequent maps, but they are more likely ridges that look like islands when viewed from the mainland. From a vantage point on the mainland, the curve of the earth obscures the low points, such as Siskiwit Swamp—and ridges, such as Feldtmann Ridge, look like islands on clear fall days.[53] The Jesuits also positioned Minong, more or less, in its relative position in "Lac Tracy or Superieur." But perhaps most impressive, the Dablon and Allouez map correctly portrays the rough shape of Lake Superior, demonstrating some experience with the entire lake.

Dablon and Allouez's map followed earlier mapmaking conventions and plotted where Indian tribes lived around Lake Superior. Subsequent mapmakers followed this convention too. At this time, knowing who was living where was as important as what the "where" looked like. Dablon and Allouez's map did not name any tribes in the immediate vicinity of Minong, although the Cree are plotted as living near Lake Nipigon. For as long as this convention persisted, mapmakers were often uncertain about specific Native groups living along the North Shore. Later, after it clearly became denoted as Ojibwe territory, the convention of naming the tribe declined in popularity. There are no significant historic maps that indicate there was any Indian group(s) living on Minong. This lack may be explained more by the small scale of Minong in these maps, rather than being a reflection of knowledge at the time.

The Jesuit map exerted great influence on other seventeenth-century maps. For example, Venetian Father Coronelle's 1688 map of New France borrowed Dablon and Allouez's name and outline for Minong, while adding greater detail to Superior's shoreline and tributaries. The Coronelle map also stated in fine print that copper mines were believed to be on the Island. At that time, the intendant of New France was believed to have a specimen of copper on his desk brought back by the Jesuits. One French engineer is said to have inspected Minong and found large copper deposits.[54] However, there has been no evidence uncovered of French or English copper mining. In 1688, Coronelle placed the Assiniboine tribe nearest to Minong roughly at Grand Portage, while Cree are placed north of Thunder Bay.

Exerting an enormous influence on subsequent maps, the King of France's royal hydrographer, Franquelin, made a series of maps that include Lake Superior, from 1687 to 1697. These maps derived most of their information about Lake Superior from the earlier Jesuit map. But unfortunately, there was even less detail provided about Minong; in these maps it becomes more blob-like and has shed its westernmost islands. Apparently no geographic advances were made in the two decades after the Jesuits paddled by Isle Royale.

At the start of the eighteenth century, and particularly during the era of New France, "Minong" was firmly entrenched as the recognized map name for Isle Royale. Despite the continuity in name, its shape continues to shift in subsequent maps. The French mapmaker de L'Isle represents "Is Minong" generally, still longer than wide, but without its fleet of small islands. A 1742 map supposedly derived from *coureur de bois* (independent fur trader) Joseph La France leaves Minong unnamed, but places the "Ouass" Indians nearby. This was a French name meaning "Fish Indians," or one Ojibwe clan that has longtime ties to the area—particularly Grand Portage, Thunder Bay, and nearby.[55] A more widely known map, by the Frenchman Roy in 1743, backtracks on detail, and Lake Superior becomes almost rectangular. Isle Royale is unnamed, is positioned further from shore, and has split into two islands. Other eighteenth-century maps by Lahontan (1703), Popple (1733), and Fitch (1785) demonstrate that there was little geographical certainty about Lake Superior during this century. Further, specific European knowledge of Lake Superior seemed to regress and become less exacting as compared to the Jesuit map of 1672.

Into this geographic vacuum of information stepped French hydrographic engineer Jacques Nicolas Bellin's series of influential maps from 1744 to 1755. Bellin was prolific and well respected—hence his work influenced many others. Remarkably, he introduced a number of mythic islands into Lake Superior: I. Philippeaux, sometimes called I. Minong, Ponchartrain, I. Maurepas, and I. Ste. Anne. Contemporary map scholars believe that these mythic islands were introduced in Bellin's maps because Bellin was provided with fictitious information by the French copper-mine promoter Louis Deny de La Ronde. De La Ronde, trying to court favor with his superior officer, gave him a present—islands newly named after his supervisor and his children.[56] The net result of the Bellin maps was that Lake Superior was suddenly teeming with a fleet of new islands. The new islands gave the map (and lake) the appearance of being half filled with noteworthy islands, rather than with its actual vast stretches of open water. Predictably the Bellin maps created new confusions. After this time, continental mapmakers were unsure if Minong was the same as Isle Royale. And further, was I. Philippeaux the same as either Minong or Isle Royale? The pioneering quest for copper could lead to either vast improvements or regressions in mapmaking.

The Bellin maps sowed two confusions. First, they introduced the name Isle Royale to what had been Minong. The archipelago is sketched as rounded like the shape of a baby carrot. Second, the Bellin maps have the name Minong migrate to a mythic island south of where it had been located. Like a lie retold and embellished with each telling, Bellin's fictional islands caused subsequent observers further problems. A Canadian writer tried to affix specific place-names—for example "West Bay"—to either the mythic island I. Philippeaux or Isle Royale.[57] Bellin's contribution was not all spurious; he did add some detail to the chain of lakes that later become known as the Voyageur Highway.

After Bellin, Isle Royale becomes the more common name for the Island, though Minong is used on occasion. Bellin's map influenced English mapmaker John Mitchell, who produced a majestic eight-sheet map in 1755 that was in great demand during the French and Indian War. Mitchell's map became the standard map of North America during the last half of the eighteenth century.[58] The most momentous use of the Mitchell Map was during the 1783 Treaty of

Paris. A line demarcated on it set the initial geographic terms of where the border would be located between the upstart Americans and the English. The border was drawn north of Isle Royale (and the fictitious island I. Philippeaux), south of the fictitious island I. Ponchartrain, and through to "Long Lake" to Rainy Lake and Lake of the Woods. Ironically, in subsequent international negotiations about where the border should be settled, the fictitious islands did not play a confusing part. However, agreement about Long Lake and the customary canoe route to the interior did.[59]

Despite the flourishing of the fur trade in the 1770s, 1780s, 1790s, and even into the 1800s, the level of expressed geographic knowledge of Isle Royale remained crude and essentially reliant, if accurate at all, upon the Jesuit maps of more than a hundred years earlier. Despite thousands of voyageurs paddling between Isle Royale and the mainland to the great fur emporiums at Grand Portage and later at Fort William, there was little advance in formal maps of the lake during this period. Additionally, the North West Company built sailing vessels that coasted along its shores on their routes to Grand Portage and later Fort William. Still, no detailed knowledge made its way to published maps that showed knowledge of the major harbors, islands, or bays of Isle Royale. Notes from literate explorers such as Alexander Henry and Jonathan Carver began to provide real detail on some areas of Lake Superior and westward. Grand Portage and the border canoe route came into great focus, with each portage name noted sometimes in both French and English. Henry noted that "Muskegoes Nation" (Ojibwe-Cree people) live on the Canadian side of the border lakes—while the important and infamous fur trader Peter Pond's 1784 map documents Grand Portage and the region west as that of the Chippeway Indian. But the fur traders' experiences did not lead to an expansion of accurate mapping of Isle Royale.

The first European to cross the North American continent, Sir Alexander MacKenzie, contributed much geographic information to British mapmaker Arrowsmith that corrected many mistakes in Lake Superior. A series of maps by Arrowsmith, beginning in 1798 or 1799 and improved with additional geographic knowledge provided by the great North American surveyor David Thompson, removed fictitious islands from the big lake. Isle Royale, however, remains very generally rendered. Ironically, one of the last maps to name Isle Royale Minong accompanies Lewis and Clark's report. Sketched wildly because of its peripheral interest, it is labeled "Royale or Minong I."[60]

One of the greatest achievements of North American mapping hung prominently on the wall of the Great Hall of the North West Company's summer headquarters in Fort William.[61] Accumulated from lengthy and dangerous travels in the Canadian Northwest and conferences with dozens of his peers, David Thompson's large 1813 map documents a vast proportion of North America. While the map was a geographical triumph, it failed to depict Isle Royale. Ironically, the map hung in Fort William, only some thirty-five miles from Isle Royale, yet did not chart it. This lack is even more peculiar because North West Company fishermen sometimes fished lakeward from Thunder Cape towards Isle Royale, less than eleven miles away. And there is speculation that they may have crossed this watery divide and fished from Isle Royale waters (nearby Belle Isle in the northeast portion of Isle Royale). Why Thompson uncharacteristically ignored this nearby place is perhaps instructive. While speculative, it makes sense that Thompson left Isle Royale off the map on purpose—his purpose being to protect the exact location of the last North West Company vessel on Lake Superior, the *Recovery*, hidden in a backwater cove on Isle Royale during much of the 1812 War. It is ironic that the British decided to hide their last vessel during the war years on American territory. This underscores the tremendous lack of American knowledge about Isle Royale during this time.[62]

Published detailed geographic knowledge about Isle Royale remained rudimentary during the 1820s, 1830s, and early 1840s. Indeed, those who knew it—such as a few fur trade personnel—knew it by a different name: Isle Millions, sometimes Isle Milons, and occasionally Mileau Island. Clerks from the Fort William Hudson's Bay Company post would call the archipelago these alternative names as frequently as its recognized name today: Isle Royale. In the 1830s, American Fur Company (AFC) officials investigating the possibility of starting a commercial fishery also initially called it "Million Island(s)."[63] Available knowledge of Isle Royale, and indeed Lake Superior nautical knowledge in general, was so poor that AFC officials sought "decent maps" from London and had trouble procuring one. A useful lake map was so precious, and good information so hard to come by, that the AFC captain, Charles Stanard, had the chart he had been using specially mailed to his home prior to his summer reappointment.[64]

The lingering question of where exactly was the border between the United States and British Canada set surveyors from both countries into Lake Superior and the customary route of travel to Rainy Lake. American knowledge of Isle Royale was so meager that the leader of the American survey party, Lieutenant Delafield, reported the voyageur name for Isle Royale as "des Isle Mulo," and he recorded a voyageur tale of a buried treasure on it.[65]

In late September and early October, 1822, a party of American surveyors led by James Ferguson spent twenty days on Isle Royale. Based out of Fort William, they began by triangulating a position on the north side of Isle Royale. To do this, they split up their crew and started by establishing positions on Pie Island and Thunder Cape and making these positions visible on Isle Royale some twelve to fourteen miles away by starting fires at these distant points. The crew then circumnavigated Isle Royale in small boats, surveying it by log—a nautical means of ascertaining distance—to increase the accuracy of Ferguson's mapping. In a letter prior to going to Isle Royale, Ferguson reports it is "said to abound in harbors," and "Besides the main island there are groups of smaller Islands lying on its eastern and southwestern side." Ferguson and his draftsman, George Washington Whistler, produced the first accurate American map of the Island. The accuracy of their map of some locations—McCargoe Cove, Todd Harbor, Chippewa Harbor, Siskiwit Bay—suggests where they lingered or camped, while other locations are left blank: the mouth of Washington Harbor, Duncan and Five-Finger bays. Ferguson and crew were the first official Yankees on Isle Royale, and they may be the authors of some decidedly American place-names that then appear, such as Washington Harbor.[66] Ferguson and crew's hard-won knowledge of Isle Royale was mapped, but languished in government boundary-survey papers. Few knew of their work. On their carefully drawn map, they labeled the Island "Isle Royale or Isle Minongue."[67]

To augment the British international border-survey work, a British naval lieutenant, Henry Bayfield, and his crew were sent to chart Lake Superior in the mid-1820s. He and his crew are responsible for the last major step forward in documenting Isle Royale's coastline. Working from a new vessel, the *Recovery II*, and small boats, they charted and made soundings of major geographic features, including Isle Royale. Bayfield likely benefited from interactions with North West Company vessel captains, and Ojibwe and Métis guides employed by that company. His frequent stays and re-equipping at Fort William meant that he regularly interacted with men with much knowledge about the lake.[68] Bayfield concluded his admiralty survey of Lake Superior and had published a lake chart in 1828. However, like the American survey maps, it, too, was hard to acquire and thus had limited influence on others. In 1832, the British Society for the Diffusion of Useful Knowledge published a map of Lake Superior from the admiralty survey, with a clear rendition of Isle Royale. Major geographic features are rendered and even named, such as Siskiwit Bay, McCargoe's Cove, Canoe Rocks, Rock Harbor, Gull Island, Batteau Rock, and Passage Island. These names stem from the fur trade era—names known by men such as Captain Robert McCargo, who sailed Lake Superior for many years and must have had substantive knowledge about Isle Royale.

Despite this accurate rendering of Isle Royale by Bayfield and the Society for the Diffusion of Useful Knowledge, detailed American maps of Isle Royale would wait until the copper fever of the late 1840s. For example, John Farmer's 1836 map of Michigan gets the basic outline of Lake Superior and Isle Royale correct, but the position of the Island in Lake Superior is far to the north. Isle Royale appears to almost wall off the opening of Thunder Bay. Farmer's map is full of wonderful annotations about specific portages, canoe routes, and river names, but it is mute about Isle Royale place-names. Further, the American Fur Company's headlong attempt to establish commercial fishing stations at Isle Royale in 1836 and 1837 was originally stymied by their lack of knowledge of the Island, and whether or not it was American territory.[69] Even unsure of its name and unable to procure decent maps, the AFC geographical knowledge of Isle Royale remained spotty until the "copper rush" in the 1840s, and even then the interior of the island was sometimes left blank. In little more than one decade, between 1832 and 1845, the specific geographic knowledge of Isle Royale rapidly expanded, after languishing as terra incognita for almost 170 years.[70]

Ojibwe contributed significantly to the advancement of geographic knowledge about Isle Royale. The Jesuits Dablon and Allouez either traveled with Ojibwe or heavily consulted with them. Later knighted by the British Queen, Sir Alexander MacKenzie traveled with local guides, as did David Thompson. The American Fur Company factors interested in starting a commercial fishery on Isle Royale sought out Ojibwe help on finding the fish and locating promising fisheries. An Ojibwe man, Bahgwatchinnini, frequently guided HBC officials, or took Jesuit fathers to Isle Royale.[71] However, Ojibwe contributions to geographic knowledge about Minong did not result in many Ojibwe place-names. Only two—Siskiwit Bay and Chippewa Harbor—come from the early period. Unhappily, the long-term geographic and linguistic confusion about Minong would also be paralleled in whites' confusion about Ojibwe stories about Minong, the topic of the next chapter.

# **2** MINONG NARRATIVES

## Oral Tradition

Islands play a seminal part in Ojibwe oral tradition. In a determining myth, after the great flood a muskrat retrieves soil from the bottom of the lake and in doing so nearly drowns, but struggles and brings the mud to the surface. From that small clutch of soil an island is formed. The Ojibwe trickster Nanabushu breathes all over the newly created island, growing the earth. In at least one version, the mud from the bottom that re-creates the earth comes from near Isle Royale. In another myth, the narrator states, "The place where Minnabozho descended was an island in the middle of a large body of water." An island, too, is the grave for the Ojibwe trickster spirit.[1]

These narratives demonstrate that "islandness," in both a symbolic and specific sense, are essential to an Ojibwe worldview. In another legend, Nanabushu duels with an evil spirit, Hewer-of-His-Skin, who dwells in an island "in the centre of the great Sea." Eventually, through helpful advice, Nanabushu kills the evil manitou who had killed his parents and is "bent on destroying the

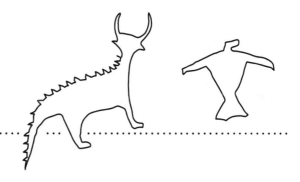

earth." Nanabushu then releases his parents and elder brother and replenishes the earth. The island on which this critical battle takes place is not specified, except that no one has ever gone there.[2]

The first sources about Isle Royale, as a specifically named place, are Ojibwe sacred stories. And since so little was known about the Island for many years, these narratives exerted a tremendous influence on what people thought about Isle Royale. But these narratives were not always understood or faithfully recorded. There is a tradition of Euro-Americans interpreting Ojibwe myth—in effect, asserting what they thought Ojibwe thought about Minong. These are divergent narrative streams about Isle Royale, although they are related. One narrative stream is authentic Ojibwe *aadizookaan*, or sacred stories.[3] A second type of narrative is derived from the first, but has a tradition of its own in print. Non-Indian renderings of the traditional Ojibwe narratives and beliefs make up this second stream. These have moved far from the original narratives, as they often mix stories, emphasize some elements over others, and interject new concerns, characters, and plotlines. These renderings have also been clipped into snippets and then retold almost like punch lines. All have had their effect on characterizing Isle Royale. To begin, we will look at the most authentic Ojibwe stories, then move to those retold and re-created by others.

Ojibwe storytellers told stories that include Minong, but it was rarely the central focus. Rather, Minong is more an appropriate place for critical events and adventures of the Ojibwe trickster Nanabushu.[4] There is a fundamental irony about Minong and storytelling. Ojibwe sacred stories were only properly told during the winter months. However, most Ojibwe used Minong during the summer months, and few Ojibwe were there in the winter. Hence, unlike most places in the region, there is not a strong storytelling tradition—that is, a tradition of sacred narratives told on Minong. Traditional stories were only told during the winter, because there was a "strong traditional belief that if stories were told in the summer, the animal manidoes (or spirit beings) would then hear themselves spoken of. Frogs, toads, and snakes were feared particularly . . . snakes may have been held in awe because of association with the mythological theme of the continuous warfare between the giant snakes and the Ojibwa culture hero, Nanabozho."[5] Despite the handicap of few storytellers overwintering on Minong, its distinctive geography, visible from the North Shore mainland yet distant enough to be otherworldly, made it a storytelling topic.

Stories were teachings. On long winter nights, the *aadizookewinini* (storyteller) would often act out the *aadizookaan*. And at one time, gift giving and a feast preceded storytelling, underlining its importance. Others began these myths with a sacred invocation.[6] During the times of *aadizookaan*, animals could talk and Nanabushu roamed the earth. There was a continuity between the natural and spiritual world. Through story, sacred matters were made evident in the natural world.[7]

Stories were also alive, each storytelling situation and audience calling forth a particular telling. Yet variation in telling remained in a traditional framework. Or in the words of one storytelling eyewitness, "It was clear to me, though, that every narrator added much of his own, and altered a good deal according to his taste. The same story has been told me by two different persons, and I have noticed considerable variations, although the groundwork and style of composition remained the same."[8] Stories were told to fit the situation, including nearby geography. Hence, Ojibwe writer George Copway would remark: "There is not a lake or mountain that has not connected with it some story of delight or wonder, and nearly every beast and bird is the subject of the story-teller." Both *aadizookaan* (sacred stories) and *dibaajimowin* (news or tidings) were thought to be true and were about "real events that occurred in the distant past."[9] It is the *aadizookaan* stories, often imperfectly recorded, that mention Minong. Minong being part of the yearly orbit of locations where North Shore Ojibwe might go, it naturally became a part of their storytelling focus. Or as one enthusiastic nineteenth-century traveler noted, Isle Royale "according to the Indians . . . is home of all the spirits of their mythology."[10]

Most influential in shaping knowledge of Minong, and also ripe for misunderstanding, was the earliest recorded "copper island" *aadizookaan* or myth chronicled by Jesuit Father Claude Dablon:

> The savages say that it is a floating island, which is sometimes far off, sometimes near, according to the winds that push and drive it in all directions. They add that a long time ago four savages came thither by chance, having lost their way in a fog by which the island is almost always surrounded.
>
> It was in the times before they had yet had any commerce with the French, and when they did not use kettles or hatchets. These men, wishing to prepare themselves something to eat, adopted their usual method. Taking some stones that they found at the water's edge, they heated them red-hot, and threw them into a bark dish filled with water. . . . While selecting these stones they found that they were almost all pieces of copper. Accordingly they made some use of them.
>
> Before setting out, they loaded themselves with a good many of these stones, large and small, and even with some slabs of copper, but they had not gone far from shore when a powerful voice made itself heard to their ears, calling in great wrath: "Who are these robbers carrying off from me my children's cradles and playthings?"
>
> That voice astounded them greatly, as they knew not where it was. Some say that it was Thunder, because there are so many storms there; and others that it was a certain spirit whom they call Missibiz, who passes among these

people for the God of the Waters, as Neptune did among the Pagans. Others say that it came from Memogovissiouis; they are, they say, marine people somewhat like the fabulous tritons or sirens, who always live in the water and have long hair reaching to the waist. One of our Savages told us he had seen one of them in the water.

However this may be, that astounding voice inspired such terror in our travelers' souls that one of the four died before reaching land. A short time afterward, a second was taken off and a third; so that only one was left, who, after returning to his country and relating all that happened, died very soon afterwards.

The Savages, all timid and superstitious as they are, have never dared to go there since that time, for fear of dying there, believing that there are certain spirits who kill those who approach them, and in fact, in memory of man, no one has been known to set foot there, even willing to sail in that direction.[11]

This last paragraph—largely an afterword—has been particularly influential and convinced many. Nor does it matter to subsequent re-users of this legend that originally it appears to be about Michipicoten Island (in eastern Lake Superior) rather than about Minong.

This story begs many questions: Who told the story to the Jesuits? And how widely known was the story—for example, was it heard at the Sault or during their exploratory trip around Lake Superior? Nor do we know the protagonist who is speaking. Is it a thunderer or Mishipizheu or perhaps even Nanabushu or some other spirit? The Jesuit narrative does not tell us who these important spirits are. Is it merely a story about what happens when Ojibwe are greedy for copper and they enrage its protectorate? Is it a warning that bad ends come to those wanting copper? And why is another version of this story not recorded later on? Clearly it includes Ojibwe characters, customs, and motifs: floating island, heating stones to cook, aboriginal belief in protecting copper unless properly handled, Mishipizheu, and marine people.

Mishipizheu, or Missibiz, is an important and frequently threatening Ojibwe spirit being. Alternately called the Great Lynx or underwater panther,

Mishipizheu is the controller of waters. When angered, Mishipizheu can roil the lake waters into deadly seas, or deluge the earth with a great flood. He can also calm the waters and is the keeper of fishes who can permit good fishing. Endowed with a serpent-like tail made of copper, Mishipizheu gave copper to the Indians. Understandably, then, Mishipizheu is associated with Isle Royale. And it was its tail of copper that was the strength and fury of Mishipizheu. Living in the deep waters plunging off the north shore of Isle Royale and Thunder Cape, and even off Hat Point at Grand Portage, he is an important spirit to address for any Ojibwe going to or from Isle Royale. Mishipizheu is also credited with having important medicinal powers. Through the Midewiwin—the principal Ojibwe religious ceremony—Mishipizheu gives powers to heal. For those participating in Midewiwin, receiving powers from Mishipizheu was useful and only became evil when matters got out of balance.[12] Mishipizheu is the most powerful of the underwater spirits, and in league with the snakes.

The Thunder Birds, once strongly associated with Thunder Cape and Mt. Josephine and Hat Point at Grand Portage, are the great enemies of Mishipizheu. With Mishipizheu in nearby waters, Thunder Being nearby in the air, and as we will see, Nanabushu on Minong, Isle Royale is the habitat of Ojibwe deities, some named and some not.[13] Importantly, in this *aadizookaan*, rendered to us by Jesuit fathers, Mishipizheu does not destroy the copper thieves in a storm when crossing the lake, its ultimate means of exercising power. Instead, his voice is enough to kill the first one, and after recounting the events, the fourth dies—both acts exemplifying the power of the spoken word. But the four who removed the copper failed in one critical matter: approaching the guardian of Michipicoten or Isle Royale copper with respect. Permitting the last to tell the story and warn others of the consequences of removing copper for frivolous purposes more effectively protects the copper in the future.

Unlike the story recorded by the Jesuits and from an unknown Ojibwe storyteller, we do know about the next Ojibwe narrator. John B. Penassie was a prominent and respected Ojibwe leader who eventually settled on the Fort William Reserve. He was born circa 1828 and died in 1910. He was of the Bullhead clan, a common clan among the Grand Portage and Fort William Ojibwe.[14]

He told the following story to linguist (and pioneering Indian anthropologist) William Jones. Jones entitled this "The Origin of Likeness of Nanabushu."

And so there for a long while continued Nanabushu. Now, once on a time to another place moved Nanabushu and his wife, and by his grandmother were they accompanied. Ever was Nanabushu in quest of game, for beavers too he hunted; a harpoon Nanabushu made, and that was what he used when he speared the beaver; spine-of-a-pickerel-fin is the name of the bone (point) which he made.

Now, once he found a place over here in the sea where the great beavers dwelt, they were very huge. Thereupon he said to his wife: "I am going after these beavers." Two were the place where those beavers dwelt: one was over here at Isle Royal [Minung], and the other was at Michipicoten Island. Now, those were the places where the beavers dwelt. He destroyed the beaver dwellings. Thereupon he wandered away, following the shore of this sea; some of the small beavers he killed, one large beaver too; but one other large beaver he did not find. So at last he thought: "Therefore I will destroy the (beaver) dam, no matter if this sea should go dry, for then I shall find the beaver."

Thereupon he had his grandmother go with him to yonder (beaver) dam [head of Sault Ste. Marie]. And when he had demolished the dam, "In this place do you remain, do you watch that the beaver does not float by with the current." He said to her, Ah! And then out the water flowed. So once more Nanabushu set out, following the shore of this sea. And then across to Michipicoten Island he leaped; and while he was standing over there, he saw an otter where the water was running low. Accordingly back across he leaped, whereat he slipped and fell in the mud. And so, when he rose to his feet, he laughed at the spot where he had left an imprint of his bottom; precisely like the form of his was the way it looked. "No matter, let my grandchildren that shall live hereafter have it to laugh at."

And when he pursued the otter, he pierced it with the fin spine of his harpoon. He was eager to eat, they say. "Accordingly before (proceeding further) I will eat the otter," he thought. And so, when he had flayed it, he built a fire; thereupon he roasted it on the spit. And when he had finished cooking it, he then sat down. He stuck (the spit into the ground) with (the otter still) on it. And then with a knife he sliced off one of the otter's ears, he then heard the sound of his grandmother whistling off yonder at the Sault. Thereupon leaping to his feet, he started off a-running. And when he came running to yonder Sault, "What (is it)?" he said to his grandmother.

Thereupon said the old Toad-Woman:[15] "It is gone, floating with the current went the beaver."

And so angry was Nanabushu, that he then smote his grandmother (till she was dead). And everywhere was the mountain reddened with blood. "Toad Mountain shall it be called," said Nanabushu.

Thereupon off yonder he wandered, looking in vain for the beaver, but he did not find it. So again he turned his way homeward, still yet was he roaming from place to place to find if yet there were any beavers; but he found none. Everywhere he went wandering, but without success; there where he had broken up the beaver dwellings, all that he saw were the logs which the beavers had gnawed to pieces.[16]

Nanabushu is an intrinsic part of Ojibwe *aadizookaan*; a cycle of narratives relate his many deeds. He is wise and foolish, brave and cowardly, haughty and bumbling, a taboo breaker and life giver. His adventures came in a mythic time before our own. Beavers were larger then and very desirable as food. Penassie is also relating in story one attribute of Minong in the early nineteenth century; namely, it was thought to be endowed with wonderful resources: beaver, reindeer, and fish—siscowet and whitefish. For example, a fur trader's letter in 1834 makes this clear:

Among Mr. Chapmanns crew here [at La Pointe] there is an old man who tells me that he knew the place well, he says the island is large say 50 or 60 miles, the Indians used to make their hunts there on account of the great quantity of Beaver and Reindeer. . . . It is there where the largest white fish are caught in Lake Superior.[17]

In Penassie's story, Nanabushu is behaving rashly and providing an example of actions not to do, such as trapping out beaver, beating his grandmother, and being distracted and losing track of his prey. Penassie made a distinction in this *aadizookaan* that so many non-Indians have not. Many have confused stories about Michipicoten with those about Minong. But Nanabushu uses both.

Nanabushu is also linked to Minong in other stories. In another tale, Nanabushu fights and defeats a giant who possessed Mount McKay and nearby Indians. In the course of the fight, the giant hurls "a great boulder across the water at his foe," or Nanabushu, who is on Minong. "This boulder became wedged below one of the cliffs of Minong. . . . This boulder, unlike all other rock formations on the Island, has been, to this day, the wonder of white men." After the fight, Nanabushu guards "the treasures of Minong."[18]

Talking with headman Penassie at his Fort William Reserve home, Indian scholar William Jones recorded two versions of the same story about Thunder Cape.

> Off toward the lake is a mountain. It is called "Thunder Cape." Clouds always hang about its top. It was common report that Thunder dwelt there, for the sound of it was always heard. Two men once thought that they would go and find the Thunder and see what it looked like. So they blackened their faces and went into a fast. In due time they set out for the mountain. Coming near, they decided that one go first, and the other afterward. So off one went. A heavy cloud hung over the top; but, strange to behold! The cloud parted, and the man saw two big birds with a brood of young. Fire flashed from the eyes of the big birds. The man had a good look, and everything about the birds was clear and distinct. Of a sudden the cloud closed together, and the view of the birds was shut off. He retraced his steps to his companion, and told what he had seen.
>
> The companion, of course, wanted to see too. He went up along to look. Presently the thunder cracked. The man went, and saw his companion dead, killed by the Thunder-Birds. Then he came home alone. Indians fear to ascend the mountain. They fear the Thunder-Birds.

The second story begins much like the first; however the ending is quite different. The first youth saw flashes of fire/light when the birds opened and closed their eyes. "One youth was content with what he had seen; but the other was curious to see more, and in an attempt to satisfy his desire he was killed by lightning. Thereupon the Thunder Birds went away from the place. One was seen for the last time upon Thunder Mountain (McKay Mountain). After the departure of the birds, the people ceased to be afraid when paddling about in Thunder Cape."[19] Is Penassie confused about the endings, one ending in fear and the other not? A closer examination reveals that the stories are not contradictory. Together they impart the lesson that one should be both wary of and reverential toward Thunder Birds on the mountain. The superficial variability of the stories is highlighted when we understand more about Thunder Birds.

Thunder Birds are powerful spirits. They once lived on Thunder Cape and Hat Point in Grand Portage, and though generally thought to be benign, they were not to be trifled with.[20] Reverent fear of the Thunder Birds was appropriate, even though they were most often helpful deities. As the preeminent spirits of the sky, the Thunder Birds often fought against the underwater spirits, particularly Mishipizheu, or underwater lynx, sometimes called an underwater panther. The Thunder Birds vanquished Mishipizheu and other underwater spirits with lightning. On occasion, Nanabushu and the Thunder Birds might fight together, threatening underwater spirits. As powerful spirits, Ojibwe warriors would seek their aid. As spirits of the sky, they are associated with the four winds and were sometimes appealed to for their help with medicine.[21]

The very different spirit beings—the Thunder Birds and Mishipizheu—express a duality in character. Thunder Birds were powerful spirit beings who often made life secure for the Ojibwe, but they were also to be feared. Even Mishipizheu, more often a dangerous life taker, also gave food in the form of fish to the Ojibwe. Fear and reverence often went together in Ojibwe *aadizookaan* and were not viewed as contradictory.

One *aadizookaan* told by an elder of White Earth, Minnesota, appears to link a spirit cedar tree, Nanabushu, and an island far out in Lake Superior—Isle Royale? In an aside to a story about a man trying to see his daughter who was dead, he seeks Nanabushu's help. Nanabushu is alive on "this island, far in the great lake (Superior). There they found Nanabushu. He was too old to travel, and on his head was a beautiful cedar tree. Beside him was a great round stone." The story tells, in part, the importance of cedar to Ojibwe and its association with Nanabushu. It also suggests that Nanabushu lives on an island in Lake Superior, such as Isle Royale, that is an intermediary step to other spirit places.[22]

Perhaps the most widely known part of a traditional Ojibwe narrative about Minong is the segment about it being a floating island. As a substantive part of the narrative recorded by the Jesuits, it is clearly an authentic part of the myth.[23] Yet the mythic assertion of the narrative, that the Island moves, defies acceptance in our rational and empirically based world. For those folks who have been to Isle Royale, the most characteristic feature of Isle Royale is its rocky nature. A Swedish-American fisherman with lifelong roots at the archipelago, Milford Johnson, used to call Isle Royale "the Rock." The Rock captured two essential qualities of Isle Royale, its isolation and its ever present bedrock, both above the lake and looming up from the bottom of the lake.

Most non-Indians who learn about "the floating island" quickly dismiss this as factually off-base and a romantic notion. This condescending conclusion is best encapsulated in one radio address: "The Island . . . was not properly anchored; when the wind blew from the north it floated across to the Keeweenaw, and when the south wind came, it drifted back to be near the Sleeping Giant on Thunder Bay. An island with such disgusting habits was no place for an Ojibway, who likes his terra very firma, so Uncle Sam was very welcome to it."[24] The floating-island notion is judged, if any thought is truly brought to bear, on whether this is a factual statement or not. It is rarely put in the context of sacred story, or perhaps of a symbolic statement common to oral tradition. It is rarely understood as "stories [which are] a circle of dreams and oratorical gestures showing the meaning between the present and the past in the life of the tribal people of the woodland."[25] Rather than viewed through Ojibwe mythic thought and as coming from a mythic time when transformations were possible, its chief function for a non-Indian audience has been to ridicule Indian thought about Isle Royale.

Floating islands, as a fantastic notion, had great appeal for non-Indians during the late nineteenth century. For example, the *Duluth Minnesotan* gleefully reported about a half-acre island with shrubbery, trees, and eventually one planted American flag moving around Duluth harbor in 1875. One such "floating island set sail from its anchorage a couple miles down the bay . . . [and] went through the canal out onto Lake Superior." Later, two floating islands were reported on Lake of the Woods in a normally staid Ontario mining publication.[26] The conclusion of this regional coverage was that the abnormal, that is, floating islands existed, but they were small curiosities and of trivial importance.

A different kind of explanation for the idea of "floating islands" is found in the German Johann Kohl's account of paddling on Lake Superior during the nineteenth century. While touring Lake Superior and making observations about Ojibwe life, he wrote:

> Twenty miles further to the north, glistened the broad expanse of the great lake at the entrance of the bay. There lay a tall, bluish island, with which the mirage played in an infinity of ways during our voyage. At times the island rose in the air to a spectral height, then sank again and faded away, while at another moment we saw these islands hovering over one another in the air. That the watchful Indians not only observe this optical delusion, but also form a correct idea of its cause, is proved by the name they give to the mirage. They call it "ombanitewin," a word meaning so much as this, "something that swells and rises in the air." They also make of it a very convenient and excellent verb, "ombanitie"—i.e., "there is a mirage around," to express which the French and English require considerable circumlocution.[27]

Mirages, if not floating islands, seemed to have been a favorite among early chroniclers. Thus, a government geologist would write, "When they said it was a floating island, it is probable they may have been misled by the vapors which surround it; they being rarified or condensed by the variable action of the sun's rays, made the island appear sometimes near and sometimes far off."[28] The same geologist wrote poetically of one mirage he witnessed in 1847.

I know not whether the season, when I had the opportunity for making my observations, was one remarkable for the frequency of Mirage. . . . At Rock Harbor, on several occasions, I observed the little islands and points on its outskirts most perfectly represented with inverted pictures of their entire forms, hanging over their summits, the images of the spruce and other trees which crown them, being seen with beautiful distinctness directly over their terrestrial originals, while the picture of a little skiff was one day seen represented beside the phantom island, the boatman in the sky appearing to row his bateau as unconcernedly as his original on the bosom of the lake.[29]

Many would be enchanted by mirages and their frequency at Isle Royale. Despite their charm and the frequency with which they were seen, a cultural gulf existed between the romance of mirages and the folly of "Indians talking about floating islands." Few whites appreciated how the keen observational powers of Ojibwe—noting mirages and thus floating islands—were incorporated into their stories.

For paddlers laboring to Minong, changing conditions made it effectively a "floating island." If lake conditions were ideal, or flat, the crossing was less laborious, shorter in time, and less harrowing. With smooth water, some paddlers were at Minong by noon on the day they left. If during a crossing, wind and seas grew, it made the trip longer in terms of time and effort and made landings more precarious. Despite these rational supportive arguments, in Ojibwe *aadizookaan* it was a floating island.

In another reworked published account, Minong is linked with the widespread myth of the great flood. Mishipizheu floods the earth, and Nanabushu creates a great raft, or Minong. A floating island, rather than Noah's Ark, is the means by which animals survive the flood. In this Ojibwe myth, after some failed attempts to bring earth from the bottom of the flooded world, a muskrat heroically brings a bit of dirt to the surface and the earth is remade. In this telling, the first earth comes from the lake bottom below the raft/floating island, called by the storyteller, Minong.[30] As a place of refuge from the great flood, Minong literally becomes "the safe place."

## Reworked Narratives

Exemplified by Longfellow's *The Song of Hiawatha*, there is a tradition of whites "mining" Ojibwe stories and rewriting them into their own. And like *The Song of Hiawatha*, almost all the stories available to us have some level of reworking or recasting of the original story. Just the act of ossifying a spoken story into writing creates a number of changes. Beyond this transformation of oral to written word, there is a wide-spread range of the degree of changes and liberties an author makes of a once authentic Ojibwe story. These stories range from radical inventions to others that use small portions of traditional elements in almost wholesale individual creations. Other changes are more nuanced where different (Euro-American) storytelling conventions creep into the retelling, perhaps even without the teller's being aware of the changes. Some quietly change the endings or tamper with characteristics of main characters. The following stories are so changed that they are quite distant from authentic Ojibwe stories.

The official tourism website for Thunder Bay refreshes and reworks elements of Ojibwe storytelling with a surprising assertion—namely, that there "once lived a great tribe of Ojibway Natives" on Isle Royale. In a subsequent detail, the story says, "Because of their loyalty to their Gods, and their peaceful and industrious mode of living, Nanabijou, the Spirit of the Deep Sea Water, decided to reward them. One day he called their Chief to his great Thunder Temple on the mountain and warned him if he told the secret to the white man, that he, Nanabijou would be turned to stone and the Ojibway tribe perish." The story contains errors, confusing Nanabijou and Mishipizheu, as well as new inventions such as a novel plot. The story plot turns on the loss of the secret to a Sioux scout and the whites' liquor-induced acquisition of the secret from the Sioux. The secret is the location of a great silver vein, what is now known as Silver Islet. Prior to the theft of the secret, the Isle Royale Ojibway used the silver to make silver ornaments, which were so beautiful they inspired greed among the Sioux. The result of the loss of the secret is Nanabushu turned into stone, in what is now known as the Sleeping Giant of Thunder Cape.[31]

Flowery in its language, the website story links Nanabushu and Isle Royale with a new addition: Sioux enemies. But much of the story dwells on the treachery, with the loss of aboriginal secrecy about where minerals are located. A similar story was told, with the same deathly consequences, about any North Shore Ojibwe who might lead whites to a silver mine in the Thunder Bay area.[32]

Henry Schoolcraft, Indian agent and student of Indian customs, provided another reworked Ojibwe narrative, though more modestly changed than the one above. Schoolcraft heard a tale about Mishosha, a magician of the lake, and his ability to fly by canoe in minutes to distant islands in Lake Superior. Mishosha is an "enemy of mankind," and through his sorcery, he threatens a boy on various islands. In one later printed version of the story, Minong is identified as an island where the boy is threatened by a giant sturgeon—which, however, he convinces to help him.[33] The boy thus escapes Minong to fight Mishosha on other islands. The problem with this later interpretation is that real places—Lake Superior and Minong—replace unnamed mythic ones. (Schoolcraft does not name any islands in the lake in either his original printed version or in his notes.) The mention of silver on the unnamed island, instead of copper, suggests that Minong is not inferred in this story. In this later, reinterpreted version, locations are identified with some well-known attributes that are not part of the original narrative. This later record fuses other Ojibwe mythic elements with Schoolcraft's Mishosha narratives. Thus, when you read a later Mishosha story, you think the South Shore Ojibwe were telling stories about Minong; but in reality, the modern writer has made these connections, not the Ojibwe storytellers of Schoolcraft's day, during the 1820, '30s, and '40s.[34]

As in the Mishosha tale, islands as a general idea become important symbolic entities for the Ojibwe. Nanabushu may descend from or live on an island on massive waters. A giant sturgeon or Mishipizheu is nearby, but mostly unseen in surrounding lake waters. These symbolic islands are a different type of place, even one that may move or appear to float on the surface of the waters. Minong geographically personifies islandness, a place of otherworldliness, a place of copper and the beings associated with copper. Crossing the lake becomes a figurative and, as we will see later, a literal test for Ojibwe. The symbolic character of Minong is enhanced by the very real transition it takes to go there. The importance of watery and symbolic transition from one place to another in Ojibwe thought is best illustrated by the names of two of the officiating priests at a Midewiwin ceremony. The *naagaanid*, or (canoe) bowsman, and *weedaakeed*, or steersman, guided segments of this life-giving ceremony.[35] For maritime peoples such as the North Shore Ojibwe, Minong was rife with symbolism and spirits in both a specific and general sense.

White authors borrowed from Ojibwe stories. The expression of the very real isolation of the first American copper miners and lighthouse keepers on Isle Royale led to the metaphorical borrowing of parts of traditional Ojibwe "windigo" stories. For example, the U.S. geologists doing the first report on Isle Royale were stranded for twenty-four days after they completed their investigation, waiting for a steamboat to take them to the Keweenaw Peninsula.[36] Being alone and away from help and society added a stress to living on Isle Royale, particularly in the second half of the nineteenth century, when there were three different mining eras. Apparently Ojibwe narrators told some windigo stories set on Minong. But there are no direct links between the quintessential windigo story and the heavily altered stories about Charlie and Angelique Mott.[37]

The legend of Charlie and Angelique Mott stresses themes of abandonment, hardship, native ingenuity, and stamina. The Mott legend helped characterize nineteenth-century Isle Royale as a place where fears of abandonment and starvation were very real.[38] The Euro-Americans reworked the meaning of traditional Ojibwe narratives when they reworked their content. Gone in the written versions were traditional Ojibwe concerns about the identity, sanity, and dangerous (cannibalistic) and asocial powers of a windigo.[39] In Ojibwe stories, the windigo threatens society and typically is killed to protect society from its cannibalistic threats. In this written story, Charlie Mott's windigo-like craving threatens one individual, his wife. Inverted in these written versions of the story is the near-windigo in the Mott legends as a French-Canadian, Charlie, instead of an Indian. The hero is Angelique Mott, an Ojibwe from Sault Ste. Marie who is wise enough to escape her husband's threats. The key point is that traditional Ojibwe narrative elements were used, reshaped, and fashioned into stories that the increasing number of Euro-Americans found interesting. These stories "say" that when Isle Royale was compared with the mainland, it was remote, different, and rudimentarily civilized.

When I and my husband Charlie Mott were first married we lived at LaPointe. Mr. Douglas, Mr. Barnard and some other "big bugs" from Detroit had come up there in the schooner *Algonquin*, looking for copper. From LaPointe Charlie and I went over with them, on their invitation, to Isle Royale. After landing with the rest I wandered a long way on the beach until I saw something shining in the water. It was a piece of mass copper. When I told the *Algonquin* people of it they were very glad and determined at once to locate it. They said if Charlie and I would occupy it for them Charlie should have $25 a month and I $5 a month to cook for him. Having agreed to the bargain we returned to the Sault to lay in a good supply of provisions. There I first met Mendenhall, the man who brought us into all this trouble. He said there was no need of carrying provisions so far up the lake and at so heavy an expense as he had plenty of provisions at LaPointe. When we got to LaPointe we found that this was not so. All we could get was a half barrel of flour (which we had to borrow from the mission), six pounds of butter that smelt badly and was white like lard, and a few beans. I didn't want to go to the island until we had something more to live on, and I told Charlie so, but Mendenhall over-persuaded him. He solemnly promised him two things: First, that he would send a bateau with provisions in a few weeks; and then, at the end of three months, he would be sure to come himself and take us away. So, very much against my will, we went to Isle Royale on the first of July. Having a bark canoe and a net, for a while we lived on fish, but one day about the end of summer a storm came and we lost our canoe; and soon our net was broken and good for nothing also. Oh, how we watched and watched and watched but no bateau ever came to supply us with food; no vessel ever came to take us away; neither Mendenhall's nor any other. When at last we found that we had been deserted and that we would have to spend the whole winter on the island, and that there would be no getting away until spring, I tell you such a thought was hard to bear indeed. Our flour and butter and beans were gone. We couldn't catch any more fish. Nothing else seemed left to us but sickness, starvation and death itself. All we could do was to eat bark and roots and bitter berries that only seemed to make the hunger worse. O, sir, hunger is an awful thing. It eats you up so inside, and you feel so all gone, as if you must go crazy. If you could only see the holes I made around the cabin digging up something to eat you would think it must have been some wild beast. Oh god, what I suffered there that winter from that terrible hunger, grace help me. I only wonder how I ever lived it through.

Five days before Christmas (for you may be sure we kept account of every day) everything was gone. There was not so much as a single bean. The snow had come down thick and heavy. It was bitter, bitter cold and everything was frozen as hard as a stone. We hadn't any snow shoes. We couldn't dig any roots; we drew our belts tighter and tighter; but it was no use; you can't cheat hunger; you can't fill up that inward craving that gnaws within you like a wolf.

Charlie suffered from it even worse than I did. As he grew weaker and weaker he lost all heart and courage. Then fever set in; it grew higher and higher until at last he went clear out of his head. One day he sprang up and seized his butcher knife and began to sharpen it on a whetstone. He was tired of being hungry, he said, he would kill a sheep—something to eat he must have. And then he glared at me as if he thought nobody could read his purpose but himself. I saw that I was the sheep he intended to kill and eat. All day, and all night long I watched him and kept my eyes on him, not daring to sleep, and expecting him to spring upon me at any moment; but at last I managed to wrest the knife from him and that danger was over. After the fever fits were gone and he came to himself, he was as kind as ever; and I never thought of telling him what a dreadful thing he had tried to do. I tried hard not to have him see me cry as I sat behind him, but sometimes I could not help it, as I thought of our hard lot, and saw him sink away and dry up until there was nothing left of him but skin and bones. At last he died so easily that I couldn't tell just when the breath did leave his body.

This was another big trouble. Now that Charlie was dead what could I do with him? I washed him and laid him out but I had no coffin for him. How could I bury him when all around it was either rock or ground frozen as hard as a rock? And I could not bear to throw him out into the snow. For three days I remained with him in the hut, and it seemed almost like company to me, but I was afraid that if I continued to keep up the fire he would spoil. The only thing I could do was to leave him in the hut where I could sometimes see him, and go off and build a lodge for myself and take my fire with me. Having sprained my arm in nursing and lifting Charlie this was very hard work, but I did it at last.

Oh that fire, you don't know what company it was. It seemed alive just like a person with you, as if it could almost talk, and many a time, but for its bright and cheerful blaze that put some spirits in me, I think I would have just died. One time I made too big a fire and almost burned myself out, but I had plenty of snow handy and so saved what I had built with so much labor and took better care for the future.

Then came another big trouble—ugh—what a trouble it was—the worst trouble of all. You ask me if I wasn't afraid when left alone on that island. Not of the things you speak of. Sometimes it would be so light in the north, and even away up overhead like a second sunset, that the night seemed turned into day; but I was used to the dancing spirits and was not afraid of them. I was not afraid of the Mackee Monedo or Bad Spirit, for I had been brought up better at the mission than to believe all the stories that the Indians told about him. . . . But the thing that most of all I was afraid of, and that I had to pray the hardest against was this: sometimes I was so hungry, so very hungry, and the hunger raged so in my veins that I was tempted, O, how terribly was I tempted to take Charlie and make soup of him. I knew it was wrong; I felt it was wrong; I didn't want to do it, but some day the fever might come on me as it did on him, and when I came to my senses I might find myself in the very act of eating him up. Thank God, whatever else I suffered I was spared that.

One time in particular I remember, not long after Charlie's death, and when things were at their worst. For more than a week I had had nothing to eat but bark, and how I prayed that night that the good God would give me something to eat. . . . The next morning when I opened the door I noticed for the first time some rabbit tracks. It almost took away my breath and made my blood run through my veins like fire. In a moment I had torn a lock of hair out of my head and was plaiting strands to make a snare for them. As I set it I prayed that I might catch a fat one and catch him quick. That very day I caught one.[40]

Angelique Mott is the only Indian character, let alone hero, that populates Isle Royale literature. Later, John Linklater and his wife become known to a few, but Angelique is the dominant Ojibwe character. However, her ingenuity and perseverance do not lead to a reward of a lasting relationship with Isle Royale. Instead, when given the chance she leaves the Island and never returns. Contrary to what might be expected, Angelique, the Indian, lives, and the white man, Charlie Mott, dies. The end result, however, is that Isle Royale is not a home to either. The timing of Angelique is remarkable; she stands between two eras, that of the aboriginal prehistoric miners that remain unnamed and that of the Euro-American miners who possess the Island and stake their mining claims. As an individual, she heroically survives; but because of greed and treachery, she is dispossessed of the Island.

Much like the case of mapmakers drawing Lake Superior and Isle Royale from afar, most of the writers of the Mott legend came from down-state or the South Shore—while the people who might be telling authentic windigo stories set on Isle Royale lived on the North Shore. We have no authentic examples of windigo stories set on Minong, despite a well-known place-name "Windigo" on the southwestern end of the Island. This wide geographic separation between story making and subject permitted free interpretations and wild renderings of parts of an Ojibwe storytelling tradition.

In contrast to the Mott legend and Mishosha tale, narratives appearing in print substantiate that there are many positive connotations about Michipicoten/ Minong. It is a good place, a place of huge beaver and copper, a place safe from the deluge, and sometimes Nanabushu is there. For some North Shore Ojibwe, fish from Minong were particularly pure and had a superior taste.[41] Talking with Ojibwe and clerks at the Hudson's Bay Company post, the U.S. border surveyors "expected to eat a lot of fish" while on the Island. The meticulous land surveyor of Isle Royale, William Ives, confirmed its reputation as rich in resources. For example, in his survey records he writes: "The surrounding reefs are said to be the best places for siskowit that are known in Lake Superior." A year later, working on the western end of Isle Royale, he writes: "There are a number of the ridges that have very handsome sugar bushes on their summits." And while in Washington Harbor, Isle Royale, he notes: "The bay in the N.W. corner of section one had been used for a fishery by the American Fur Company. There is considerable many fish around the islands and in the harbor, such as trout, white fish, siskowit, herring, sturgeon, pike, etc. and all of the best kinds."[42]

For North Shore Ojibwe, Minong was a place of many "good" resources: fish, reindeer (or really woodland caribou), and beaver. Traditional Ojibwe narratives also recognized a darker side of Minong, sometimes with threatening powers. Thus, in the narrative recorded by Jesuit father Claude Dablon, it was also a place where people might get hurt if they behaved improperly, either while voyaging to the Island or while on Minong. Grand Portage elder Ellen Olson reported that if caught there and forced to overwinter, the people might get hungry. And windigos might reside there.[43] In short, Minong, like Mishipizheu and even the Thunderers, exhibited a duality of character. It was both good and threatening. It was rich in resources, yet you had to be careful not to be stranded there. It was rich with copper, but copper had to be handled carefully to be useful. It was an arduous paddle or dangerous crossing on the ice to Minong, yet it was also a place where Nanabushu might come to trap or battle with giants. Mishipizheu might cause a great deluge, but Minong was safe ground for the primordial animals, thus making the way for humans. And Mishipizheu frequented the inky blue-black deep waters off Minong, but guarded the Island from unprincipled exploitation.

Out of these remakings and misunderstandings of traditional narratives came another corollary, namely, that Lake Superior Ojibwe believed copper to be taboo, best left alone and thus not used. But copper, much like Minong, is multivalent in meaning and not easily reduced to one polar attribute. For example, there is an equal tradition of copper being very positive. An account in the *Jesuit Relations* about Lake Superior and its resident "savages" states:

One often finds at the bottom of the water pieces of pure copper, of ten and twenty livres' weight. I have several times seen such pieces in the Savages' hands; and, since they are superstitious, they keep them as so many divinities, or as presents which the gods dwelling beneath the water have given them, and on which their welfare is to depend. For this reason they preserve these pieces of copper wrapped up, among their most precious possessions. Some have kept them for more than fifty years; others have had them in their families from time immemorial, and cherish them as household gods.[44]

Copper was carried in Ojibwe medicine bags, and "wonderful power is ascribed to them."[45] In a legend of long ago, a young Thunder Bay Ojibwe brave, armed with extra spirit and a special tomahawk of copper, kills a great serpent fighting for the Sioux, leading to a rout of the Sioux. In this case, the copper tomahawk is a specially powerful weapon which helps preserve area Ojibwe.[46] Ojibwe historian William Warren's accounts make it clear that copper was highly revered, used in the Midewiwin ceremony, and used in one instance to record sacred clan history.[47] One Fond du Lac headman held a small piece of copper—Mishepizheu's tail—to remain healthy and free of bad dreams, and for help in hunting bear.[48] A German visitor to Lake Superior in the 1850s, Johann Georg Kohl, recorded a revealing tale of a trader and an Ojibwe chief concerning copper. The chief, wanting to demonstrate his friendship, even hoping for kinship, reluctantly reveals the location of a large copper mass to the trader. Even after propitiating the copper boulder with tobacco and all the goods he had been given by the trader, the chief felt extreme misgivings about his role in revealing the copper boulder. Further, he felt he experienced many misfortunes because of showing the trader the copper boulder. According to the biased account, only conversion to Christianity brought the chief peace.[49]

Despite this Ojibwe tale warning against revealing secrets about minerals, we know Ojibwe were not fearful to work with copper. For example, at a minimum, four Grand Portage Ojibwe worked at the first copper mine at Todd Harbor, Isle Royale. And they brought their families with them and overwintered there. Grand Portage elder Ellen Olson remembered Ojibwe men who worked at the Isle Royale mines and liked it. The Jack Scott family, who were part Ojibwe, mined copper at McCargoe Cove. There are other Ojibwe families who participated in the mining ventures. And a few Portage men were guides helping prospectors find copper and silver deposits, particularly on the mainland. Clearly, North Shore Ojibwe were not fearful of copper and indeed, when available, took jobs working in or around the Isle Royale copper mines.[50]

Despite the great interest in copper and participation in copper mining on Isle Royale, a shift in the Euro-American interpretation of Ojibwe evaluation of copper begins with the first Jesuit narratives. For some, they believed the point of the story was that copper was poisonous and thus best avoided.[51] This belief is often grafted together with the observation that the utilitarian use of copper by Lake Superior Ojibwe stopped with the availability of European-made kettles and other metal objects.[52] Thus, according to this interpretation, since copper made one sick, and there was an alternative once traders arrived in the area, historic use of copper ceased. A good example of this view is expressed in an official record of the Michigan Department of Conservation.

> The recent Indians very evidently felt an awe of the island and did not make it a habit to frequent it, whether from some untold incident . . . such as a storm on the way to the Island, a pestilence on the island or from some obscure tradition handed down from the dim past we do not know. Perhaps this awe might be ascribed to that far-off day with some cause dictated the abandonment of the mines by the primitive copper seekers.[53]

Could there be an alternative explanation to why segments of Ojibwe narratives about Minong appear to ward off interest in the Island because of its dangerous nature? Could these narrative segments or motifs have been used to scare off others—other Indians and whites—so as to ensure unhampered use of the Island? Another descriptive section from the Jesuit Relations answers these questions in great part. Father Dablon, writing between 1669 and 1671, wrote that on the same North side, is found the Island which is most famous for copper, and is called Minong [Isle Royale]; this is the one in which, as the Savages had told many people, the metal exists in abundance, and in many places. It is large, and is fully twenty-five leagues long; it is distant seven leagues from the mainland, and more than sixty from the end of the Lake. Pieces of Copper mingled with the stones, are found at the water's edge almost all around the Island, especially on the South side; but principally in a certain inlet that is near the end facing the Northeast. . . . In the water even is seen Copper sand as it were; and from it may be dipped up with ladles grains as large as a nut; and other small ones reduced to sand. This large Island is almost all surrounded with Islets that are said to be formed of Copper. . . . One, among others, is only two gunshots distant from Minong; it is between the middle of the Island and the end that faces the Northeast. Again, on this Northwest Side, far out in the lake there is another Island, which, because of the copper in which it abounds, is called Manitouminis [Island of the Spirit]; of this is it related that those who came here formerly, upon throwing stones at the ground, made it ring, just as brass is wont to ring.[54]

This narrative makes quite clear that early Native stories of the rich copper deposits were told openly to the Jesuits and likely other Frenchmen. Indeed, there appears to be both a tradition of touting the copper riches, and some individuals who felt reluctance to talk about it. And it appears some Natives and Frenchmen talked about it positively, hardly warning off others. The narrative is also interesting in that no group is associated or specifically named with Minong. It is unclear if this is because Father Dablon knew it was open for use by any group, or simply that he did not know who was using it at the time. But on the whole, this narrative would likely hasten use of Minong rather than retard it. It clearly contradicts the notion of Minong as a malevolent place and copper as dangerous.[55]

Faithful reports on the Ojibwe sense of awe and respect for copper get "stretched" into an interpretation that its sacred nature meant it was totally off-limits. Thus, an early historical account states, "It is a common belief among the Indians that there is a great abundance of copper on the island; but they dare not go there."[56] This rewording and reinterpretation of what Minong and copper meant to the Ojibwe was particularly active during the nineteenth century, when the miners/entrepreneurs' enthusiasm for the copper resources of Isle Royale and the Keweenaw Peninsula of Michigan was running high. Certainly there was an economic incentive to downplay the value of copper resources on Minong during treaty negotiations (as discussed in chapter 4), but there also appears to be another collective symbolic action by Euro-Americans to discount Ojibwe interest in Minong and copper.

Non-Ojibwe did not comprehend the breadth of possibilities, character, and depth Ojibwe understood in their manitous, resources, and Minong. Non-Ojibwe truncated and simplified the richly symbolic spirit beings such as Mishipizheu, Thunderers, copper, and even Minong. A radical reduction took place. For non-Ojibwe commentators, Minong could not be both good and bad; rather, they would choose one attribute. Its reputation ran on superlatives at one moment—unending supplies of fish, or an island made of copper—to a desolate island with resources so poor that no one could live on it.[57] This sorting and seizing upon one quality appears to have been more radically employed in non-Ojibwe interpretations about Mishipizheu, which might be an evil manitou or a foolhardy superstition. For example, a copper miner's wife from Island Mine had this to say about the many Ojibwe she saw during the 1870s: "In 1877 quite a few Indians lived on the island, which they normally refused to do unless white people were there too because they had become superstitious about the copper and believed the island to be occupied by an Indian Devil."[58]

The influence of Christianity impacted Ojibwe religion and deities such as Mishipizheu and Thunderers. During the 1850s, Catholic priests put pressure on traditionalists such as Attikons (Addikonse) to renounce their "pagan" faith and become Catholics. Jesuits convinced converted family members to not speak to those who had not converted. The Mt. Rose Catholic Church—the oldest log church in Minnesota—was built on top of the former grounds of a Midewiwin lodge. Practitioners of traditional Ojibwe religion were literally driven away from Grand Portage and ridiculed by Catholic priests. The telling of *aadizookaan* was discouraged. For several Ojibwe, some of the traditional spirit beings lost their original significance. As Christian conversion advanced, there was a narrowing of meaning of traditional symbols and understanding about traditional spirit beings. The growing negativity about aboriginal beliefs made for some changes. Thus the Spirit Little Cedar Tree becomes in English, "The Witch Tree." Mishipizheu became the "Matchi-Manitou" or evil spirit, leaving aside its original Ojibwe character as the keeper and provider of fish or medicine. Other traditional ideas were trivialized, such as a literal interpretation of "the floating Island." While from an Ojibwe perspective, Minong and Mishipizheu had to be approached respectfully, as mysteries and risks were part of crossing to the Island and residing there and living upon its resources.[59]

One dominant assertion in non-Ojibwe commentary about Ojibwe use of Isle Royale stresses Ojibwe fear of the lake and of the Island. The presence of Mishipizheu—now converted to the evil spirit—and other mysteries in these narratives appear to have given fuel to the misunderstanding that Ojibwe feared the lake. And since mystery was an unacceptable explanation to these commentators, they supplied their own. They assumed that if Indians could get hurt in the crossing or in the use of Minong, they would stay away.[60] Among these non-Ojibwe, Isle Royale became a "spooky place."[61] Other Ojibwe narratives were corrupted or wildly misunderstood. In one, Isle Royale becomes "haunted" for Ojibwe.[62] It transformed from a safe place and good place to a place where supposedly Ojibwe were fearful to venture. Certain whites would try to capitalize on these fears when a copper miner on the Suzie Island archipelago (off Grand Portage) tried to frighten Ojibwe residents, warning that if they went to Isle Royale, they would not come back.[63]

Before long, the darker interpretation of what Minong meant to Lake Superior Ojibwe overwhelmed its positive connotations. Stories were repeated over and over until virtually everyone "knew" that North Shore Ojibwe and their kinsmen rarely dared to paddle across the lake to live or fish or hunt on Minong.[64] What was reverence, awe, caution, and belief in animistic spirits for the Ojibwe was interpreted by many non-Indians as being scared of the lake and the Island. In effect, "sacred" became "scared." The good place or beautiful place of North Shore Ojibwe became, in whites' accounts, a place where the Ojibwe believed the devil dwelled and was thus avoided.

This misunderstanding is encapsulated in a conversation I had with Mrs. Ellen Hanson.

Mrs. Hanson and her husband were close friends of the Linklaters—a friendship nurtured through her husband's and Jack Linklater's work together as game wardens in Northern Minnesota. Together the families bought a fishery in the 1920s on Birch Island, within McCargoe Cove on Isle Royale. Mrs. Linklater, or Tchi-ki-wis, was Ojibwe and had family roots at Minong. Mrs. Hanson recounted that she and Mrs. Linklater were afraid of the lake: "It was too much water for me." Mrs. Hanson observed that Mrs. Linklater was "superstitious" about Lake Superior. But they would paddle a canoe down McCargoe Cove regularly to go berry picking or on their way to the ridges for lunch, or merely to poke around at the abandoned copper mines and pits. Although it was very sheltered from the big lake, Mrs. Linklater always paddled close to shore or followed the shoreline. Why Mrs. Linklater preferred to travel close to shore is the point. Mrs. Hanson thought it was because she was fearful of the lake, while at another point she noted that Tchi-ki-wis always kept a lookout for plants to harvest for making cedar mats and other items for sale and use at home. Mrs. Hanson was surprised that Jack Linklater supposedly talked his wife into co-purchasing the fishery because of her "fear" of the lake. Despite these "fears," Tchi-ki-wis regularly traveled to Isle Royale, as her grandparents had done decades before she and her husband bought the Birch Island fishery.[65]

Conventional wisdom and written narratives have their own kind of logic. For example, it is an easy step to infer that if the Ojibwe did not live on the Island, that meant they were scared of it. A high-water mark of assertions about Ojibwe being afraid of the lake, scared of Isle Royale, and not frequenting Minong is when, during the 1930s, the drive to establish Isle Royale as a national park was in full swing. Articles repeatedly portrayed the Ojibwe as superstitious, as the following quote illustrates: "The Indians called it Minong and believed it to be a floating island where lived the Great Spirit. They seldom visited it, turning their canoes away from its rugged walls. Often, they believed, in fog or haze, the Island would disappear, to be seen in another location."

Following this line of argument, if no one lived there in historic times, then no one usurped this Island archipelago from its original owners.[66] Or, from a non-Indian perspective, if Indians truly believed the Island to be "floating," this belittles their relationship to it. Belittling Indian knowledge of it makes it easier to appropriate it through "rational" thought, such as ownership.

Ojibwe *aadizookaan* and non-Ojibwe narratives have been entangled to create a public story of Isle Royale. This intermixing public dialogue has been disinclined to recognize authentic Ojibwe myths. Rather, it has been more likely that *aadizookaan* were corrupted and reshaped than appreciated as is. Few authentic Ojibwe myths are well known, leading to an unexamined assumption that Isle Royale was not particularly well integrated into an Ojibwe religious worldview. This is not an accurate conclusion. Ojibwe sacred narratives envelop and incorporate Minong. Thunder Cape was a place of hierophany for Thunder Birds. Mishipizheu swam in waters off Isle Royale and likely was a steward of its copper. There are likely Ojibwe sacred places on Minong especially associated with copper. For example, tobacco was regularly placed on large masses of copper, such as those found on Minong.[67] The Island would be freer for the symbolic appropriation by non-Ojibwe if it was bereft of a sacred meaning for North Shore Ojibwe. It would be freer for others' use, too, if it was free of Ojibwe use. The next chapter will demonstrate the intricate and long-standing use of Minong by North Shore Ojibwe.

# 3 ON MINONG

ake Superior was a precarious road to Isle Royale for Ojibwe of the North Shore.[1] It had also been a pathway for the precursors of the Ojibwe. But the road was not obvious to the latecomers, the Euro-Americans. The stir of finding ancient mining pits scattered throughout the Island gave whites a rationale for why people might venture over the sometimes ferocious watery road to isolated islands. An unvoiced logic was afoot; it was only worth it for people to venture to Isle Royale for copper. That logic bonded the Euro-American miners with their aboriginal predecessors. Initially it helped obscure the notion that there might be more reasons to travel to Isle Royale than just copper.

Scholars and amateur archeologists have been fascinated about prehistoric copper mining on Isle Royale and the Keweenaw Peninsula for over a hundred years. Archeologists from the Smithsonian Institution, universities, state government, and the National Park Service have examined and pondered the Island's remarkable prehistoric past. Indeed, one of the principal recommendations for including Isle Royale as a national park was based on its distinguished and

numerous mysterious archeologies.[2] Early interpretation of these pits with copper veins led to extravagant claims of lost races, a Viking fort, and Egyptian miners.[3] In contrast, the historic descendants of these copper miners have not fired popular or scholarly interest. Instead, until now, most have even assumed that the Ojibwe did not use the Island. As supposed nonminers, they were thus nonusers of Isle Royale.

Most striking in the archeological evidence of this late prehistoric period is the use of Isle Royale by multiple groups, perhaps even at the same time.[4] If used at the same time, Isle Royale could have been, in effect, like Switzerland for the various groups. No one group assumed exclusive use, each having peaceful access to the copper resources. Or if one group made a claim, it did not own these resources exclusively for long, or perhaps permitted others to go there and use them. These different groups were likely ancestors of some historic Indian groups that became traditional enemies, such as the Dakota, Ojibwe, Huron, and Cree. The evidence of different prehistoric groups on the Island fits well with recently discovered archeological evidence on the Canadian North Shore.

A number of groups moved east and west along the North Shore, especially to trade. When a prehistoric group paddled to the Island, they brought stone tools made from rocks such as jasper taconite and gunflint silica collected in the Thunder Bay area. Some even brought their own pottery, while others stayed long enough on the Island to find clay, and shape and fire pots. While on the Island, they ate beaver, caribou, loons, painted turtles, lake sturgeon, trout, whitefish, snowshoe hares, blueberries, strawberries, and bearberries. Returning to the mainland, they often carried copper in the shapes of rectangular bars, awls, beads, and even hooks. These late prehistoric peoples traveled to the Island relatively frequently, and traveled throughout the Island, living in many locations that are campgrounds today.⁵

At the dawn of the historic period, there was much change afoot. Groups were moving, or had recently moved. Archeologists believe the numbers of Native Americans using Isle Royale diminished, perhaps with a regional decline in population. About this time another change occurred: Isle Royale became the exclusive domain of Ojibwe, versus the diverse groups of the late prehistoric period. The few datable objects from the early historic period are a French clasp knife, beads, tinkling cones, gunflints, and a couple of Jesuit rings.⁶ Ojibwe might acquire Jesuit rings as an inducement to convert to Christianity. Or, a ring might be acquired as a trade item from a priest who did not have other desirable goods to trade. Because they became a trade item with area Native Americans, finding one distant from known missions means they were likely brought to the location by Native Americans rather than Jesuits. Ojibwe using Isle Royale between 1750 and 1800 probably brought the two rings found at McCargoe Cove. The rings exemplify cultural change, trade, and travel from the east to the west and to the Island, and they underscore the importance of McCargoe Cove as the entry point to Isle Royale.⁷ The two brass rings, one with clasped hands and the other with glass inserts, also exemplify what we do not know about who brought them there and exactly what they were doing.

During the historic period, a few sites on the north side of Minong were used most often. Earlier, prior to the arrival of whites, there appears to have been a more widespread use of the archipelago. McCargoe Cove remained the primary entry point to the Island. Groups of paddlers entering the narrow cove must have been relieved to be in sheltered water with a number of good campsites. They would also be pleased to meet up with those who had been on the Island, and to hear where caribou might be hunted, where fish were plentiful, and in later years where a job might be had.[8] Archeologist Caven Clark believes the early historic use of the Island continues the prehistoric pattern of primarily using and living on Minong in the spring through the early fall.[9]

Small Ojibwe extended family groups canoed to Minong, stayed there for the summer, and returned prior to autumn, when the lake is more commonly dangerous. For example, "Illinois" and his band (mostly his family group) left Fort William for Isle Royale on June 2, 1831, and were back at the Hudson's Bay Company post by August 2, 1831.[10] Crossing back at this time also permitted the family group to travel inland to harvest wild rice.[11] Because the groups were small, use of the Island appears to be light or nonintensive. However, the historic records from the early 1800s suggest that trips to the Island were frequent, perhaps a yearly event. The lack of any evidence of wild rice or maize brought to the Island suggests an intermittent and seasonal use of Minong.[12] By the time of the historic copper mining, in the late 1840s, Ojibwe material culture was very difficult to distinguish from Euro-American material culture.[13]

Euro-American use intensified in the late 1830s and 1840s with the first commercial activities (fishing and mining) on Isle Royale, and documentary sources became more plentiful. It is possible that the patterns of use of Minong by North Shore Ojibwe may have changed by this time, but with little documentation we are hard pressed to comment on any hypothetical changes. From a Euro-American perspective of the 1840s, Isle Royale was a backwater as compared to the South Shore settlement and mines, particularly on the Keweenaw Peninsula. For example, during the winter of 1849–50, Isle Royale and the North Shore were cut off from communications with the outside world. This isolation made the gift of a precious rooster and hen from the Todd Harbor miners to their visiting priest more noteworthy.[14] With the intensification of copper mining and the coming and going of lake vessels, by 1854 the isolation had temporarily abated with a regular exchange of employees. One consequence of this increased traffic was the arrival on the Island of the same illnesses found on the mainland.[15]

Up until the 1830s and '40s, Americans knew little about Isle Royale, or who used it. For example, in 1839 Indian agent Henry Schoolcraft wrote a paragraph-long report about the "Chippewas and Kenistenos [Cree] of Grand Portage and Isle Royal." In it he laments the poor state of geographical and ethnographic knowledge. "The number of Indians occupying these islands [Isle Royale, and other islands lying east and south of 'Keministiquoia, or old Grand Portage'], their means of subsistence, and the condition of the trade, whether carried on exclusively by American citizens in conformity with law, or by foreigners in violation of it, constitute topics of pertinent inquiry."[16] Only a year later he made a startling assertion that there were two hundred Chippewa living on Isle Royale.[17] All now accepted his statement that it was Chippewa or Ojibwe, rather than Cree, occupying this area. But his assertion that Chippewa were specifically occupying Isle Royale was immediately disputed. Hence, a U.S. Indian Service annual report stated:

> Isle Royale was first resorted to as a fishing station in 1837, and since then has been used in the autumn and spring, by the white and half-breed population in this vicinity as such, but has never been inhabited [sic] by Indians. Indeed, a barren rock island of 45 miles in length, by about 8 to 15 miles from the mainland, covered with small scrubby timber, destitute of game, with the exception of a solitary herd of reindeer, and almost no soil, it is incapable of supporting even an Indian population.[18]

A Methodist minister and newly appointed Indian agent at La Pointe, Alfred Brunson, espoused a view echoing Schoolcraft's. Three years later, Brunson wrote that there was a band of Ojibwe living on Minong who must be factored into treaty negotiations.[19]

## Ojibwe Subsistence Use of Minong

North Shore Ojibwe used Minong in two very different ways: for subsistence use, and as a place where they could find employment and earn cash. Subsistence use means harvesting Minong's resources for food, material culture—clothing, shelter, canoes/boats, trade—or for religious purposes. Subsistence use was typically during the summer months. Occasionally a small family group would reside on Minong for a full year. In one important respect, subsistence use was directly related to looking for work on Isle Royale. Quite often, Ojibwe were employed in jobs on the Island that were in some part built upon subsistence knowledge of where specific resources were (fish and timber) and how to harvest them, or a more generalized knowledge of "making do" in the woods. For example, we know that Ojibwe mining families used cross-Island trails to walk from one site to another in the 1840s. They likely had a major role in establishing a number of the trails, or perhaps they used trails already in existence.[20] Ojibwe also used subsistence derived knowledge to trap beaver, otter, and other animals while working for commercial enterprises on the Island. Subsistence activities included plant gathering, hunting caribou, trapping, and maple sugaring—plus spearing, netting, and setting fish weirs.

"The greater part of the Indians went off to fish for their livelihood along the lake"—so wrote a Fort William clerk in 1824. Few fish were caught in early June and summer near Fort William, so many Ojibwe dispersed to better fishing grounds. And summer fishing was comparatively good at Minong. Indeed, fish were so common that the early copper miners heavily relied upon it, to the point that when it was not served at the Todd Harbor boarding house in 1854, it was remarked "the fish was missing."[21] Ojibwe fished Minong waters with an ingenious variety of gear, depending upon exactly where they were fishing (deep waters, small streams, or in shallow near-shore waters).[22] For example, Ojibwe caught or speared shallow-water-dwelling fish such as pike, walleye, sturgeon, and white and redhorse suckers during the summer months. While fishing, they might also opportunistically catch painted turtles. At other encampments, near deeper water, Ojibwe might net trout, whitefish, bourbot, or longnose suckers. Ojibwe would troll for trout as they paddled their canoes from one location to another. Trolling with hooks was common enough that a Fort William clerk sent off a noted fisher, Scandagance, with forty hooks and line to catch trout in mid-July. Inland, Ojibwe made small fish traps or weirs to catch brook trout in streams. The cold (and deep) water fish of Isle Royale were appreciated for their "wonderful taste" and were relatively abundant and easy to catch. Ojibwe appreciated the fish as being especially pure.[23]

There were many productive locations for fall fishing off the mainland coast and islands. Hence, most Ojibwe left Minong by early August, precluding them from catching the deeper-water fish such as trout and whitefish that are dispersed (often in deeper water) in the summer months.[24] Most Ojibwe caught their "lean" and siscowet trout and whitefish in gill nets from mainland family fishing locations. Gill nets were the most productive fishing technology used by Ojibwe in Lake Superior waters. And traditional ways of preserving fish persisted as late as 1905, when a Grand Portage family caught trout and dried and smoked them on wooden racks erected at Isle Royale. They then transported the dried siscowet or "fat trout" in barrels to birch bark–lined pits in Wauswaugoning Bay, where they would be preserved in the cool or frozen subsurface conditions.[25]

It is highly likely that North Shore Ojibwe used other gear—such as wooden decoys, gill nets used under the ice in the winter, and spears for torch-lit nighttime fishing from a canoe. For example, there was a brisk trade at Fort William for "fish darts," the metal ends of spears used for fishing.[26] Hook-and-line fishing was also frequently used in the wintertime, off thick ice into open water. Ojibwe fishers would have to be more than a quarter mile offshore to be in wintertime trout habitat. We do not have records of hooks and lines being used at Minong, but it would be unusual if they were not used there.[27] Nor do we know if North Shore Ojibwe harvested the relatively plentiful wild sarsaparilla on Minong to put on their nets to make them more effective.[28]

The lack of fibrous plants in the area that were typically used to make gill nets was a fishing hardship. Two of the three preferred plant species customarily used for making nets (nettles and basswood) are not found on Isle Royale and were only found on the periphery of their traditional use area. Fortunately there was plenty of northern white cedar on Minong and nearby. The inner bark of the northern white cedar was made into fiber and then knitted into gill nets. Besides making their own nets, North Shore Ojibwe also likely traded with their kinsmen outside the area for net twine made of nettle or the inner bark of basswood. When traders came, new net fiber was introduced, and this material was popularly received. North Shore Ojibwe made it a priority to trade for cotton twine nets that were an even more effective fishing technology than those nets made of native materials.[29] Despite the advantages of using purchased net twine, knowledge of making nets from native plant materials persisted well into the 1900s.[30]

North Shore Ojibwe knowledge of fish stocks was extensive. They knew and could report to the Fort William clerk that large trout typically spawn off the eastern side of Thunder Cape at the Shangoina Islands from October 7th to the 18th. Or, they would tell the clerk in charge that "little trout" began to spawn off the Kaministiquia River–mouth shoal roughly on September 19.[31] This detailed knowledge of fish biology and behavior is best illustrated by North Shore Ojibwe knowledge of siscowets, or fat lake trout, found at Isle Royale.

Ojibwe prized siscowet trout. One Ojibwe wrote in 1850, "Sis-ka-way . . . is the sweet fish of the lakes . . . [and] esteemed a very great delicacy."[32] Rich in oils, siscowets were a welcome addition to their sometimes lean diet and could be used for a variety of purposes. Once rendered in kettles over a fire, sometimes 70 percent of their weight would be made into oil. Traditionally, siscowet oil was used as a balm for dry skin, a base for medicines, a leather softener to make it pliable, a food mixed with berries and meats, and a substitute for bear grease for other purposes. Mixed with charcoal and tree pitch, it was used to gum birch-bark canoe seams. Thus critical repairs to canoes could be made on Isle Royale with siscowet-oil-based pitch, a life-or-death matter for those paddling the lake.[33] In other words, its versatility made it highly sought after. However, the deep water–dwelling fish were beyond the reach of most Ojibwe fish-catching techniques during most of the year. They typically inhabit Lake Superior waters deeper than 200 feet, or deeper than other trout, whitefish, or sturgeon. Indeed, during the summer months, most siscowet live in water depths of 400 or 500 or 600 feet.[34] And, when most trout concentrate and spawn in relatively shallow waters, siscowet typical spawn in water deeper than 180 feet. This depth was beyond the reach of Ojibwe and Euro-American gill nets at the time.[35]

Siscowet are like lean lake trout (and whitefish) in that they spawn (and thus concentrate in catchable numbers) in the fall. The fall months are the time of rough water or dangerous seas on the Big Lake. Historic fishing for siscowet, then, could either be a formula for failure (because of depth), or death, or great catches.

Despite the troubles in catching siscowet, North Shore Ojibwe led the American Fur Company to "Sickawaite Bay" because of its siscowet fishing potential.[36] The original Ojibwe place-name Siskawekaning has been reworked into the part Ojibwe and English place-name, Siskiwit Bay. The Ojibwe name casts light on the preexisting Ojibwe knowledge of a special and highly prized resource. It is also a place-name of a defining geographical feature of Isle Royale, which was heretofore unnamed by Euro-Americans. "Siscowet" was quickly adopted into English. The American Fur Company leaders were particularly interested in "siskeywet fishing," noting they were a "very fine, rich fish." They sold for a higher price than whitefish or trout, making them more desirable.[37] The overall value of siscowet to the American Fur Company is best testified to by their naming of one of their prized schooners *Siskawit*.[38] Isle Royale had a reputation for large trout, whitefish, and "siskawaite."[39] This reputation continued as Isle Royale land surveyor William Ives noted that the string of islands off Houghton Point were the "best places for catching siskowit that are known in Lake Superior." The Isle Royale siscowet were reported to be so fat that "one fisherman made two and a half barrels of oil from the heads and leaf fat alone."[40] H. H. McCullough's large operation rendered siscowet into oil by boiling them. "I stayed eight days at Siskawet Bay [*sic*], where all the people of Pigeon River and a large number of those from Immaculate Conception were assemble for fishing. The fish that the Saulteux call Siskawet are extraordinarily abundant there. . . . It is probably for the oil that can be extracted from it; this fish is very greasy and can only be eaten with potatoes."[41] Isle Royale siscowet enjoyed a special reputation and were marketed to Midwesterners salted or as rendered oil.[42]

There is a problem with this story. According to orthodox biological judgment, siscowets should not be in most of Siskiwit Bay because much of it is too shallow, or less than two hundred feet deep. Nor should siscowets be in Siskiwit Bay when they were being caught in the late summer months. Geologist Douglas Houghton noted that Ojibwe were catching siscowet in July—an unheard-of time in most contemporary biologists' opinions. The American Fur Company sought to start up their Isle Royale fisheries in mid-July, with the main station within Siskiwit Bay. McCullough's fishing operation was particularly active in late July and August, after which some North Shore Ojibwe would return to the mainland in early September. Both the American Fur Company operation and McCullough built and operated fishing stations within Siskiwit Bay—at Paul Islands, Checker Point, Wright Island, and outside of Hay Bay, despite its navigational drawbacks for deep water–drawing vessels.[43] Summer fishing for siscowets, especially in the shallow western half of Siskiwit Bay, defies biological wisdom.

The only conceivable explanation for this is that there was a discrete population of unusually behaving siscowet in Siskiwit Bay. This is not unheard of, as other early Lake Superior fish populations demonstrated more variability than those today. The nineteenth-century siscowet must have spawned earlier in the season and in shallower water than today's siscowet. It is possible, even likely, that little of this population of early-spawning siscowet survived until today—or if they did so, they are in much diminished numbers.[44] Ojibwe fishers knew of this discrete siscowet population and led commercial fishermen to them. The value of siscowets for Ojibwe subsistence and commercial fishers created the impetus to establish fish stations in harrowing places, such as the Paul Islands.[45] These two small islands provide a good boat landing in the channel between, but deep waters plunge off to the Siskiwit Bay side. It is exposed to the fury of the lake on the other side. It is a daunting but productive location. McCullough thought this location productive enough that he purchased the forlorn outpost, it being some of the first property purchased on Isle Royale.[46] The plentiful siscowet oil on Isle Royale was highly sought-after for both subsistence and commercial reasons, as fish oil soared in price—from 25 cents to $1.25 a gallon—during the Civil War.[47] McCullough ran a siscowet rendering plant to produce lubricating oils at Wright Island. So many siscowet were rendered at Wright Island that one bay was white with the trout skeletons.[48]

Learning of this unusual fish population illustrates how North Shore Ojibwe knowledge of biological phenomena on Minong was clearly detailed and highly honed.[49] They lived along Siskawekaning long enough, and experimented with fishing there, to figure out the unusual behavior of this localized stock of siscowets. The highly detailed and place-specific subsistence knowledge became the basis for a commercial enterprise that unfortunately appears to have overharvested this fish population.

Many fur traders especially esteemed whitefish as table fare. However, at certain times of the year they are difficult to catch. A rare, river-running variety of whitefish was caught in the Kaministiquia River in September and October. At one time, when the whitefish run was right, 2,297 small whitefish were caught in a seine net in the river in one day. Other large catches were also made.[50] Despite this unusual run of whitefish, they were more often in short supply during midsummer. Hence, the whitefish North Shore Ojibwe caught off McCargoe Cove and brought back to Fort William were considered a delicacy. The North Shore Ojibwe discovered the gravel bottom off McCargoe Cove, which is perhaps the single best whitefish habitat at Isle Royale. On the other hand, there is little evidence that the shimmering herring schools found in many Isle Royale harbors and bays were harvested much. There are historical records of herring being caught in gill nets and then used as bait in Thunder Bay. It is likely that this technique was also tried at Isle Royale.[51]

Sturgeon likely congregated on shoals in Isle Royale waters. They were most often found in or nearby Washington Harbor and McCargoe Cove.[52] Ojibwe speared sturgeon for both subsistence and commercial purposes. John Tanner and his party speared sturgeon on Minong in the 1790s. Grand Portage families continued, on an interim basis, to harvest sturgeon into the 1800s.[53] Though relatively rare, if caught, the size of the sturgeon made for many meals. One sturgeon harvested in Wauswaugoning Bay appeared to a teenager "as the size of a submarine."[54] And in the 1880s, Jack Scott and his Grand Portage family were hired by a Wisconsin company to spear sturgeon in "the shallows around Isle Royale. But butchering and rendering the huge, 300 to 400 pound carcasses was more than he could stomach; after a few weeks, his disgust at the slaughter forced him to quit."[55] Today, like the siscowet of Siskiwit Bay, there are few of these large and long-living fish in Isle Royale waters. At one time Ojibwe oral tradition noted the epic-sized sturgeons at Minong. But sadly, slow to mature and breed, their numbers have not recovered. [56]

Euro-Americans brought with them a new way of preserving fish—by salting them—that made Isle Royale more attractive as a summer location. With salt, the abundant fish caught in July and August could be put in a salt brine in barrels and kept for the hungry months of the winter.[57] Ojibwe would then take their barreled fish back to the mainland and move on to harvesting wild rice. Prior to the adoption of salting, fish had to be dried (that is, smoked) if caught in the summertime. Smoking took more time than salting, and spoilage remained possible if truly hot weather came. One problem that developed with salting fish was the occasional lack of useable barrels, and less often a shortage of coarse salt used for brining.[58] Salt became precious enough that it was even used as a gift from the Hudson's Bay Company to the Espagnol a North Shore Ojibwe chief in 1829. And yet coarse salt became common enough that once a bear on Pie Island adjacent from Isle Royale broke into a barrel of salt, got it wet, and ruined the supply. The "freeman"—not a direct employee of the Hudson's Bay Company—shot and killed the bear after it fought with and killed one of his dogs. The advantages of salting fish and using manufactured net materials amplified a prior pattern of use, but did not totally replace this earlier pattern.[59]

North Shore Ojibwe seem to always have hunted caribou while on Minong. But Isle Royale caribou became especially precious after the large game on the mainland was decimated in the early 1800s.[60] Mainland moose numbers dropped throughout the first half of the 1800s, making the Isle Royale caribou herd an attractive, if distant, alternative. While obviously smaller than moose, a caribou is better than twice the size of deer, with upwards of six hundred pounds in a large individual. John Tanner narrated the first report of hunting caribou on Minong from his family's sojourn in the 1790s. Even dressed caribou skins were deemed valuable in the fur trade and were actively traded at the North West Company's Fort William post in 1805. It is not known how many Isle Royale woodland caribou skins were traded there.[61] When Ojibwe hunters were on Minong, they would search for woodland caribou that are normally dispersed along shorelines—of Lake Superior and inland lakes. Once found, the animals would often attempt to flee into the water.[62] Others may have been stalked after they were found at the dozen or so natural salt licks at Minong. Ojibwe might smoke the roots of bearberry and purple stem aster as a hunting charm to attract caribou to the hunter. To hunt properly, a hunter would ask the caribou for their help in a song: "Upon the one that is hoofed do I call for help. Upon the one that is hoofed do I call for help." Ojibwe believed that after the caribou was killed and its soul released, the caribou returned to its former self and continued life as before.[63]

One Ojibwe hunted caribou—or what the HBC clerks' called "Rein Deer"—on Minong with dogs.[64] The HBC clerk at Fort William briefly noted, "The Bete and family arrived from Isle Royale. He killed only 3 Rein Deers."[65] Non-Ojibwe especially enjoyed caribou, as it was a welcome addition to a diet heavily dependent upon fish.[66] North Shore Ojibwe hunted caribou on Isle Royale in both the summer and winter, as the previous and following 1851 record illustrates: "Occasionally, in severe winters, the ice does extend from the Canada shore to Isle Royale, which is from fifteen to twenty miles distant; so that the caribou and moose cross over on it to the island, whither the Indian hunters sometimes follow them over the same treacherous bridge, liable, although it is, to be suddenly broken into fragments by surges of the lake."[67] While a number of Ojibwe hunted caribou, they were not always successful. Medishean, his oldest son, and their families overwintered on Minong and "made a very poor hunt." A few years earlier the Fort William clerk reported, "They say there are no caribou there this summer and suppose they all crossed to the mainland last winter."[68] Still, if overwintering on Minong, caribou would become a precious source of food. North Shore Ojibwe would sometimes dry the caribou meat, pound it into a powder, and mix maple sugar into it. Food was often made with dried berries and caribou (or bear or moose on the mainland) grease.[69]

Harvesting beaver, like hunting caribou, was a venerable activity on Isle Royale. The pressure to trap beaver is not surprising, given Isle Royale's proximity to Grand Portage—you can see it from the porch of the North West Company's Great Hall—and the premium put on prime beaver hides in the intercontinental fur trade. Luxuriant beaver fur—particularly the inner fur—of the cold winter months was most valuable. Beaver were commonly trapped by "breaking up the house [during which] . . . the family make their escape to one or more of their washes. These are to be discovered, by striking the ice along the bank, and where the holes are, a hollow sound is returned. After discovering and searching many of these in vain we often found the whole family together, in the same wash. . . . From the washes, they must be taken out with the hands."[70] With beaver being relatively hard to find on the mainland, still over 849 beaver skins were traded at Fort William in 1816. By the 1820s beaver was "extirpated everywhere on the shore of Lake Superior" except for Isle Royale.[71] In contrast, Minong had a reputation for large beaver. Three decades later, McCullough's "fishermen" trapped beaver on the Island all winter. Sometime after this trapping episode, Isle Royale beaver were essentially, if not actually, extirpated.[72] This lag between extirpations on the mainland versus the Island suggests a surprisingly lighter-than-expected trapping pressure on Isle Royale beaver. Perhaps this may be explained, in great part, by the fact that most Ojibwe had vacated Minong for the mainland in late summer, and trapping was a late fall and winter enterprise. In effect, the trapping pressure would be light, not because Ojibwe were not using Minong, but they were using it at a non-trapping time. And yet the effects of trapping, hunting, and migration of some animals (caribou) not only to, but also from the island meant sometimes Minong was barren, or empty of game. One year in the late 1800s, Grand Portage Ojibwe could not find hare, caribou, or beaver to hunt or trap.[73] And even when the game was abundant, it was a long harrowing trip to and from the Island, diminishing its attractiveness.

At least for significant interludes of time, North Shore Ojibwe families made maple sugar from the large stand atop and between Greenstone and Red Oak ridges. Making maple sugar at Minong appears to be common, but not an annual event. This stand and those along the North Shore are precious because they are the northern most extension of these trees and thus the availability of maple sugar. Each spring, families at Fort William and Grand Portage resorted to "their" sugar bush.[74] But a letter by Jesuit father Fremiot in 1851 suggests mainland sugar-maple groves were fewer and less productive than before. He noted the "sugaring grounds are beginning to thin out and people must travel a great distance to find new ones." And in 1830 L'Espagnol and his band were traveling as far as Grand Marais to make sugar.[75] In 1848, government surveyor William Ives frequently noted evidence of sugar-maple camps on Isle Royale. For example, on May 31, atop what is now called the Greenstone Ridge, he noted "an acre cleared and a very handsome sugar bush around it. . . . There are a number of the ridges that have very handsome sugar bushes on their summits."[76] The same year, a government geologist wrote: "We next went to the head of Siskawit Bay, and taking an Indian Trail ran up to the maple ridge."[77] Another observer believed there was an "aboriginal trail" from Washington Harbor to the sugar bush.[78] And in the 1870s, when the Island Mine was in operation, miners and their families would encounter Ojibwe making maple sugar in this same general location.[79] Indeed, in the 1870s some of the copper miners would buy or trade with the Ojibwe for maple sugar. There appears to have been continuity in use, particularly by a "Chief Yellowbird" and his extended family.[80] The expectation of returning for another maple-sugar season must have led to a family or two caching their sugar-making equipment in the bush. "Each family had their little area where they had their little sugar bush. And they kept the things there, nobody ever bothered them. They had piles of birch bark that they used. Birch bark cups and dippers . . . and their iron kettles . . . just covered them up."[81] Another stimulus to producing maple sugar was that it became a trade item that Fort William was to provide to other posts. For example, from 1837 to 1854, HBC officials stipulated that Fort William would produce typically three to four thousand pounds of maple sugar for other posts such as Michipicoten that did not produce any.[82] Freeman Michel Collin, with strong roots in Grand Portage, typically would produce "1000 [pounds?] weight" in maple sugar that was traded with the post.[83] One pioneering naturalist estimated a Grand Portage family would annually make one hundred to five hundred pounds of maple sugar.[84] Thus, there was both subsistence and trading stimulus for producing maple sugar. And while we do not have written sources about Ojibwe making maple sugar on Isle Royale prior to 1848, this is more likely because of a lack of records than the activity not occurring.

North Shore Ojibwe conducted other subsistence activities at Minong. Angelique Mott survived a winter without food by snaring snowshoe hare, or what they called simply "rabbits."[85] Typically a woman's task, men only became involved when the catch was bartered with someone. For example, Ojibwe men traded fifty rabbits at Fort William in 1835, and another group arrived with a "load of rabbits" in 1836.[86] Women typically snared rabbits in the winter. Rabbits were caught both for food and for making warm rabbit-skin blankets. On one occasion the Fort William clerk wrote: "In winter their sole dependence for subsistence is on rabbits."[87] Ojibwe on Minong traded rabbits with miners for other foodstuff.[88] The well-known fluctuations in snowshoe-hare populations also had their effect, such as during the winter of 1831 when rabbit numbers were low. North Shore Ojibwe "can hardly snare enough to support themselves."[89] Another low cycle of rabbit numbers occurred in the early 1850s, leaving North Shore Ojibwe scrambling for precious winter food.[90] To be successful, family groups would have to move their snaring locations before one was exhausted. Occasionally they would have to move great distances to another productive rabbit-snaring area.[91] If rabbit numbers on the Island were low, North Shore Ojibwe might have to leave Minong and make a dangerous winter crossing back to the mainland. More likely, any group assessed rabbit numbers prior to making the decision to overwinter at Minong. However, among North Shore Ojibwe, snaring rabbits was a complementary subsistence activity with their mainstay, fishing.

Great flocks of passenger pigeons would occasionally darken Isle Royale skies during the late summer season. Likely attracted to the acorns from the small stand of oaks on Red Oak Ridge, a flock might opportunistically descend on the Island. If Ojibwe had nets with them, they would be hastily strung up in the sky and hundreds of pigeons thus collected.[92] Ojibwe also collected and ate seagull eggs, an activity that became a tradition among some Isle Royale lighthouse keepers.[93]

Sadly, there are few notations about Ojibwe use of plants on Isle Royale. Harvesting plants was customarily a woman's activity, so few male clerks and writers noted it. And, harvested plants as part of a subsistence regime were of less interest to the commercially minded HBC clerks and early copper miners and investors. Yet plants were undoubtedly harvested as much or more than animals. We know plants were harvested for food, trade, to make beautiful craftwork, and likely for medicine. One time an Ojibwe guiding a Jesuit priest stopped and harvested "wild leeks." The plant specie, what we would call "wild chives," is rare in Minnesota. It is found, however, at Grand Portage, on Pigeon Point, Suzie Islands, on the Fort William Reserve, and on Isle Royale. Grand Portage Ojibwe sought to domesticate wild chives as it was found in their garden plots (and in rich soil) distant from its preferred "natural" location in rocky areas near Lake Superior shores. Another early naturalist claimed the French introduced it to the area.[94] Its presence in Grand Portage gardens and this claim of introduction raises the possibility it could have been brought over to Isle Royale by Ojibwe people.

Sweetgrass, an important plant for Ojibwe, is commonly found at Grand Portage, and most recently found in a moist meadow of Washington Island, the largest, closest island to Grand Portage and in an area known to be used by Grand Portage people. It was used in ceremonies, smoked for pleasure, and used in wonderfully smelling coiled baskets. It, too, could have been brought to the Island. And while there is no record of it, arrowhead, or duck potato, is common on Isle Royale, and Ojibwe likely ate this common plant. [95]

Blueberries also are common on Isle Royale and were customarily collected and then dried over a fire. They did not, however, take the trouble to go to Minong for the sole purpose of picking berries.[96] But the bulk of Ojibwe use of Minong occurred during the midsummer berry season. One Island Mine copper miner remembered, "You never lost any thing by giving to an Indian for he would always repay you back with some game, fish, or berries."[97] Berries could be dried, stored, and thus used later. A scaffold was built over a fire and the drying process begun in the morning. By evening the berries were sufficiently preserved to use later.

Indirect records of plant use are evidenced by what Ojibwe made while on the Island. Ojibwe paddling a canoe in Rock Harbor traded "a mat made of cedar bark" to miners. As late as the 1920s, Tchi-ki-wis, an Ojibwe woman married to Jack Linklater, harvested cedar bark and wove the bark strips into intricate geometric patterns in cedar mats. She then traded or sold a number of these mats, some of which are now in the Isle Royale museum collection. A grass mat, also likely made by Tchi-ki-wis, is in the Isle Royale collection. Tchi-ki-wis made her own dyes from roots and bark to color the cedar and grass mats.[98] She also regularly made miniature birch-bark canoes and paddles and worked on leather craft such as belts, pouches, and moccasins.

There are few detailed accounts of Ojibwe trips to Minong. John Tanner's account, circa 1794 or '95, of his trip to Isle Royale gives us more details than most. When destitute, Tanner and his family were befriended by an Indian who fed and assisted them. Later, Tanner and family were invited to go to Minong, where he "could provide all that would be necessary for our support." After a dawn-to-dusk paddle to get to Minong, their host immediately made good on his word and speared two sturgeon. While on the Island, they harvested gull eggs, hunted caribou, and caught beaver and otter. Tanner's description is vague, but they likely traveled to either Siskiwit Lake or perhaps Lake Desor. They also met up with a large group of relations of their host. They fared well on the Island.[99]

## Traditional Ojibwe Religious Activity

Traditional Ojibwe religion, as well as Christian faith, was practiced on Minong. Aboriginal religious expression was of many types and has great antiquity on

Isle Royale, beginning (in the sense of being documented) with a prehistoric dog burial in Rock Harbor.[100] Ojibwe continued to perform special rites throughout their travels to Minong.

Perhaps the most common religious expression was the appeal to the manitous for safe crossing on either shore of Lake Superior. Sprinkled through the records detailing lake crossings are references to offerings and sometimes prayers. One Ojibwe recalled "the gathering on the Canadian shore and the ceremonies, dance and appeal to the spirits deemed necessary before the trip [to Isle Royale] could be taken." Tobacco was offered when praying to the manitous for compassion. This practice, of asking for compassion and offering tobacco, continues today for Ojibwe traveling the lake.[101] To appease and spiritually feed Mishepizheu for the manitou's favor and calm waters, Ojibwe would on rare occasion sacrifice a dog. With the dog sacrifice, "they cannot offer their deities and spirits a finer sacrifice." It was not necessary to have a religious expert present to do so.[102]

In June 1853 a shamanistic rite was held at the mouth of Washington Harbor, Isle Royale. A Jesuit father witnessed, and approved, the physical halting of a "shaking tent ceremony" because he deemed it sorcery.[103] Joseph Memashkawash, a young Ojibwe man, with help from Pierre Attikons, was preparing a "shaking tent" divination ceremony. As a *djessakid*, Memashkawash was trained to communicate with a manitou for some essential purpose. The purpose might be finding game, finding the cause of illness, or obtaining critical knowledge. The starting basis of the *djessakid* knowledge came from a powerful dream. The ceremony was considered very powerful and could be harmful if not approached carefully. With Father Fremiot present, Memashkawash's grandfather intervened, and he destroyed his grandson's drum. Bits of the drum were thrown into the water.[104]

It does not appear that the largest—in terms of participants—of traditional Ojibwe religious ceremonies, the Midewiwin, was held on Minong. Sometimes a week-long ceremony, it was preceded by purification rituals and a sweat lodge. The Midewiwin is a complex and highly symbolic rite and includes songs, charts, medicine bags, and elaborate knowledge. The Midewiwin taught its members the ways of gaining power over sickness and healing others, and is called a "breathing life ceremony." With eight progressive levels of knowledge, *Mide* priests learned the medicinal power of plants. If the Midewiwin was ever held on Minong, it would have been during the 1850s when hundreds of North Shore Ojibwe were there fishing—but we have no record of it. The "Grand Rite" of the Midewiwin was planned for in advance, held during the summer months when large numbers of Ojibwe would gather and prominent Mide priests were present.[105] More likely, the small family groups that fished and worked on Minong would not hold a Midewiwin ceremony. And in one case, one Ojibwe family group, who were Baptists, left Fort William for Isle Royale when a Midewiwin ceremony was held.[106]

## The Case of the *Recovery:* Kinship and Alliances

Ojibwe sought out relationships with powerful allies. In many cases, this would take the form of forging real or metaphorical kinship with powerful strangers in their midst. Ojibwe and fur traders created some trust and obligation by creating these relationships.[107] This propensity to make alliances, honor kinship among real or fictive kin, and extend trust to those in these relationships helps explain the curious abandonment of the North West Company's vessel *Recovery* in McCargoe Cove during the 1812 War. At risk for the Ojibwe and British fur traders during the war was a reliable supply line by the traditional route westward across the Great Lakes. Having already lost most of their Lake Superior fleet due to conscription for the British War effort, the North West Company was desperate to retain their one remaining vessel, the ninety-ton *Recovery.*

Explaining why it was cached in McCargoe Cove and why it was not dismantled for its valuable metals suggests another type of aboriginal connection to the Island. Built in 1809 at Fort William, the *Recovery* was customarily captained by Robert McCargo. McCargo, likely with the approval of his superiors, cached the ship in the deep and narrow cove now bearing his name. It was a wonderful hiding spot, rarely used and hardly known, as the ship would have to get through the Z-shaped rocky entrance and sail a mile or more to its terminus. The ship was not visible from the open lake. "There the ship was unrigged, the masts removed, and the hull carefully covered with brush and the branches of trees." It lay cached for perhaps as many as three years.[108]

This action raises two questions, namely, (1) why did the North West Company choose McCargoe Cove to hide the *Recovery*? and (2) how did it stay untouched for three years? The answers to both of these questions likely involve Ojibwe women. A relatively new arrival in the area, Captain McCargo opportunely found the Lake Superior backwater to hide the *Recovery*—Isle Royale. Captain McCargo's knowledge of the cove could have easily come from his Ojibwe "country" wife or her family. Robert McCargo formally married Nancy McKay sometime before 1816, and prior to this time they likely had a "country marriage." More importantly, Nancy McKay's mother, Marguerite Wadin, a Métis woman, had remarried by this time to the chief factor of Fort William, John McLoughlin.[109] The important point here is that McCargo married into a native family with roots in the area, and he became a kinsman with the influential chief factor John McLoughlin. It is through these relationships that it makes sense that McCargo and the North West Company learned about "McCargoe Cove."

At this time, iron was a highly desirable and precious commodity in northwestern Lake Superior. A large vessel such as the *Recovery* would hold a large supply of iron. For example, when the first *Recovery* was abandoned, it was burned to recover the nails and iron holding her together. It is significant that the second *Recovery* was not stripped of its iron by Ojibwe while it lay unguarded.[110] Knowledge of Ojibwe kinship helps explain why the *Recovery* was not salvaged for valuable metals. McCargo's father-in-law, the chief factor, was not only powerful because of his fur trade position but also because he was married to an influential native woman. McCargo, too, was married to a local native woman. These kinship ties would partially safeguard the *Recovery*. The North Shore Ojibwe alliance with the British during the War of 1812 also helped safeguard this vessel.[111] Because of this service and a military alliance with the British during the 1812 War, North Shore Ojibwe leaders were given British medals to honor their alliance. If it had been an American vessel left at McCargoe Cove at this time, it would have been stripped of all its useful resources. At minimum, the *Recovery* example contrasts the vast geographic knowledge of North Shore Ojibwe and their allies with the dim American knowledge of Isle Royale and the North Shore at that time. Ironically, the "front door" of Minong for North Shore Ojibwe, McCargoe Cove, was unknown by name or by location to the Americans.

## Ojibwe Families on Minong

Ojibwe travelers to Minong tended to be repeat users, that is, family groups that had a tradition of living on Minong. One frequent user of Isle Royale was Illinois and his small band, including some or all of his three sons.[112] Interestingly, the Fort William clerk once noted that Illinois's sons were at one time "Nipigon Indians."[113] However, they spent most of their time in the area recognized as the domain of the North Shore Ojibwe. Illinois was also known as Miskouakkonaye, Red Coat, and John Ininway. Later, a very elderly Illinois participated in the "Robinson Treaty" negotiations in the late 1840s, signed in 1850, and was recognized as a lesser Fort William chief. Illinois liked to receive a "chief's coat" from the traders as recognition of their esteem. He preferred a coat that was "always red, with gold braid and metal buttons. . . . [He was] rudimentarily a Baptist . . . [and] fancied himself an orator." During treaty negotiations, he dressed in full regalia and carried a long pipe.[114] He would live past 1860 and reportedly beyond the age of one hundred.

Illinois and his sons were like many others moving about and searching for productive hunting and trapping areas. They were also looking for locations with a competitive edge in dealing with traders. For example, an 1824 report from Fort William states there were "too many [Indians] for that part of the country [Nipigon] & for the furs about it." And there was an incentive for the Lake Nipigon Indians to come and see our "Montreal gentlemen" at Fort William.[115] Remember, too, that some of Illinois's children (both sons and daughters) were married to North Shore Ojibwe families. And area Indians continued to move widely in this period. So, Nipigon Indians suddenly appeared at Lac La Pluie, as did the Fort William chief on one occasion. Their principal objective was to test traders and see if they could get better trading terms or receive a more liberal debt in trade goods.[116] Illinois's sons did exactly this during the winter of 1834–35, testing the traders' willingness to extend debt at both Fort William and Lake Nipigon.[117] After the 1820s, Illinois and sons are no longer mentioned as Nipigon Indians and become accepted members of the Fort William/Grand Portage Indians.

Illinois's oldest son, L'homme du Sault, or man of the Sault, regularly traveled to Isle Royale in the 1820s and '30s. From the HBC clerk's perspective, L'homme du Sault was "one of our principal Indians" and was known as a productive trapper. For example, in May 1838 he brought "upwards of 130 skins of prime furs" to trade at Ft. William. Like his father, his exact birth date is unknown, but he was a father by 1816.[118] Like many successful Ojibwe men, he had multiple wives, most likely two, with one being considerably older than the other. His family became a stalwart at the Todd Harbor copper mining operations. L'homme du Sault and his relations likely participated in the building of a short tramway, road, dam, docks, blacksmith shop, rudimentary houses, and in the mining of more than eighteen tons of almost pure copper. His death date is not clear, but a Jacob Picke (or Pishke), thought to be L'homme du Sault, died at Isle Royale in December 1851. His blessing was later held at Fort William Mission on May 15, 1852. The Pishke family remained at the Pittsburg and Isle Royale Mining Company operation at Todd Harbor after L'homme du Sault's demise.[119]

One of L'homme du Sault's daughters, Margeurite Webanbonok, married pioneering copper miner Richard Singleton on September 17, 1849. Unfortunately, little is known about Margeurite, but Singleton is easier to trace. At the age of twenty-nine, Singleton left Lancaster, England, and came to the Upper Great Lakes, where he alternated working at mines at Prince's Bay (Canadian North Shore), Todd Harbor (Isle Royale), and Bruce's Mines (Lake Huron area). Four out of five of Richard and Margeurite Singleton's children were born at Todd Harbor, Isle Royale. Alex Singleton was born at Todd Harbor in 1855 and would become a headman at the Fort William Reserve in the 1880s.[120] Elizabeth was the last child born at Isle Royale in 1859, after the first mining era had ended. Throughout the 1850s, other members of the Pishke family frequented Isle Royale. Singleton was still associated with the Island in the late 1850s and perhaps was an unofficial lighthouse keeper at Rock Harbor Light.[121] Sometime after 1859, Margeurite died, and Richard moved away from the area for awhile. He would later marry two more times and discover a minor copper vein located in Thunder Bay. He appears to have been more of a mine laborer and explorer than a mine owner or financier.[122]

In 1882, Singleton, an English citizen, came back to Isle Royale to work as a lighthouse keeper at the newly constructed Passage Island Lighthouse. A year before, he had worked at the Victoria Island Lighthouse on the Canadian side of Lake Superior. In May 1883, while in Port Arthur purchasing supplies, Singleton was run over by a train. His death left a third wife and three young children alone on Passage Island. Within a month they were taken off.[123] For at least sixty years, between the 1820s and 1883, four generations of this Ojibwe family lived and worked on Isle Royale. They began as hunters of caribou, became copper miners, then likely commercial fishermen, and finally lighthouse keepers. Throughout this time they likely subsistence-fished from Todd Harbor, Rock Harbor, as well as other locations. In this one family history, children were born on Isle Royale, and L'homme du Sault perhaps died there. There is a remarkable story of continuity of use and of residency throughout a tumultuous time.

The Bahgwatchinnini family of Grand Portage were another North Shore Ojibwe family with longstanding roots at Minong.[124] Bahgwatchinnini literally means "wild man," or has alternately been translated as "bushman." During the 1830s, Weisaw Bahgwatchinnini was a reliable hunter and guide for the Fort William HBC post. Two winters in a row, he and a companion took mail and a "packet" from Fort William to Rainy Lake.[125] The first mention of Weisaw Bahgwatchinnini on Minong is when he was hired there to fish for the American Fur Company for a one-year term in 1838. Along with the other American Fur Company fishermen, he overwintered on the Island, likely at their main station in Siskiwit Bay. He was given generous terms as an employee and rehired in 1839.[126] After the American Fur Company stations were closed, Weisaw (called Louis by some) and his family would live at the Island for part of the year and move back to Grand Portage for the winter months. On

June 22, 1853, a Jesuit priest noted that he was fishing at Siskiwit Bay. In 1853, Bahgwatchinnini, his brother, and their families overwintered on Isle Royale and continued fishing through the ice. His son, William Bahgwatchinnini was born on Isle Royale in 1854. The same year, a relative, Joseph Bahgwatchinnini, died at Isle Royale. William must have been a good boatman, because by the 1860s he was operating a sailboat or mackinaw and regularly guided the Jesuit priests from Fort William.[127] He also regularly fished from Isle Royale waters. His father continued to enjoy Minong and overwintered on the Island during the 1870s when the Island Mine and Minong Mine were in operation.

Weisaw Bahgwatchinnini became a noteworthy prospector. Indeed, he was credited by many for guiding a prospector friend to the mainland silver deposits at Rabbit and Silver mountains near Whitefish Lake—near the center of the traditional use area of the North Shore Ojibwe.[128] Many Grand Portage men became guides during this mining boom, and one trail to the Silver Mountain mines splintered off the Grand Portage trail and crossed the river just downstream from the confluence of the Arrow and Pigeon Rivers. Weisaw's and his son William's tenure at Isle Royale includes both commercial and subsistence use. The longstanding roots are sometimes poorly documented, but underscore an intimate relationship with Minong. Descendents of Weisaw and William continue to live in Grand Portage today, and this family connection is the most detailed oral history of Ojibwe use of Minong known today.

Early Ojibwe families—such as the Illinois and Bahgwatchinnini families—were clan-based. But exactly how clans functioned on Minong is an open question. Did clans function as more than a family lineage? Or, did clan leaders have authority over others to the point of having recognized territorial rights? Ojibwe from at least two clans—Bullhead and Caribou—went to Minong. The Bahgwatchinnini or Bushman family were Caribou clan members. The clan identification for the Illinois family is unknown. But the Caribou and Flatte families of Grand Portage that also frequented Minong were Fish, or more specifically Bullhead, clan members.[129] Unfortunately we do not have any records of other clans—Bear or Crane, most likely—that frequented the Island. Remarkably, these clans, Caribou and Bullhead, are the oldest documented clans for the area.[130] And we know that these and other families made repeated trips to Minong. However, we do not know if one or both of these clans held Minong as their territory.

This question of territoriality and how clans or *dodems* functioned takes us into the heart of two well-worn anthropological debates. Some have argued that clans were merely family lineages, much like a last name. For example, a border surveyor observed "an Indian letter" at a recent encampment with clan markings. "The Indian letter consisted of a canoe & three persons & some animal traced upon birch bark with a burnt coal, meaning, no doubt, that three Indians in a canoe had gone from that lodge toward the Grand Portage and the animal designated the person or family, according to Indian heraldry."[131] Other scholars have concluded that clans were more than a descent or "family" group. These writers assert that clan membership might also include social obligations among fellow clan members living nearby or afar. One obligation would be taking care of a fellow clan member. Some have pushed the idea that clans were a more potent social institution—in this case, a form of governing that had "strict territorial control by each group over strategic trade resources." Seconding this idea, another scholar wrote, "The distinctness of these totemic groups, then, was exemplified by their occupancy of hunting and fishing grounds. (The boundaries of the hunting tracts may not have been precisely delimited, but the major fisheries were unquestionably circumscribed.)" Another asserted that fall fishing places and maple sugar bush were the most territorial of subsistence pursuits.[132] Thus, for example, the Collin family frequently traveled from Fort William to Grand Portage to their sugar bush above Grand Portage. There also appeared to be some elements of territoriality to fall fishing—for example, Michel Collin often returned to his fishery at Thunder Cape. In contrast, "summer fishing places, berry patches and rice fields are free for all." The only Ojibwe elder to comment on this topic, Ellen Olson, has tentatively suggested that only a couple of clans used the Island in the early days, thus implying some limited familiarity and or territoriality.[133]

One problem in understanding what was truly going on is that the concept of ownership and territoriality was changing during this period.

Thus, Ojibwe trappers understood they alone "owned" beaver pelts, or a North Shore fisher would understand that he had singular possession of his barrels of salt fish. Both product—furs and salt fish—were actively traded and had a fluctuating value. Beaver even became a kind of currency—"Made Beaver" or MB in traders' logs. Thus, individual possession of some property was known. Trap lines appear to have changed more toward individual rights, eventually recognized by Canadians in registered trap lines. Treaties are an extreme form of territoriality, as was the eventual breaking up of lands into individual allotments or property.

But prior to these severe changes, there appears to have been some territorial predisposition among North Shore clans. For example, the Bear clan was dominant at Beaver Bay and were an important group in Chippewa City (Grand Marais). The Awause clan (Bullhead clan) were numerous at the Kaministiquia River.[134] And yet during this time, the importance of clans was diminishing for some Ojibwe. What appears to be the case in the first half of the nineteenth century is that clan membership likely played a role in the use of Minong. Continued multigenerational use of Minong by male family members, such as those of L'homme du Sault, would mean a clan presence as long as clans remained an important social institution. And the occasional appearance of Ojibwe from Nipigon or Basswood Lake—like the Linklaters—at Minong might mean continuity in clan use, such as the Caribou clan. The privilege to use Minong might extend to all clan members, not just those living on the North Shore.[135] But the coming of new economic ventures, especially mining and commercial fishing, also undermined any clan control of resources on the Island.

## Participation in Commercial Activities

At the same time a young L'homme du Sault, the Bete, Medishean, or other Ojibwe might have been hunting caribou on Isle Royale, officials of the American Fur Company were investigating commercial fishing prospects there and at Grand Portage. Fur trade profits were sagging, so the American Fur Company (AFC) was looking for another profitable enterprise.[136] AFC official policy "commercialized" the catching and marketing of the much acclaimed Lake Superior fish. They built an enterprise, in large part, upon the subsistence knowledge and many skills of Ojibwe. AFC officials in the mid-1830s were particularly dependent upon North Shore Ojibwe (and other Indians elsewhere along the lake) to locate fish stations near rich fishing grounds. Thus, AFC president Ramsay Crooks would write: "Avail yourself of Indian information" and use "Grand Portage Indians' knowledge of Isle Royale fishing" to site fish stations.[137] And indeed Ojibwe influence was so prevalent that when Charles Chaboillez and a large AFC crew were first dropped off at Isle Royale in Rock Harbor because of its safe and accessible location, they moved the central fish station to Siskiwit Bay because of its reputation for fishing.[138] This siting of the central station in the relatively shallow waters of Siskiwit Bay caused extra effort, as the large company vessels could not get in to dock. Their loads had to be "lightered" in small boats and brought to and from the dock in Siskiwit Bay.

American Fur Company officials had very high hopes for their fishing experiment, and particularly their operation at Isle Royale. Fresh from a trip to Isle Royale in their initial year in 1837, veteran trader Gabriel Franchere wrote, "The fishermen at present only employ half of their nets and get 10 barrels per day. The fish are large trout 15 c 20 for 200-pound barrel, white fish of extraordinary size and rich flavour with plenty of siskawet."[139] Seen as a fishing Shangri-La, the AFC built five fishing stations scattered around the Island. Portage chiefs Espagnol and Old Peau de Chat reported there "are upwards of one hundred men with their families fishing at the Isle Royale for the Yankees." At least twelve children were borne on the Island to Métis parents.[140] The chiefs applauded the AFC competition with the HBC that meant greater trading strategies and better deals for the North Shore Ojibwe. The AFC fishermen, coopers, and clerks came from Montreal, Mackinaw, L'Anse, La Pointe, and Fond du Lac to run their fishing operation. They also engaged local Indians for wage labor or paid them per barrel. In 1838, the AFC hired Isle Royale local fishermen Waisaw Bahgwatchinnini and Louis Rivet. They were among thirty-four fishermen at the Island—many with their wives, who dressed fish.[141] Rivet would later report at Fort William that the AFC workforce at Isle Royale cured eight hundred barrels of fish in the fall.[142] In 1839, local fishermen hired at Isle Royale included Louis Rivet (with relatively high pay and rations for wife and children), John Sayer, Jean Bte Passigard (sp), and "Yellow"—likely Waisaw Bahgwatchinnini. And like the year before, most of the local fishermen were paid slightly more than those from Montreal and most other locations.[143]

The AFC also picked up a number of Indian fishermen for their fall fishing at Grand Portage for a total workforce of fourteen. The next year, the AFC employed about twenty Grand Portage Indians. The clerk, Pierre Cotte, provided salt, nets, and barrels, and paid them $3 per barrel. Scaling back at Grand Portage in 1839, the AFC hired two Indians for $35 each to fish from August 13 to November 15.[144]

A number of the AFC fisheries at Isle Royale were paired with North Shore Ojibwe encampments. Thus, there was one station on Card Point (in Washington Harbor) near an Ojibwe encampment at Grace Island. The main station at Checker Point, Siskiwit Bay, was near an important subsistence-fishing area, trail head, and thus encampments. The AFC also established a fishery at Belle Isle, known early on as "Fish Island," a few miles distant from McCargoe Cove. Whether the encampments came first, then the AFC stations were located nearby is not known, but probable. There was much bartering between stations and encampments. This trade likely included potatoes, ground corn, cedar mats, fish, moccasins, and furs. While the AFC was precluded from fur trading with Ojibwe because of their agreement with the Hudson's Bay Company, they were allowed to "trade with our own people." Likely a brisk trade on Isle Royale beaver, otter, and perhaps marten ensued, particularly since the large AFC workforce overwintered on Isle Royale during the 1837–38 and 1838–39 winters.[145]

A number of chronic difficulties, such as lack of salt and barrel wood, extra effort in collecting barrels from five remote locations, spoilage, and a scarcity of reliable markets made the AFC experiment less profitable than hoped. A national recession made marketing fish difficult. With poorer than expected returns, the AFC abruptly removed their fishermen from Isle Royale in the early fall of 1839. The next year the AFC rotated fishermen from Fond du Lac, to Isle Royale, then to La Pointe. Leaving the Island in early October 1840 became the literal and symbolic undoing of the AFC fishing operation on Isle Royale. In a fierce nor'wester, the schooner *Siskiwit* dragged her anchor, crashed on a reef, and seas broke over her. After the squall calmed, the AFC crew hauled her up on the beach, leaving her to the mercy of fall storms and winter abandonment.[146] The AFC investment at Isle Royale was over. Most Métis fishermen returned to their homes southward, or to other fishing stations. A few stayed, married Grand Portage women, and were absorbed into the Grand Portage Band.[147]

Some have presumed that Ojibwe were not substantially involved in historic copper mining on Isle Royale, as they had "left" the Island prior to this development.[148] Perhaps this is a result of the legacy of misunderstanding that Ojibwe were fearful of using copper. Or maybe it was a mistake created by the low number of firsthand accounts of the labor force at the pioneering mines on Isle Royale. But the evidence suggests that North Shore Ojibwe were part of the mining workforce. Remember, for example, that Angelique Mott, alongside her husband Charlie, was employed by a copper mining company to ensure that no claims-jumping occurred. North Shore Ojibwe hungry for wage labor or trading prospects frequented many of the mining operations. The Pishke family appears to have been a mainstay at the Todd Harbor mine, while the Cawinabinesis were regulars at the Siskiwit Mine.[149] While the Ojibwe were not dominant in numbers, they brought skills and knowledge that were useful to the operation. One mining captain's wife at Ransom townsite, now known as Daisy Farm, wrote, "The weather being pleasant and the waters of the Bay so quiet that Mrs. Mathews and myself ventured out in a boat alone with a half-breed woman, she managed the boat just as well as a man. We went out around the point of the Island and went ashore at a place where the Indians had camped."[150] The Jesuit diarist at the Fort William mission noted on September 3, 1849:

Two young men from Sault Ste. Marie, one a Metis [and] the other an Indian, who had come with the Indians from Ile-au-Cuivre [literally Copper Island or Isle Royale] where they were working in Mr. Smith's mine, offer their services to Father Chone to saw planks.[151]

A couple of years later, while on a proselytizing trip, another Jesuit father noted how the miners, be they Indian or White, looked after one another:

Four Native families of Pigeon River spent the winter at Tott's [Todd] Harbor. The men and the young lads were employed at work outside the mine and earned a salary that made them quite well off. One of them, a father of a family with only very young children fell sick. God knows how wretched would have been his lot if he had not received help from people other than his fellow tribesmen. The Irish Catholics . . . although they were few in numbers, they started a subscription in aid of the sick man, and collected a sum of 14 dollars for him. His brother, who had been left a widower with a little child, lost a finger that winter and was thus prevented from working for a while. Once more our good Irish people came to the rescue and got up a subscription to buy him a barrel of flour, some bacon, and everything he needed for himself and his child.[152]

On the other hand, some early mining families felt ill at ease around the Ojibwe in both the first copper mining wave (late 1840s–'50s) and the second wave (1870s). A young woman in the 1850s would later recount, "The Indians terrorized us on the island and each season they would come over from Canada in bands, erecting their wigwams directly before our doors. All the women in the camp remained in doors and felt at ease only when their husbands returned from work."[153] But friendly relations were more commonplace. Indeed, one mining official would greet the Indians they would meet along the Island Mine road with an Ojibwe phrase, *bozhu-neeji*, or "hello, friend." Miners learned the hard way that North Shore Ojibwe did not like to give their names directly to a stranger.[154]

During the 1870s, it appears that Ojibwe on the Island were more likely to trade with the miners than be employed by the companies. Thus, one miner remembered:

We wore German stockings all winter and moccasins too. They were obtained from the Indians. Our overshoes went over these. I don't know what hide the Indians used to make the moccasins. They must have brought the hide from the mainland. They had a large camp on the Island.[155]

And another miner at Island Mine remembered:

There were Chippewa Indians living on the Island at the time, but it was Mr. Shea's opinion that they left for the main shore during the winter. They made maple sugar that the white folks bought. As youngsters they use to go over to the Indian's camp with or without adults. The Indians were very friendly and often came up to the settlement for "handouts." They apparently lived by hunting and fishing and would often bring fish, ducks, or snowshoe rabbits to those who gave them something to eat.[156]

The Indians would regularly supply the miners with fish and game, even going to small streams to get trout. On occasion, miners and Ojibwe would travel to visit one another. In one instance, miners brought gifts of tobacco and canned food that were traded for maple sugar. This exchange and others built upon a strong Ojibwe custom of sharing food and hospitality at their camps. A return visit by the Ojibwe led to this exchange:

The Indians had been pleased by our visits and one day in the late spring returned our call. It had grown warm enough to have the windows open. At the end of our sitting room was a bay window. One day while sitting at the piano, with my back to the window, playing simple little tunes, I heard a grunt. I turned to see in every window the head and shoulders of an Indian buck and behind him his squaw. There were several couples and I was a little startled, but quickly realized they were harmless. One of the bucks thrust in an arm, motioned toward the piano and grunted with no uncertain meaning. A little disturbed I began to play my little tunes, "Pure as Snow," Can You Forget That Night in June," "Danube Waltz," and "Maiden's Prayer."[157]

After listening intently and thanking the piano player, the Indians left and soon departed from the Island. And during the heyday of the 1870s copper mining with established towns, Grand Portage Ojibwe had the contract to deliver mail to the mining settlements during winter.[158]

Just like the American Fur Company fishing operations, the copper miners were reliant on Ojibwe and prehistoric miners' knowledge of where copper veins were located. It was a well-known technique for Euro-American miners to look for prehistoric mines and exploit them.[159] Ojibwe were knowledgeable about other minerals as well. For example, fishermen from Pigeon River confidentially told a navy surveying party where silver could be found on Isle Royale.[160] Grand Portage Ojibwe were also knowledgeable about and collected "greenstones" from Isle Royale beaches. Circa 1895, "an aged Indian, his squaw and his grown son came to and camped on the Amygdaloid Channel of Fish Island for several weeks. They said they came to search for greenstones."[161] North Shore Ojibwe used a flexible economic strategy to incorporate a minor economic activity such as finding and trading/selling greenstones to earn hard-to-come-by cash.

During the late 1840s and '50s there was a second economic boom—beyond copper mining—on Isle Royale. From 1848 to 1857, Hugh H. McCullough operated a large-scale fishing enterprise at Isle Royale.[162] Scores of North Shore Ojibwe were his workforce, and whenever possible he reoccupied areas and buildings constructed by the American Fur Company and mining companies. North Shore Ojibwe fished from Siskiwit Bay, near Hay Bay, and Fish (now Belle) Island, where he owned properties.[163] The stark isolation of one fishery, between a narrow pair of red rock islands off Houghton Point, suggests the preferred fishing locations of his Ojibwe workers. Fishing from canoes and small boats and perhaps mackinaw boats, they wanted their fish station to be very close to a productive fishing grounds to minimize travel effort. On the down side, this fishery location was also very exposed to rough seas. Ojibwe fishers could be wind-bound depending on the direction and height of the waves.

Isle Royale was not McCullough's only operation, nor was he only interested in fishing. In addition to Ojibwe fishermen, he hired up to thirty-six "packers" to haul supplies to his distant posts. At the height of his business, he operated trading posts all along the border lakes as far west at Lake of the Woods. Posts nearby Grand Portage were located at Mountain, Saganaga, and Basswood Lakes. His fishing operation included sites at Two Island River, Grand Marais, Grand Portage, Siskiwit Islands and Fish Island on Isle Royale. His main warehouse on the Island appears to have been at Siskiwit Bay, though its exact location is unknown.

McCullough's Ojibwe workforce stayed on the Island later into the fall to catch fish—trout and whitefish—that concentrate in spawning grounds. Thus, Ojibwe fishing for McCullough could not harvest wild rice inland and became further reliant on foods such as flour. Through exchanges such as this, some Ojibwe became more dependent on a cash economy and moved away from an exclusively subsistence lifestyle. Few Ojibwe stayed on the Island through the winter, so most had to make a more dangerous lake crossing in October or November.[164]

McCullough was trading for furs on the Island as well. An HBC clerk at Fort William wrote, "John Finlayson and Wm Corbeau were sent off in the direction of Pigeon River to look out for Stor [unintelligible] Rouge and to prevent his furs [from] falling into the hands of a trader who is prowling about the place from Isle Royale."[165] And at the height of McCullough's operation, trade goods were shipped from Isle Royale to the Hudson's Bay Company's post at Fort William.[166]

It is the size of McCullough's operation that makes it noteworthy. Perhaps as many as three hundred North Shore Ojibwe, really entire families of both groups from Grand Portage and Fort William, came to Isle Royale to fish for McCullough.[167] Or as one of the Jesuit fathers would lament, "All the savages from here [the Fort William mission], except for some women, leave to fish at Isle Royale."[168] Most Ojibwe fishermen worked on a per-barrel basis, and were usually paid $2–$3 per barrel, minus charges they had made for goods in

# Ojibwe Deaths at Isle Royale Noted in Jesuit Records

| NAME | DATE OF DEATH |
|------|---------------|
| Paul Undomkomiskishang | c. 1844/45 |
| Peter Wickop, age 10 | October 5, 1849 |
| *His grave was blessed at Pigeon River on October 12, 1849* | |
| Marie Wickop | September 10, 1850 |
| *Her grave was blessed at Siskiwit Bay* | |
| Catherine Okabenwinzok, age 40 | December 29, 1850 |
| *Her grave blessed at Todd Harbor* | |
| Unnamed, "young man" | October 29, 1851 |
| *Death at Siskiwit Bay, grave location unknown* | |
| Jacob Piske (?L'homme du Sault) | December, 1851 |
| *Death at Todd Harbor, grave blessed at Fort William Mission, spring 1852* | |
| Josette Debwewitawok | December 15, 1851 |
| *Her grave blessed at Fort William Mission, spring 1852* | |
| Joseph Bahgwatchinnini | December 24, 1854 |
| *His grave blessed at the Fort William Mission, Spring 1855* | |
| Unnamed | May 5, 1855 |
| Josephte Aiakodjiwang, age 12 | February 21, 1857 |
| *Her remains taken to Fort William Mission on February 27th and blessed* | |
| Lisette Bishke [?Pishke] | September 19, 1857 |
| *Her remains were taken back to Fort William* | |
| Adam Roach LaPlante | 1933* |
| *His remains were taken back to Grand Portage* | |

*Fort William Mission Death Records compiled by Father William Maurice, St. Anne's Catholic Church, Fort William Reserve; Mission of Immaculate Conception Diary, May 20, 1849, October 12, 1849; and interview with Mrs. Violet Miller, by Tim Cochrane, in Ahmeek, Michigan, October 12, 1988.

McCullough's trading establishments.[169] With the tempting prospect of hard cash for fish, so many came that the Jesuit fathers on the mainland became frustrated that there were no Indians to convert or educate. It is through working for, or trading with, McCullough that many additional Ojibwe learned about and used Isle Royale resources.

## "Blood Equity" on Minong

Rediscovering the presence of Ojibwe on Minong also means that important life passages occurred there. Important symbolic and literal connections are made with the death, or marriage, or birth of a loved one on Minong. Up to the point of this effort, few considered that North Shore Ojibwe might be buried at Minong. But they are. Subsistence pursuits, fishing, mining all led to several Ojibwe who were born, baptized, married, and died on the Island. Using only the Jesuit records from Fort William, we can document that ten or more Catholic Ojibwe died on Minong.

The Catholic records also note who was present at the grave blessing. For example, Paul Memashkawash was present at Marie Wickop's burial. Memashkawash was a common Grand Portage family name, and a number of Memashkawash were Grand Portage chiefs, including one who signed the 1854 treaty. Numerous descendants live in Grand Portage today. Pierre Isk-kwikijikweshkang [alternate name Caribou] and Susanne Ogabewinjog were married on September 15, 1853, at an unnamed place on Isle Royale. Caribou is another common Grand Portage name, and the family has included a number of prominent leaders. On September 12, 1850, in "Ciskawet Bay," Father Fremiot baptized four Ojibwe infants—all four less than one year old. The mother of one child, Therese Collin, is an ancestor of the former First Nation chief at Fort William, Peter Collin.[170]

The height of Ojibwe presence at Isle Royale during the McCullough fishery and first copper mining boom appears to be 1850. For example, six (Catholic) Ojibwe children were born on Minong in 1850, compared with three non-Ojibwe children. The year 1850 saw the highest number of Ojibwe

Catholic baptisms on Isle Royale, with six. The early years, especially 1850–51, have a sprinkling of mixed ethnicity in baptismal "sponsors." Thus, the child might have a Cornish, Irish, or Ojibwe sponsor. Other Ojibwe were born on the Island, but not being Catholic or not being born during an infrequent visit by the priest, their births went unrecorded.[171] And after the first mining boom and the end of McCullough's fishing operations in 1857, few vital records were kept of Ojibwe on Minong.[172] For example, a year later a mineral prospector on Isle Royale met the Rock Harbor lighthouse keeper, "who came over in his boat, said that no vessel had put in there last year, except with his supplies. There are a few Indians on the Island and the lighthouse keeper married one of his squaws. He is the only white person on the island."[173] Gaps in documentary sources means there were likely more Ojibwe families with blood equity on Minong.

## South Shore Ojibwe on Minong

All the examples of Ojibwe on Isle Royale so far demonstrate that they came from the North Shore. This contrasts with a wild claim that crossing the lake from the South Shore was done frequently.[174] The historical record does show a number of South Shore Ojibwe came to Isle Royale, often as employees of a larger business concern. Usually they did not stay, as did Angelique Mott or the La Pointe area Ojibwe fishermen working for the American Fur Company operations at Isle Royale. Most commonly they came and left, severing any long-term connection to Minong. However, a few Sault Ste. Marie Ojibwe came to Grand Portage and Isle Royale, married into the band, and became part of the Ojibwe on the North Shore.[175]

There are two reports of South Shore Native Americans crossing the lake to use Isle Royale in early times. Pierre Radisson's account of his 1659–1660 explorations on Lake Superior was eventually poorly translated. In it, Radisson generically reports of "wild-men" paddling across the lake. It is dubious for a number of reasons. His own trip itinerary is disputed because of the generic nature of his statements. It is also not clear if he is just reporting the trip was possible, or that he had talked with "wild men" who had made the trip.[176]

The second report, made by a Fond du Lac Ojibwe chief, Loon's Foot, in 1852, is equally frustrating in its generality. While talking with his "Canadian nephew" about ancient North American copper mining, he reportedly said:

> A long time ago the Indians were much better off then they are now. They had copper axes, arrowheads, and spears; and also, stone axes. Until the French came here, and blasted the rocks with powder; we have no traditions of copper mines being worked, and don't know who did work them. Our forefathers used to build big canoes and cross the Lake over to Isle Royale, where they found more copper than anywhere else. The stone hammers that are now found, in the old diggings, we know nothing about. The Indians were formerly much more numerous, and happier, than they are now."[177]

The statement is vague on a couple of critical points. His statement does not detail where—from what shore—his ancestors may have crossed over to Isle Royale. And we do not know the specific time period Loon's Foot is referring to—only that it happened in the past. It is unclear if he is speaking about ancient or relatively contemporary times. More importantly, how might Loon's Foot know anything about finding copper on Isle Royale? Was this knowledge common in oral tradition at Fond du Lac, or did he learn this some other way? There are at least three possible ways Loon's Foot learned about copper on Isle Royale. We do know that Loon's Foot was a member of the Loon clan and a Midewiwin practitioner. He also possessed a circular plate of virgin copper in which generations were counted that have lived in or nearby Mon-in-wun-a-Kaun-ing, or Madeline Island in the Apostle Island area.[178] The Loon clan, like most Ojibwe clans, believed their ancestors last came from the Sault Ste. Marie area prior to moving westward. Is it possible that his ancestors who visited Isle Royale came from the Soo in the prehistoric period? A style of pottery found on Isle Royale, what archeologists call "Juntenen" pottery, was made by people believed to be from the Soo area. Hence, it is literally possible that the ancestors of the Ojibwe that made Juntenen-style pots may have traveled to Isle Royale from the Soo, and Loon's Foot is recounting this history.[179]

Loon's Foot could also be speaking metaphorically. The Loon clan may have had an affinity for copper that other Ojibwe clans did not. Thus, they might have prided themselves on knowing about copper. A very plausible explanation is that Loon's Foot may have learned about use of Isle Royale copper from his "Canadian nephew." Indeed, we know that Loon's Foot—or Mongazoid, as he was sometimes called—worked and intermixed with North Shore Ojibwe one winter. During the 1824–1825 winter, Mongazoid worked for the American Fur Company in Grand Marais. He worked for wages for the AFC, but he also camped and trapped with Little Englishman, a North Shore Ojibwe *ogima*, or leader.[180] He had plenty of opportunity to learn about Minong and its copper while in the Grand Marais and Grand Portage area. In any case, there is no specific information in Loon's Foot's account about who went to Minong and when, or specific information about the trip. In short, there is too much unexplained to make this an exacting record characterizing use of Minong by South Shore Ojibwe.

The expanse and sometime wild nature of the lake preclude much connection of South Shore Ojibwe to Minong. A trip from the south shore might encounter the "Keweenaw Current," which would carry a small watercraft to the east away from the Island with a volume of water analogous to the outflow of the Mississippi River.[181] A fifty-mile crossing would be deadly to many and likely vividly remembered by those who did cross the breadth of the lake. And the resources available on Minong (copper, fish, and beaver) were available much closer nearby to the Wisconsin and Michigan Ojibwe. There is not sufficient reason that outweighs the risk for South Shore Ojibwe to historically travel to Isle Royale.

South Shore Ojibwe chiefs confirmed during the 1843 Isle Royale Compact negotiations that Minong was the province of the Grand Portage Band. Thus, Balsom, the head chief of Fond du Lac, stated: "My father, We did not sell Isle Royale; we only sold these island close to the mainland on this shore of the Lake. That Island we did not sell. It belongs to my brother; there he sits: (point to the Grand Portage Chief). He may take it and sell it for what he can get." At the same negotiations, Buffalo, head chief of La Pointe, would remark: "My Father, we did not give away Isle Royale [during the 1842 Treaty]. . . . We only sold the Islands round this place. It is not possible that all these chiefs [during the 1842 Treaty] should steal that Island, and sell it." And an interpreter speaking for the Keweenaw chief stated: "My Father, We deny selling Isle Royale. . . . The Island belongs to the Indians living nearest to it [the Grand Portage delegation present when these comments were made]."[182] Even during the stress of land-cession negotiations and the temptation of being a "co-owner" of Minong that would give them some negotiating leverage, the chiefs acknowledged that Minong was the territory of North Shore Ojibwe. These South Shore Ojibwe chiefs were merely acknowledging what is now obvious—that there are no credible traditions of Fond du Lac, Keweenaw, Madeline Island, or other South Shore Ojibwe using Isle Royale going there for their own exclusive purposes or having a tradition of use of Minong.

## Conclusion: North Shore Ojibwe Roots at Minong

In contrast to their kinsmen on the South Shore, Ojibwe from the North Shore made repeated visits to Minong. A number of North Shore Ojibwe were born and married there. Others died there; some were then buried there, while others' remains were hauled back to the North Shore for burial. Many North Shore Ojibwe worked there, and some developed trading relationships with mining and fishing companies. By the time we have detailed records of use, dramatic changes had enmeshed North Shore Ojibwe, including the gradual importance of a cash economy. Some North Shore Ojibwe families have multigenerational connections to it, and many of their descendants still live in Grand Portage and Fort William. Other families with strong connections, such as the Memashkawash, have family members in Grand Portage and Pays Plat, on the Canadian North Shore of Lake Superior.[183]

Many North Shore Ojibwe had detailed knowledge of Minong resources. They demonstrated ingenuity in fishing at Minong, which likely involved varied types of technologies and was based on a keen knowledge of the Island's fisheries. This same knack for being keen observers of environmental conditions improved the likelihood of safe crossings to and from Isle Royale. For example, when crossing during the winter, they used an ice bridge between the mainland and Minong where there is some of the most reliable ice on Lake Superior. Or, in another instance, this environmental knowledge was rewarded with higher pay than that of their fishing peers, French-Canadians, working for the American Fur Company.

And yet theirs was only a modest level of use. There is, for example, no definitive confirmation of plant introductions on Isle Royale such as Indian corn, wild rice, partially domesticated wild chives, or Jerusalem artichokes.[184] The latter two plants may have been brought to the Island, but the evidence is unclear. No permanent settlements were maintained. However, Ojibwe traditionally moved throughout their territory many times a year. Place-names, oral history, records of use, and historical data suggest a continuous but modest pattern of use. For some families it was part of their seasonal round, a well-known location resorted to for specific reasons such as the early siscowet fishing in Siskiwit Bay. Ojibwe knowledge of Isle Royale led the way for Euro-American voyageurs coasting its shores, fishermen, copper miners, border surveyors, and even small family resort owners. Modest subsistence use became the basis on which some commercial enterprises began. The use of salt brine to preserve fish increased the attractiveness of Isle Royale fish, which could now be preserved for the long route to market or stored for the winter months. And in the case of McCullough's large fishery operation, large in terms of the Ojibwe workforce, many more North Shore Ojibwe learned of Minong's resources.

Through the historical period, most Ojibwe use of Isle Royale was by small family groups for subsistence purposes and with minimal impact. Portages were barely recognizable from one year to the next. The primary attraction was the abundant fish. Some Ojibwe associated Minong with purity compared with the mainland, and as a good place to live. While changes—such as religious changes—were rampant during the last two centuries, the Ojibwe respect for the lake, evidenced by the offering of gifts to the lake manitous, persisted. The memory of paddling and sailing across to the Island remained with select families even as they moved from the North Shore to the interior of Minnesota—for example, John Linklater and Tchi-ki-wis. Grand Portage and Fort William Ojibwe made frequent use of Minong prior to and after the three treaties that challenged their use of Minong. The effects of the treaties and a suite of changing conditions leading to a waning Ojibwe use of Minong is the topic of the next chapter.

# **4** REMOVED FROM MINONG

A succession of external forces removed North Shore Ojibwe from Minong. The cumulative effects of treaties—the Copper Treaty of 1842, the 1844 Compact, those of 1850 and 1854—did impact Ojibwe traveling to Minong. But even more forces were afoot. Through time, cumulative national, regional, and local changes slowed, and nearly ended, the use of Minong in the second half of the nineteenth century and early twentieth century. Grand Portage coalesced from dispersed clan groups into an Ojibwe settlement—in part because of the advantages of being there to trade with whites and having control of the portal into the West. Later, after the treaties, they were supposed to be confined on reservations and stop their travels to distant parts of their former territory, such as Minong. The arrival of white settlers in the region accelerated change.

Attempting to answer a larger question about Native Americans' experience, writers have argued whether change inevitably leads to cultural extinction, determined cultural persistence, or some creative result in between. Our interest is more modest in this chapter. We seek to explain how change—sometimes slow in coming and sometimes rampant—eroded the practice of Ojibwe use of Minong. Their once large home tract of densely forested lands, lakes, and open water diminished as they became unwelcome to harvest resources in places now frequented, or owned, by others. The disruption of use of Minong is only a special instance of cessation of use in their traditional territory—far to the inland, west, northwest, and even along the stony coasts of Lake Superior.

Perhaps the greatest impact on the North Shore Ojibwe was the coming of new, deadly diseases. "The Small Pox, at one time, nearly annihilated these Indians" along the border lakes.[1] The terrible toll of the disease led to a change in ratio of Ojibwe to whites. After the 1782–83 smallpox epidemic, they were much less numerically dominant and at times were outnumbered. Other diseases were unleashed.[2] Measles in 1871 killed fifty at Rainy Lake and fifteen at Grand Portage and Fort William. Despite these new diseases, there was a steady increase of area Ojibwe in the nineteenth and twentieth centuries.

Another change was the growing tendency towards more centralized villages for parts or all of the year. The first to make this change were the women, children, and men who worked for the fur trading posts. Relations with traders and clerks, along with the availability of traders' food stores in tough times, made living near large posts attractive at "hungry times." Smaller, traditional residential areas—at Beaver Bay, Arrow Lake, Gunflint Lake, and even Saganaga—were used less often.

Before their more remotely located kinsmen, North Shore Ojibwe were deeply familiar with powerful whites in their midst, with the summer headquarters of the North West Company in their heartland. The size and scale of the fur trade operation dwarfed those anywhere nearby, and North Shore Ojibwe saw firsthand the power of the company to construct sailing vessels, docks, and warehouses, and to amass goods—as well as the explosion of whites in the country during Rendezvous times. The powerful whites were also clearly fickle. In 1798 the Northwesters sought out, negotiated, and concluded a land lease with Grand Portage clan leaders, made necessary because of a newly devised "border."[3] The lease paved the way for the Northwesters to move to Fort William (and leave American soil) once their new fur emporium was completed in 1803. Yet the fact that a deal was formally concluded illustrates that the North Shore Ojibwe were a group to be recognized and accommodated.

The presence of a succession of competing fur trade companies, first the North West and "XY" companies, then the North West and Hudson's Bay companies, and finally the American Fur Company, sharpened the trading acumen of the North Shore Ojibwe. The pressure to trap, for whatever company, eventually greatly diminished the numbers of beaver available.[4] Beaver was the most sought-after and valuable fur. By the early 1800s, the better beaver trapping was far westward, and some North Shore Ojibwe went west to trap. Many would eventually come back.[5] These experiences gave North Shore Ojibwe a first-hand experience of the hierarchy and power, as well as folly, of whites.

The onset and participation in the fur trade meant significant changes in diet and activities, the introduction of a cash economy, and new goods. As the fur trade lingered on, North Shore Ojibwe had to go farther and be gone longer to procure furs. Once-exotic foodstuffs, such as flour, potatoes, and sugar, became integrated into their diet. For example, in the late 1800s, common provisions for a two-week trapping trip for three men would be "2 lbs flour, a day to a man, 1 lb bacon a day to a man, 1 can baking powder, 5 lbs sugar, 5 lbs salt."[6] Clothing changed dramatically. Wool blankets made in England replaced fur blankets, formerly made of woven rabbit fur. Manufactured and often imported fishing gear—"New Holland" twine and "codhooks"—replaced gill nets made out of the inner bark of cedar or from basswood fiber once harvested on the perimeter of their traditional territory.[7] Since cotton-fiber fishing gear was available through trade, North Shore Ojibwe traded less often with their kinsmen in the west for basswood-fiber nets.

North Shore Ojibwe warfare with the Dakota was over by 1800.[8] Earlier wartime leadership of Portage clan leader Waubojeeg against the Dakota was a distant memory—as was the 1718 battle with Dakota in which seventeen Ojibwe were killed near Kaministiquia. By the 1800s the threat of Dakota raids against North Shore Ojibwe was also over. And while its impact was not fully understood right away, the conclusion of the War of 1812 was the last time Great Lakes tribes would militarily threaten the young United States. It is likely that some North Shore Ojibwe participated in the 1812 War, fighting alongside their allies, the British.[9]

Not all Ojibwe bands acculturated, or resisted change, at the same speed. Some groups were noted traditionalists, such as the Rainy Lake and Nipigon Ojibwe's faithfulness in maintaining Midewiwin ceremonies.[10] Grand Portage Ojibwe thought that their kinsmen at Fort William were particularly known for their devotion to Christian faiths. According to traders and Indian agents, the Grand Portage Band was reportedly the most civilized tribe of the Lake Superior area. For example, one Portage leader was writing fluent letters in French and English in the 1840s. Grand Portage Ojibwe were reportedly "distinguished from others of the same tribe by their desire for civilization and education."[11]

More localized changes also impacted North Shore Ojibwe. The large-scale American Fur Company fishing operation on Isle Royale was shut down by 1840.[12] The first copper mining frontier on Isle Royale closed in 1855. A year later, the McCullough fishing operation closed. Boom-and-bust economic opportunities swirled around them, such as mining jobs at Rove Lake (in the present day Boundary Waters) and Silver Islet, and paid labor to construct breakwater piers for Grand Marais Harbor. Often these local operations would cease, in part, because of a national economic downturn—the 1841, 1857, and 1873 "panics." From a North Shore Ojibwe perspective, there was little predictability in how long such an enterprise would last.

Even fishing was changing. Once the most reliable means of harvesting food, it now also became a way to earn cash. Hundreds of Ojibwe and their families resided on Minong and fished on a two, three, or four dollars per-barrel basis for the McCullough operation.[13] Fishing for hard-to-come-by money was a welcome enterprise, as fish were plentiful and the Ojibwe were already knowledgeable about both fish and fishing techniques. While there, the same Ojibwe would also fish to eat, harvest plants such as birch bark for panels on dwellings, hunt for caribou, and trade with miners. The welcome access to cash for fish did not, however, dramatically change established use patterns of the archipelago. For example, it still was largely a summer use, though it now extended into the early fall. Small family groups stayed together, as in the past. And there is limited evidence that some family groups had preferred fishing grounds that they would return to year after year.

After McCullough's fishing operation closed in 1856, Ojibwe use of Minong appears to have waned.[14] A plethora of changes and influences, sometimes speedy or incremental in effect, were making their mark on North Shore Ojibwe lifeways. No single influence can explain the diminishment in Minong use. They had already endured many changes.

North Shore Ojibwe had limited experience with governing entities prior to directly participating in treaties. They were used to the annual treating with the powerful HBC governor Simpson—called the "Little Emperor"—at Fort William. It is also likely that Portage chiefs, such as Attikons and perhaps Espagnol (the Spaniard), witnessed, but did not sign, the 1826 Fond du Lac treaty.[15] Attikons or "Little Caribou" was one of many leaders sketched at Fond du Lac. Attikons and other onlookers would eventually learn of the mineral clause of the treaty that would permit whites to remove precious minerals. Within their traditional territory, Isle Royale copper was now vulnerable, despite the likelihood that they did not understand this liability.

Disturbing to all the Ojibwe in the region was the repeated discussion of removing them westward, away from the whites encroaching on their homelands. Increasing numbers of whites moved into southern Michigan and along Lake Michigan's southern shores. Eventually they would move northward and into Lake Superior country. Further, the U.S. government flirted with the idea of removing Lake Superior Ojibwe beyond the Mississippi River. Aware of this increasing likelihood, some Ojibwe looked to move north to the British lands, and one British Ojibwe leader encouraged their movement across the border to find refuge.[16]

North Shore Ojibwe leaders wanted to remain in their homes. In the spring of 1840, a small delegation of Grand Portage chiefs traveled to La Pointe and met with American Fur Company officials. The closing of the Isle Royale fisheries and the diminishment of the Grand Portage operation alarmed the Ojibwe. Fishing had provided a welcome economic opportunity at a time when returns from furs were lagging. Portage headmen were seeking an economic means to stay at Grand Portage. They offered exclusive trading privileges to the American Fur Company in exchange for helping them gain a livelihood. In their talks with the company, they seemed to have a prescient realization of what the future would bring. "The reason for all this they gave as simply a wish to remain on their own land which they believe will soon be demanded by the U.S. Government, and of which they are afraid that others who have no right might dispose of [it] without their consent."[17]

Later in the summer, the leaders sent a messenger to La Pointe to confer with American Fur Company officials and receive their answer. In an economic downturn and uncertainty, the AFC was unable to promise much, so they sent the messenger away with some trading credit. That fall the AFC would cease its fishing operations at Grand Portage, leaving North Shore Ojibwe in tough economic conditions.

Prior to the outbreak of "copper fever" and the 1842 treaty of La Pointe, North Shore Ojibwe were led by Espagnol (the Spaniard), Joseph Peau de Chat (Joseph Skin of the Cat), Attikons (Little Caribou), Shawgwawnawsheence (Little Englishman) and other headmen. Espagnol, born during the smallpox epidemic of 1783, was recognized as the principal chief, and estimated by fur traders to be a great "rascal" because of his trading shrewdness. He would die before treaty negotiations, leaving the North Shore Ojibwe to be led by Joseph Peau de Chat. Less than thirty years old, he was the son of a former chief, Jean Bapiste Peau de Chat, who is sometimes called in the fur trade records Peau de Chat the elder. North Shore Ojibwe had to live by their wits and negotiating skill, as there was little agricultural potential nearby and they were remote from markets to sell their one plentiful resource—fish. The great portage into the interior, geographical knowledge, and of late, the border became their chief bargaining resources of interest to whites.

To create a trading monopoly and increase their profits, the HBC negotiated a secret deal with the American Fur Company. In March 1833, William Aitken, an American Fur Company employee, entered into an agreement with George Simpson, governor of the Hudson's Bay Company, whereby the HBC would pay the AFC 300 pounds sterling to not trade with Ojibwe residing in border country west of Lake Superior.[18] This agreement would last until 1847, or fourteen years. The agreement remained secret enough that most AFC employees did not know of it, as illustrated by AFC men at La Pointe sending a trading outfit to Grand Portage in August 1836. Learning of the competition, the HBC objected. The AFC factor in La Pointe had to remove the fur trade outfit from Grand Portage.[19] Without the AFC trade competition, the local value of their furs declined, and more North Shore Ojibwe went northward to trade with HBC clerks at Fort William. The agreement also emboldened the Fort William clerk to demand that the Ojibwe be "released" from fishing at Isle Royale and Grand Portage and "sent off to their hunting grounds" so as to trap furs and continue trading with the HBC.[20] The Americans ignored this wish. There was an unopposed economic magnet to the north that encouraged travel to, and trading with, the British.

To improve his trading advantage, Espagnol "played the border" before and after the HBC-AFC agreement. For example, in the 1820s, not wishing to invoke the direct ire of the HBC by trading with the Americans himself, he directed his stepsons to do so. Or, often, he made it hard for the HBC traders to find him, as he and his band were encamped far inland on American lands. On one occasion, the HBC sought to curry his favor to the degree that they had chocolate brought to him while he was in the highlands inland from Grand Marais. In the late 1830s, he fished for the AFC at Grand Portage.[21] Yet he wished to settle near "the [HBC] forest so that the smoke of their homes might thence forward rise among Canadian forests; and that, being all Catholics, they should like to have a priest among them."[22] Still, the AFC fishing enterprise and a scattering of independent traders appearing in Grand Portage brought welcome economic opportunities to North Shore Ojibwe.

In truth, the North Shore Ojibwe lived on both sides of the border, sometimes trading at Grand Marais as well as Fort William. Jobs at posts provided food or trading credit, but the posts might be in what became Canada or the United States. Wild rice was harvested at Whitefish Lake in the British territory as well as at Rose Lake on the border. Caribou were hunted on American and Canadian lands. Religious instruction was sometimes available in Grand Portage, and in other years at Fort William. Families would resort to their maple sugar bush, recognized as a domain of a specific family on both sides of the border. North Shore Ojibwe lands spanned what became an international boundary that eventually complicated negotiations with the Americans and then the British.

## Three Treaties and the Isle Royale "Compact"

The great rumors of the Ontonagon Copper Rock, a copper isle and copper riches on the South Shore, drove the United States government to remove Indian claims to lands in the "copper district." The publishing of Douglas Houghton's "The Copper Report" in early 1841 started a "copper fever" among whites.[23] To remove obstacles to mining, the superintendent of Indian Affairs for Michigan was directed to commence negotiations with thousands of Lake Superior and Mississippi River Ojibwe at La Pointe, Wisconsin Territory. Replacing longtime Indian agent Henry Schoolcraft in April 1841, Robert Stuart became superintendent of Indian Affairs for Michigan, including Wisconsin Territory.

Negotiations began in late September 1842 at the village of La Pointe on Madeline Island. Many Ojibwe were invited, but the Grand Portage Ojibwe were not. Instead, when the treaty was being negotiated, most of the Grand Portage Band were helping Jesuit Father Francis Pierz build a chapel and schoolhouse on the Pigeon River, and harvesting crops, especially potatoes.[24] At the same time, a couple of Grand Portage leaders were on Manitoulin Island in Lake Huron, receiving presents from British officials.[25] Others were harvesting wild rice, taking credits for a fall hunt from Fort William traders, and making ready for the coming winter. There is no record that any Grand Portage Ojibwe were aware of the ongoing treaty making.

Three to four thousand Ojibwe gathered in La Pointe. In the opinion of one missionary, more Ojibwe would have attended except for the lateness of the season.[26] Unfortunately, commentary about what exactly transpired at the treaty is scarce and sometimes contradictory. Robert Stuart made a "sketch" of what was said on September 28, 1842, while negotiations were ongoing. His sketch presents his actions in the best possible light.[27]

The treaty began in high style. Groups arrived and were recognized with salutes of cannon fire and a return of musket fire. Perhaps the most impressive group to arrive was led by the celebrated chief Hole in the Day. One eyewitness described this arrival: "Upon the top of this Batteau a sort of deck or scaffold was raised, upon which the warriors were dancing to a war song, sung by a company of Indian musicians. When this party had landed they proce[e]ded to the council ground in truly martial order. The leader at their head bearing the American colors, succeded [sic] by the warriors and these followed by musicians consisting of drummers & singers and rattlers, that is men with rattles."[28] Indian agent Robert Stuart began the negotiations by offering tobacco and an introductory speech.

Sticking points quickly arose, especially the Ojibwe wariness of being removed from their homelands. Stuart agreed that the Ojibwe could stay on their homelands. Another troubling point was payment to "halfbreeds," and if so, the proper amount.[29] Formal negotiations and informal Indian councils went on for six days. Each day a council was summoned by the sound of cannon fire. More than forty-one Ojibwe headmen from as far away as Crow Wing River to Mille Lac to L'Anse, as well as the powerful Ojibwe delegation from the Upper Mississippi River country, attended the parlay. A number of

American Fur Company officials also witnessed the ceremony and would be paid significant Indian debts from the treaty money.

It is unlikely that the assembled Ojibwe understood the geographic bounds of the treaty. In his introductory speech, Stuart proposed purchasing the mineral district beginning at Chocolate River (near present-day Marquette, Michigan, where the previous treaty had left off) to Fond du Lac (site of present-day Duluth). Stuart then pointed out the country he was proposing to purchase upon a large hand-drawn map. Unfortunately, the map is no longer to be found.[30] Stuart, himself, had recently proposed different treaty boundaries to his superiors. The map he submitted to Indian Affairs commissioner Crawford in April 1842 only included the Upper Peninsula and not the territory along the Wisconsin South Shore. On a later map in September, Stuart included territory "up to Pigeon River," or the Minnesota North Shore, but does not identify Isle Royale by name.[31] Nor does it appear that Stuart specifically said either Isle Royale or Minong to the assembled Indian delegation.[32] Further, the exact geographical terms defining the area being treated differ between Stuart's opening speech of September 29th and his later ones, whose terms are incorporated into the treaty. The geographical uncertainty about the inclusion of Isle Royale was high because few whites knew exactly where it was located. Few maps were publicly available. For example, as late as 1837, officials of the American Fur Company wondered if the "Royal Islands" were in American territory, and they were stymied in their attempts to find a good map of the Island.[33] And since this treaty, like so many others, was largely a verbal agreement (and that through translators), versus a written one, and Isle Royale was unnamed, few Indians present likely knew that it was included.

Even if they knew Minong had been ceded, few of the Ojibwe present at La Pointe knew much about it. Few, if any, had been there. There were also some differences between the Ojibwe at the treaty and those at Grand Portage. The North Shore Ojibwe spoke a different [northern] Ojibwe dialect, and its members came from largely different clans than those at La Pointe. Further, if Isle Royale was depicted and labeled on a map, it is questionable if any chiefs present would have recognized its shape, its exact location on Lake Superior, or its distance from the mainland. If any Ojibwe knew it by name, it would have been Minong not "Isle Royale" as used by whites.

A number of Lake Superior Ojibwe remained reluctant to sign the treaty, worried that it would lead to their removal from their homelands. Stuart labored hard to convince them that they would be able to stay, but these terms were not included in the treaty language. Once the issue of payment to "half-breeds" was settled and Hole in the Day affirmed that he would "come to tie the knot," acceptance of the treaty was virtually assured.[34] The treaty was concluded with "the touching of the pen" on October 4, 1842. Each leader who "signed" would touch a pen signifying that he assented to the terms of the treaty—or the words presented to them by translators, Indian agent Robert Stuart, and the assembled traders with strong relationships with some Ojibwe leaders.

The 1842 Treaty sets a number of terms that define and shape North Shore Ojibwe use of Minong. Article 1 of the treaty begins:

> The Chippewa Indians of the Mississippi and Lake Superior, cede to the United States all the country within the following bounderies [sic]; viz: beginning at the mouth of Chocolate river [sic] of Lake Superior; thence northwardly across said lake to intersect the boundary line between the United States and the Province of Canada; thence up said Lake Superior, to the mouth of the St. Louis, or Fond du Lac river [sic] (including all the islands in said lake); thence up said river to the American Fur Company's trading post.

Article 2 of the treaty states: "The Indians stipulate the right of hunting on ceded territory, with the other privileges of occupancy." Article 5 asserts:

> Whereas the whole country between Lake Superior and the Mississippi, has always been understood as belonging in common to the Chippewas, party to this treaty; and whereas the bands bordering on Lake Superior, have not been allowed to participate in the annuity payments of the treaty made with the Chippewa of the Mississippi, at St. Peters July 29th 1837, and whereas all the unceded lands belonging to the aforesaid Indians, are hereafter to be held in common . . .

And Article 7 states, "This treaty shall be obligatory upon the contracting parties when ratified by the President and Senate of the United States."[35]

Exactly how the treaty area pertained to Minong was problematic. There is no explicit mention of Isle Royale or Minong, only the literally parenthetical statement, "all the islands in said lake." Stuart later would claim he traced a yellow line on a rough map illustrating the treaty area.[36] No Ojibwe would remember any such map in which the Island was identified.[37] Perhaps few of the three or four thousand looked at or could see the map or understood its legend and labels. Only one Ojibwe headman present, Mong o zet, or Loon's Foot, of Fond du Lac, likely had some knowledge of Minong. Mong o zet could have learned of Minong from North Shore Ojibwe during his employment with the American Fur Company at Grand Marais.

Ojibwe at the treaty assumed that "rights to hunting and other usual privileges of occupancy" would include fishing, gathering, maple-sugaring, and other typical uses of their traditional lands.

The treaty language in which "all lands [were] held in common" and that the assembled groups represented "one nation" was a strategic ploy of Indian agent Robert Stuart. Asserting all lands were held in common provided the numerically dominant Mississippi River Ojibwe a larger "vote" or influence on lands in which they were less involved than those living in their homelands along Lake Superior. In effect, Stuart was exploiting what he noted in his speech: "Your Great Father is sorry that there are divisions among his red children." Asserting that all treaty Indians held in common lands traditionally used by a few is remarkable in that Stuart is asserting rights for those who did not traditionally use areas. For example, if taken literally, Sandy Lake Ojibwe would have the same rights as those Ojibwe living on the Keweenaw Peninsula to hunt there. Stuart and the treaty sought to create use rights that did not exist at the time. The incentive for "western" or Mississippi River Ojibwe was treaty annuities.[38]

During the same month of the treaty, Methodist minister Alfred Brunson was named the new Indian subagent at La Pointe. Because of prior obligations and difficulty in travel, Brunson only arrived in La Pointe in January 1843. He quickly learned that his predecessor had stripped his office of all maps, copies of treaties, and correspondence.[39] Once in place and engaged in official duties, Brunson's version of what transpired at the treaty would clash markedly with that of Robert Stuart.

President John Tyler ratified the treaty on March 28, 1843.[40] The U.S. government then sprang into action to hasten copper exploration. With explorations at a high pitch, many assumed Indians would be removed from the area. The United States Mineral Land Agency was established in Copper Harbor, Michigan, in the spring of 1843. Rules were inserted to impose order on the "copper fever." The copper rock at Ontonagon was to be taken in possession by the U.S. Army. Speculators and miners were told they must lease mineral lands. Indians were told not to molest miners.[41] Whites poured into the copper district and searched for copper veins. During the summer of 1843, United States mineral agent Cunningham made two trips to Isle Royale, and during one trip he met a party of Ojibwe in Rock Harbor.[42] Noted professors were hired by hopeful mining investors and traveled to Isle Royale in the summer months. Professor Locke explored the northeastern end of Isle Royale for the Isle Royale and Ohio Mining Company.[43] Between thirty and forty leases were made on the Island, each lease typically being three-by-three miles square. While these claims were made on Isle Royale, little mining was done.[44]

During the same summer, trying to figure out his duties and obligations towards Indian schools, subagent Brunson received a written request from Reverend Baraga to start a school in Grand Portage. This simple request alerted Brunson to a number of vexing questions. He was supposed to visit the school as part of his duties, but without a map from the Webster Ashburton Treaty, he was unsure where the international boundary was in relation to the proposed Pigeon River School. Seeking clarification, he learned that there was a dilemma about the recent treaty and Isle Royale. The problem was that the Ojibwe who claimed it—Grand Portage Ojibwe—did not sign the treaty, indeed had not been invited to the treaty.[45] Brunson also learned that no one at La Pointe doubted that Isle Royale belonged to the Grand Portage Band.

Brunson even initially declared from La Pointe that "I was informed here that Mr. Stuart did not intend to purchase that Island, & therefore did not send for the Grand Portage Band who claim it."[46]

August 1843 was an anxious time at Grand Portage. The band and its leaders heard that Isle Royale had been sold, and perhaps even parts of their mainland home as well. Not connected to Stuart and other involved officials, band leaders were unsure of what had been done and agreed upon.[47] Learning that the first treaty payments were to be held in La Pointe in September, Grand Portage leaders Joseph Peau de Chat, Attikons, and Shawgawnawsheence determined to go. They sought to learn what had transpired, and if necessary plead their case. Arriving at La Pointe with little fanfare, Peau de Chat and the delegation pieced together information that Isle Royale was considered ceded by most U.S. government officials. But their fellow kinsmen, assuming the Island had not been sold, argued that the Grand Portage Band should be excluded from treaty payments as they were not parties to the treaty.[48] Firmly declaring they had not sold Minong, but also realizing it was unlikely they would be able to maintain possession of it, the Grand Portage delegation sent a counterproposal to the U.S. government:

> We the undersigned Chiefs of Grand Portage, Lake Superior, understand, that a portion of our land (: Royal Island and 18 small islands:) was included in the Treaty made last fall at La Pointe, Lake Superior; and mines have already been found on Royal Island, and occupied by a mining Company of Americans. We even understand, that probably the mean-land [sic] of Grand Portage is also included in the said Treaty.
>
> We now declare, that all this has been done without our consent, even without our knowledge; and our land cannot be considered as ceded, by the afore said treaty, to the United States. But if Government wish to possess the Islands, which abound with copper mines, we will sell them. The price we ask for them, is seventy-five thousand dollars, payable in annuities of three thousand dollars, during twenty-five years, to be paid half in cash, and half in goods.[49]

Four days after their original proposal, and apparently stymied from getting treaty payments and not detecting any change in the U.S. government's position, the Grand Portage delegation moderated their proposal. Instead of selling Isle Royale for $75,000, they reduced their proposal to $60,000. Being more explicit with their second proposal, they added: "The said chief and head men further propose, that if the President and Senate of the United States accept and ratify this proposal, it shall be forever binding."[50] Unable to meet, because so many Ojibwe were conferring with Brunson and his time was taken up with dispensing annuities, Peau de Chat wrote an additional letter. He added, "I do not wish to have anything to do with the other Inds. who have already ceded their lands. . . . And in case you would buy the Island, I want to be paid as early as possible and I wish to be paid at the Grand Portage and no where else."[51] The 1843 treaty payments ended without the Grand Portage Ojibwe receiving any payment, because the "Leech Lake and western bands all refused to allow them to participate in the money, goods, and provisions . . . saying their [Grand Portage] lands were not sold."[52]

Brunson had now become convinced the treaty was deeply flawed, and he began correspondence with his superiors, seeking to persuade them to correct its defects. He first wrote to General Walter Cunningham on September 27th informing him that the Ojibwe denied selling Isle Royale, and argued it would be best to accept their offer of $60,000 for its sale. He further intimated that if something agreeable were not done, it would lead to "serious trouble—it is on the British line, where men would gladly fan the flame of discord, if once ignited and supply the Indians with the means of offensive and defensive war. . . . The Indians have justice and equity on their side."[53]

Stung by Brunson's assertions of Indian rights and intimation of possible hostilities, Cunningham quickly wrote to the secretary of war, James Madison Porter, discrediting Brunson, saying he "thought him insane." He also noted that he already had given out many mining permits and "he [had] already taken the possession" of Isle Royale. And there was more: While passing through La Pointe, Cunningham had heard Brunson assert that "there was a Band of Indians living upon Isle Royale."[54] Writing a follow-up letter to the secretary of war, Cunningham laid the blame on Brunson for not squelching this alternative view of whether Isle Royale had been sold or not. Cunningham seethed and wrote, "One day [of withholding payments] would have brought them all to their knees." While irked, he concluded that nothing could be done about this trouble until the next year. But the secretary of war did not wait and removed Brunson from office that October.[55]

His reputation tarnished, Brunson defended himself and several unpopular positions, including the position that Isle Royale had not been legally ceded. In his defense, he wrote that he was threatened with the information "that Isle Royale will be claimed, by force, if necessary, and that probably I shall be removed from office, on the charge of not carrying out the policy of the government." He added: "But if it is the policy of government to defraud the poor unlettered Indian of his lands, and that, too, without even the pretense of treaty with the rightful owners, I must beg to be excused from sustaining such a policy."[56] That fall and winter, additional government correspondence continued to blame Brunson for "the Isle Royale difficulty." Declaring that the Island had been properly ceded, still they recognized that something must be done to squelch the question, "as the Indians [are] perfectly crazy on this subject."[57] Robert Stuart, the author of the treaty, proposed additional gifts to the chiefs at the next annuity payments to settle the question. He estimated these would cost approximately $500 to $1,000 at the most.[58] Later, he figured that "$500–$400 worth of Powder and say $100 for a pair of oxen to feast upon" would be enough to straighten out this problem.[59]

Subagent Hurlburt, Stuart's new employee, brought to the forefront in private correspondence what had been a latent argument. He asserted that "the Grand Portage Indians have no right to Isle Royale, because they *in fact* are all British Indians—that is they trade with them and go annually to the English at Fort William. This has been the case since 1834."[60] His choice of 1834 was ironic because that was the year in which the secret and likely illegal agreement between the HBC and AFC began. Stuart seized on this point of whether Grand Portage Ojibwe were British or American Indians in his correspondence with his superiors as to why they had not been invited to the 1842 Treaty. "That a small Band of about 20 men, residing about the Grand Portage, and trading with the Hudson Bay Co., were not notified to attend the treaty, because they were believed to be British Indians." His argument that they were British was clever in that it was complicated and was not likely to be fully understood at the time. Perhaps somewhat uneasy about how his argument might be accepted by the Ojibwe, he also requested "troops in the country to quell any troubles." [61]

However, a number of witnesses present at the treaty, and perhaps Stuart himself, knew about the relationship between the North Shore Ojibwe and Isle Royale. The question of whether they were "British Indians" is complicated by the secret AFC-HBC agreement that economically lured Ojibwe to trade northward. If some of the band were drawn across the border to trade because the post was much closer than an American post, would that make them British?[62] Or, conversely, if some of the band lived on British lands and yet "owned" Isle Royale, would they have any standing in an accord?

There is no direct evidence that Stuart knew of this covert agreement between the AFC and HBC. However, with his knowledge and privileged position as a senior AFC official and then Indian agent, he was in a position to know about such business deals.[63]

Stuart's assertion that Portage Ojibwe were British subjects, which held sway in much correspondence, was contradicted by many actions of the United States government, which, in effect, recognized them as Ojibwe residing on American territory.[64] Perhaps most damning to his position and innocence was the fact that he knew that the U.S. government was paying a schoolteacher at Grand Portage in 1842, because he managed this arrangement.[65] North Shore Ojibwe only learned of the treaty because of correspondence about the school. Catholic Fathers Baraga and Pierz were seeking back pay for teaching and had begun writing to Stuart. In addition, U.S. Indian agents regularly licensed traders for Grand Portage as late as 1841.[66] U.S. censuses were taken of the numbers of Grand Portage Indians, including one in September 1840 in which then agent Schoolcraft asserted that there were two hundred Chippewa on Isle Royale.[67] And even while the secret agreement between the HBC and AFC was in effect, the American Fur Company received a license for these fishing operations at Grand Portage and Isle Royale, with the U.S. Indian agent in charge.

Stuart's assertion that Grand Portage Indians were British Indians is duplicitous in another respect. While an AFC official in Mackinac from 1817 to 1834, Stuart met and corresponded with members of the United States Border Survey, particularly in 1822 and 1823. Indeed, Stuart even outfitted the U.S. Survey crew whose mission was to designate the border north of Isle Royale and west of Lake Superior. Stuart also served as a witness to contracts made with voyageurs providing the muscle for the survey crew.[68] He worried, in his correspondence, that the AFC might lose a lucrative contract if the survey crew received supplies from the Hudson's Bay Company at Fort William. All the while, he was advising the Border Survey crew. He was in a strategic position to learn what the United States Border Commission would argue with their British counterparts, namely, that Grand Portage was within the United States border. Clearly then, Grand Portage Indians would be American Indians, and Stuart likely knew this long before the 1842 treaty.[69]

Quite a number of the witnesses and claimants to the treaty knew about United States licensing of Indian trade at Grand Portage and North Shore Ojibwe connections to Isle Royale. However, there is no record that anyone came forward with the information during the treaty. Cyrus Mendenhall, a witness, was the co-owner of the Cleveland [North Lake] Company, which owned a schooner, the *Algonquin*, that sailed regularly to Grand Portage and Isle Royale. He also leased mining tracts on the Island. His company claimed that $1,485.67 was owed to them from the Indian trade, and treaty payments were a way to recover this money. Pierre Cotte lived in Grand Portage for four years, provided lay religious instruction to residents, and intimately knew of North Shore Ojibwe fishermen on Isle Royale. He claimed the Indians owed him $732.50—likely the majority of these debts would have been incurred when he ran the AFC operation at Grand Portage. Other claimants in the treaty—James Scott, George Johnston, George Bonga—knew of the intimate connections between Grand Portage Ojibwe and Isle Royale. While there were plenty of treaty witnesses and claimants who knew of the North Shore Ojibwe connection to Isle Royale, they did not make any existing statements affirming that connection.[70] Nor does it appear that they wanted to cross the imperious Stuart with concerns about the Grand Portage Band's long history with Minong.

Ironically, most of the clerks at Fort William considered a good many of their clients to be American Indians. And they kept close watch on these Indians, and others who might defect to American traders, often treating them to gifts that others might not receive. Espagnol was frequently called an "American chief," as was Attikons. One Fort William clerk would write: "There are many of them whose hunting ground lies beyond the Boundary Line and extends with in fifteen leagues of the American establishment at Fond du Lac"—or most of the way to Duluth![71]

In 1844, Grand Portage headmen were aware that difficulties lay ahead at the La Pointe negotiations. However, the murder of a community member near La Pointe added another level of unease. Louis Rivet, whose two children were born on Minong, disappeared near La Pointe during the spring of 1844. Portagers alleged he was murdered by "some Indians of the interior of that place. . . . [And] put the corpse under the ice of a small lake."[72] Unsure of what had happened to their community member and by whom, the Grand Portage delegation went to La Pointe.

British Indians or not, Stuart traveled to La Pointe for the 1844 treaty payments to solve the question of Isle Royale cession. Arriving in September, he "found the Indians assemble[d] at La Pointe, & under considerable excitement in relation to Isle Royale."[73] Gathering the Ojibwe together, Stuart concluded a compact to resolve the Isle Royale question. The compact reads:

> Whereas a difference of opinion has heretofore existed between the United States and a portion of the Chippewa Indians of the Mississippi & Lake Superior, in relation to the cession of Isle Royale, by the treaty concluded with them on the 4th day of October 1842, at La Pointe, in the Territory of Wisconsin. Be it therefore known, that the said Indians hereby declare themselves satisfied with the explanation now made by the commissioner of the United States, of the said Isle Royale having been included in the cession of that treaty, and by these presents, they ratify and confirm said cession. In consideration of which, & the regard which the President of

the United States bears to his red children of the Chippewa nation—Four hundred dollars worth of gun powder, & one hundred dollars worth of fresh beef, shall be delivered to the said Indians, on their signing this compact—In witness whereof, we hereunto set our hands, at La Pointe, this 20th day of August A.D. 1844.

Forty-one of the fifty-three Ojibwe chiefs made an "X" at their name, including Shawgawnawsheence, or Little Englishman, and Attikons, or Little Caribou, from Grand Portage. Because of illness, Joseph Peau de Chat was unable to attend.[74] The $500 in gunpowder and beef were shared equally among all assembled, and likely little of it remained when the Grand Portage delegation paddled back to Grand Portage. In reality, their share of the payment for Isle Royale was so meager and mixed in with other payment proceedings that it is unclear if the Grand Portage delegation understood they had been paid. The Grand Portage delegation received more valuable goods previously from the AFC, who sought to keep their trade from moving to the upstart Cleveland Company, than from the 1844 payment.[75]

Commissioner of Indian Affairs Crawford wrote in a congressional summary that the Isle Royale difficulty, which was "very improperly raised, and utterly without foundation," was resolved. Or, in his words, "I am gratified that the encouragement of the groundless pretension set up, and its possible consequences, have been so quietly and cheaply put by."[76] Assuming the compact was merely an addendum to the 1842 Treaty, the government neither sought to have, nor did have, the compact ratified by the Senate and the President. Whether it was legally concluded without such ratification is for legal scholars.[77] However, it did not die so quietly among the Grand Portage Ojibwe. Through time, they repeatedly protested the nature of the events and questioned whether their title to Isle Royale had ever been truly extinguished. As late as 2006, a candidate for the Reservation Tribal Council wrote in a campaign letter, "We still have a tie to Isle Royale. Our Grand Fathers were not present or were not a signatories on the document that gave Isle Royale to Michigan. Our ancestors traveled to and from Isle Royale for generations before anyone else set foot on the island."[78]

The Isle Royale treaty question and overlapping leases made investing money in Isle Royale mining a complicated business. Walter Cunningham, the mineral agent, elected to suspend awarding leases in 1844 to "shew [sic] to the Indians that it [the U.S. government] did not place so high a value upon it and was not so very anxious to retain it—and further that the Whites and Indians should be kept apart from each other and thereby avoid any collision or occasion for it."[79] The copper rush was mismanaged. Problems arose because speculators could apply for leases at the Copper Harbor Mineral Office and Washington, D.C. This inevitably led to claims and counterclaims for the same leased ground. Duplicate permits tangled up the process and retarded investment in mining. Some mining on Isle Royale began in 1846 and increased in 1847, with eleven mining ventures ongoing. However, from 1845 on, no more leases were issued; they were suspended first by administrative means, then because of a U.S. Supreme Court decision that stated there was no authority to lease mineral lands on Isle Royale. In December 1851 the General Land Office at Sault Ste. Marie for the first time sold Isle Royale lands, on which mineral prospects might be located.[80]

The Isle Royale Compact was the first of a succession of treaties that would enmesh the North Shore Ojibwe and strip them of most of their lands. The 1850 Robinson-Superior Treaty negotiated by Joseph Peau de Chat and twenty other tribal leaders and the British Canadian representative, William Robinson,[81] would cede most of the traditional territory of the Portage Band to the Crown. Beginning on the Pigeon River and going inland as far as the watershed divide or the height of land, all the lands in the Lake Superior drainage basin were ceded to the British government. The treaty negotiations took place at Sault Ste. Marie in late August and early September 1850. Peau de Chat played a lead role in the negotiations, yet was again very ill during the deliberations.[82]

Joseph Peau de Chat was described in 1849 as "dressed like the white men, as were most of the Indians. He is a man of about 40, tall and well built, with a vibrant, sonorous voice. His eloquent enthusiasm and vehement impetuosity have caused the Indians to elect him as their chief." While relatively young for a chief, he was chronically ill.[83] Further, these negotiations occurred during personally trying times. A cholera epidemic near the Sault Ste. Marie cut short a British pre-treaty fact-finding party, and at the same time Joseph Peau de Chat's father died. Never recovering his health, Joseph would die less than two years after his father and only one year after the Robinson-Superior Treaty was concluded.[84]

In many significant ways, the Robinson-Superior Treaty was similar to the 1842 Treaty of La Pointe. Canadian North Shore Ojibwe, like their South Shore kinsmen, kept hunting and fishing rights on public lands, and the treaty was a surrender of land for cash. It was also similar to the American treaty in that the British sought to treat with a mass of assembled tribal leaders. Peau de Chat again sought to treat separately, but again failed to achieve this desire. Even one treaty clause would be hauntingly familiar to the North Shore Ojibwe, namely, that they would be dispossessed of "the Islands within the said Lake within the boundaries of the British possessions therein."[85] And both treaties would be concluded with the "touching of the pen" signifying tribal leaders' affirmation of the treaty as they understood it.

And yet the Robinson and La Pointe treaties were also quite different. Mining had already begun on the Canadian side of the lake prior to the treaty making.[86] Ojibwe were indignant about this injustice, and they protested by publishing a full-page plea in the *Montreal Gazette* in 1849. Also, an Ojibwe raid had shut the Mica Bay Mine down. To calm Canadian North Shore Ojibwe prior to treaty making, the governor general, Lord Elgin, pardoned two Ojibwe leaders, Shingwuakonse and Ninina-goo-ging, and two Métis leaders for their efforts in this Mica Bay Mine affair.[87]

The Robinson Treaty negotiations were also different in that they were conducted in light of the earlier American treaty. Terms of the Robinson Treaty were compared either favorably or unfavorably with the prior American treaty. Thus, to make their position more palatable, British government officials reminded the Ojibwe that they were not decreeing that Ojibwe would be removed westward. At the same time, the Ojibwe negotiators noted that the Americans paid more per acre.[88] By the time of its conclusion, most Fort William Ojibwe assumed they were to be given clothing for life as a treaty provision. A year later, they learned clothing was not included, which many believed Robinson had promised.[89]

The Robinson Treaty was different than the prior American treaties in the region in that it created "reserves" for Ojibwe to reside within. Tragically the Fort William Reserve, the location selected by Joseph Peau de Chat, was remarkably small.[90] One feature of the Robinson Treaty was unique in that Indians would be paid an adjusted amount for mining claims. Not pleased with Peau de Chat, the British government sought to unseat him as the primary Fort William chief.[91] And Peau de Chat, coming to the negotiations as a relatively important tribal leader, rather than an afterthought at La Pointe, sought to increase his leadership across to other bands. He did not succeed in these attempts.[92] He was successful in reaching a treaty agreement in which Hudson's Bay Company clerks would dispense treaty payment at Fort William prior to August 1, which meant it was at a convenient time for the band.[93]

Interviews between Peau de Chat and the various British officials are revealing of conditions at Fort William at the time. While fielding questions from Indian agents, Peau de Chat remarked: "I am the chief of the Catholic Indians." Peau de Chat's Catholic band was the largest of the Fort William groups, and hereafter religious affiliation would be mixed with geographic predisposition among the North Shore Ojibwe bands. Thus, some of the band would identify themselves as either a Catholic band or a smaller Baptist band in British territory, or a "Pagan" band in the United States.[94] Clearly, the presence of three ambitious and active missionaries in their midst accentuated religious matters, including religious identification.

During an interrogation about the general territory of the North Shore Ojibwe, Peau de Chat confirmed that the band's territory straddled the border. When asked about receiving treaty payments also in the United States, he answered: "What is it you wish to know? Would it be a crime for the Americans to give me money? Would it be a crime also for the English to pay me? . . . Is it not my land that is in question in this deal? The English land is also my land."[95]

Four years after the Robinson Treaty, and three years after Peau de Chat's death, the Americans sought a treaty to cede all the Ojibwe lands in Northeastern Minnesota. In a tragically familiar story, accounts of valuable minerals in the area led to white trespass and the desire for the mineral-rich lands to be available for claims. At the same time treaty-making preparations were going on, a new trader, H. H. McCullough, established a new store at Grand Portage, making it a more economically attractive place. The Grand Portage Ojibwe were pleased with this development, as they knew McCullough from his mining and fishing operations on Isle Royale. Grand Portage Ojibwe liked McCullough to the degree that they hoped to have him named their Indian agent.[96]

The importance of McCullough's fishing operations is illustrated by the fact that most Portage Ojibwe were fishing at Isle Royale rather than participating directly at the treaty negotiations.[97] Across the lake at La Pointe, the crowded and chaotic atmosphere of the 1854 Treaty engulfed the small Grand Portage Ojibwe delegation. After the treaty, and hearing what the Grand Portage headman reported about it, a Fort William Jesuit wrote:

> In a first council the chiefs from the lake [Lake Superior bands] resolved to say no. Atikons[98] was put in charge of talking, he related very well . . . the former decisions of savages. . . . (Mr. Gilbert) the agent of the government had said then that they would not address them anymore, but to those [Ojibwe] from the Mississippi. For a whole week, it was a constantly growing confusion of notices, councils, threats, frights, etc. The merchants were putting themselves in the party, taking sides, to attract payments towards their business. The agents shouted at the chiefs a few times in the presence of the whole assembly of savages. Many were armed with small axes and appeared to threaten whoever was speaking of giving away the land. A few times the chiefs were taken aside to an apartment, above the big room. Finally the fear of losing both their lands and the advantage of being on the lake compelled [them] to consent [to the treaty]. . . .
>
> After the conclusion of the treaty, the Agent distributed meals to the chiefs and subchiefs. Almost all those who received them appeared to be very proud of them, but the 3 chiefs of Grand Portage refused those which were offered to them. . . .
>
> La Pointe, during those three weeks was a theater of debauchery and libertinage. Mr. McCullough told me that the band from Grand Portage

was noted for better conduct and a more dignified attitude during the whole time of the councils. . . .

Now Grand Portage has become once again an important place. 185 savages are inscribed on the list of its inhabitants. And the 400 of the Bois Blanc [Bois Forte Band] are supposed to come there every summer for the distribution of the annuities. . . .

The Little Englishman in a visit recounts one part of the treaty details. He admits the superiority of Atikons for speaking. The Little Englishman and Memachkawash had resolved to say nothing and to let Atikons answer along all the requests of the government envoy.[99]

An eyewitness account of the 1854 Treaty deliberations reported that

Atte-konse may appropriately be styled the Roman of the Chippewas. With his nation, as well as with the white people, he sustains a reputation for good character, wisdom, integrity and inflexible firmness. . . .

His costume was always plain, though elegant quite uniformly, each day in his native dress; his size and height are full, rather more, his features quite regular and prominent. Perhaps no one at the payment, red, or white man, surpassed Atte-Konse in genuine dignity of mien and manner. He gave his age as sixty-six, though appearing much younger. He made several speeches during the payment. . . . His cool manner—sensible words, and self-possession in council, were subjects of general remark.

He was the last to yield title to their lands, purchased by our Government. Among the chiefs and Indians assembled at the treaty, Atte-Konse long stood, *solitary and alone*, pitting himself, nobly, against the Government orators, and insisting that the proffers of annuities, etc, were inadequate, and not sufficient for the cession or sale of the lands of the Chippewas—though finally a compromise was effected, the Government yielding to the satisfaction of the chief.[100]

The 1854 Treaty provided cash (and goods) for ceded lands. It also prescribed reservations on homelands for all of the "Lake Superior Chippewa," including

Grand Portage, rather than removal. Contrary to the objectives of Robert Stuart in the 1842 Treaty, the 1854 Treaty recognized a difference in ownership between the group of bands living along or nearby Lake Superior and those from the Mississippi River:

> The Chippewas of the Mississippi hereby assent and agree to the foregoing cession, and consent that the whole amount of the consideration money for the country ceded above, shall be paid to the Chippewas of Lake Superior, and in consideration thereof the Chippewas of Lake Superior hereby relinquish to the Chippewas of the Mississippi all their interest in and claim to the lands heretofore owned by them in common, lying west of the above boundary-line.

Article 4 of the treaty provides for

> household furniture and cooking utensils; three thousand dollars in agricultural implements and cattle, carpenter's and other tools and building materials, and three thousand dollars for moral and education purposes, of which last sum, three hundred dollars per annum shall be paid to the Grand Portage band, to enable them to maintain a school at their village.

Articles 5 and 11 provided for a blacksmith and assistant to be furnished at reservations, and provided for treaty payments at Grand Portage and other Lake Superior locations. Further, Article 11 provided "such as them as reside in the territory hereby ceded, shall have the right to hunt and fish therein, until otherwise ordered by the President."

Four Grand Portage leaders signed the agreement: "Shaw-gaw-naw-sheence, or the Little Englishman, 1st chief," "May-mosh-caw-wosh, headman," "Aw-de-konse, or the Little Reindeer, 2nd chief," and "Way-we-ge-wam, headman."[101] However, they expressed some symbolic reluctance as they refused to accept the "peace medals" offered to them at the treaty conclusion, in contrast to other Ojibwe signatories who accepted medals. Discord spread when treaty payments were unevenly distributed, with some Grand Portage Ojibwe getting nothing. And only days later, an unnamed sickness spread from La Pointe to Grand Portage, Fort William, Isle Royale, and Rainy Lake.[102]

Attikons and others had successfully won a key provision, namely, the disbursement of payments at their home location. This minimized the effort to get to annuities and thus permitted the continuation of some traditional activities at home during this time. Eventually, however, the timing of treaty payments in late August and early September would cut into wild rice harvesting time. And for two years, hundreds of Bois Forte Ojibwe would canoe and portage to Grand Portage to receive their payments. This led to many feasts, lacrosse, and the reinvigoration of traditional religious practices—to the dismay of the Jesuit fathers.[103]

## More Struggles

Annuity payments were made in cash—really coin—goods, furniture, cooking utensils, agricultural implements and cattle, building tools, schools, guns, beaver traps, ammunition, and clothing. An obvious goal of the treaty was to civilize the Ojibwe, as measured by dress, schooling, individual ownership of land, and agricultural pursuits. Farming at Grand Portage is difficult, as elder Ellen Olson made clear: "So when you look at Grand Portage, there's a pile of rock there and trees and a lot of water, but not much else to make a living with. It's a hard place to live."[104] Still, the Indian agent often measured progress by the acreage under cultivation. In 1859 "twelve acres of ground" were under cultivation. By 1878, there were fifteen to twenty acres under cultivation. Occasionally there was a remarkable harvest—in 1860, for example, 3,000 bushels of potatoes were grown and lots of fish were salted in barrels for the winter because of the good supply of salt available. In 1901 a remarkable harvest produced 1,375 bushels of potatoes, 240 bushels of turnips, 75 bushels of onions, and 30 bushels of beans. More often, however, an Indian agent would remark that they were "the poorest Band in the agency," or of all the Lake Superior Ojibwe.[105]

An Indian agent declared to a Jesuit father at Grand Portage that "the plan of the government was to fix the savage bands on fairly narrow reservations, and to force them there to some degree of civilization." To this end, in 1855, a number of Grand Portage Ojibwe were given cooking stoves for their cabins so they would "refrain from their wandering life."[106] However, their "roving habits" kept them moving off-reservation to hunt and gather food, as well as for employment. Despite efforts of the missionaries and Indian agents, their "roving disposition" and "following the chase" continued for quite some time.[107] This frequent movement in pursuit of food or employment meant it was difficult keeping track of who lived at each reservation. To sort out these issues for treaty payments, "it is settled that only those who will reside on the reservation will be recognized as belonging to these different bands." By this forced inducement, it became imperative to declare yourself either a "Grand Portage" or "Fort William" Chippewa.[108]

The limited amount of annuity goods produced a temptation to reduce the number of claimants. The imposition of the border became one way to eliminate Ojibwe from being on both American and British annuity lists and payments. The growing calls for, and even advantages of, residing in one reserve or another, or near the Mission of Immaculate Conception, made for heart-wrenching years. Instead of being able to play the border for positive advantage, the border now became exclusionary. One chief would jockey to deny another band's options to come north or south to also receive payments. For example, in 1849, when the only treaty payments in the region were at Fort William, Little Englishman requested that his band move to Fort William. Initially Peau de Chat resisted this request, but later relented. Earlier, Fort William Ojibwe kinsmen at Nipigon and Rainy Lake also tried to get put on annuity payment lists at Fort William.[109]

The HBC clerk at Fort William did not want more Indians near his post, as he was worried they would exhaust the nearby game and post provisions. A succession of clerks would lament in their reports that the bands nearby were reliant "On fish, potatoes & Indian Corn" available at the post. During one hard winter, "two thirds of the poor Indians must abandon their lands and resort to this establishment." Or, as during the winter of 1833–34, many of the nearby Ojibwe would resort to Fort William from January to March.[110] The fur traders' interest in keeping Ojibwe dispersed, but able to travel to

Fort William, would be superseded by the interests of the missionaries and government officials on both sides of the border.

The immediate consequences of the treaties is best described by North Shore Ojibwe—in this case, the Fort William Band—responding to the consequences of the 1850 Robinson-Superior Treaty:

> Father, we abandon to you our lands, our rivers, our lake and the islands which bathed them. But in doing that, have we renounced our lives and the lives of our children? We told you that we wanted to keep our fisheries. And you wrote on your paper: my children have given up all their islands, without reserve. Did you not think that when the white skin find our fish good, he will go and ask you for it? And you will give them up to him: and it is written on your paper that the red skin will no longer have the right to go and stretch his nets there.
>
> Father, you told us: My children, leave hunting to work the earth and make your food come out of it. Father, the animals which we hunt are well dressed, the Great Being gave them that advantage, and they only have to seek and stalk their prey. Our children are naked, and you, you replace for us the Great Being, above all since we surrendered to you that which was given to us; and do you not have pity of their misery. If we do not hunt, they will die of hunger and above all of cold.[III]

"Hungry years" preceded and followed the treaties. In the words of a veteran trader at Fort William:

> All this part of the country, in former times produced a good many Beaver & Otters—the Indians now complain of a scarcity in those animals—there are still many martins & cats, but foxes, fishers & bears are not numerous & the Musquash [sic] not so much so as in other parts of the Country, near the Lake. Formerly there were Moose Deer—at this time not one is to be seen, being literally extinct—Carribou [sic] was also at a former period, and not a great many years since very numerous—few now are seen. The scarcity of those Animals is greatly felt by the Indians. In winter their sole dependence

for subsistence, is on Rabbits & Partridges of various kinds. In the Summer & Fall the Indians are furnished with nets & in the fall they are supplied with a good stock of ammunition. Notwithstanding these supplies they are often necessitated to have recourse to the establishment when we give them fish, potatoes & Indian Corn.[112]

Caribou numbers on Isle Royale hung on longer than on the mainland, making trips to hunt Minong caribou more attractive. However, the increased numbers of hunters on the Island and in the region soon depleted the remaining big game.[113] In 1851, Indian agent Henry Sibley reported:

"The Sug-wun-dug-ah-win-iin-e-wug [living along the north coast of Lake Superior] are miserably poor, depending for subsistence upon the precarious supplies of the chase; they rely for their winter's support upon the rabbit and reindeer. Last year the rabbit almost entirely disappeared, having been swept off by a distemper. Great distress ensued, and during the winter thirteen of their number literally starved to death. This season the rice crop has failed, and these people anticipate with aching hearts the sufferings and deprivations of the approaching winter. Our government has shown them but little attention, and their predilections are in favor of the British, who have treated them with much kindness."[114]

A few years later, a Jesuit priest would write, "Hunger torments them [the Ojibwe]," chasing the savages from Grand Portage to Fort William. Another failure of the wild rice left them again vulnerable. More reliably, fish continued to be their mainstay, but they were largely reliant upon cash to purchase gill nets. But factors such as high winds, or not having enough salt to preserve the fish might greatly diminish their catch. Time spent on trapping animals for their fur and cash often meant not harvesting wild food. The hungry years became hungry decades, especially with the scarcity of fish and game, including the desertion of fish from shallow waters of the interior.[115]

The hungry years were also those of heightened missionary activity at Grand Portage, Fort William, and Isle Royale. From the summer of 1848 onward, there were resident Jesuit fathers nearby. The Mission of Immaculate Conception started at Pigeon River in the summer of 1848 and a year later moved to the Kaministiquia River upriver of Fort William. Three fathers—including one devoted to frequent travel, Father Nicholas Fremiot—made frequent trips to Grand Portage and Isle Royale proselytizing Ojibwe, miners, and indeed anyone who would hear them. Fremiot took regular canoe trips to Isle Royale to provide Catholic services, baptisms, marriages, and death rites.

Traditional Ojibwe religion persisted, but now in a highly charged atmosphere. Jesuit fathers charged those who did not convert as "infidels" and used many means such as shaming and demeaning their religious traditions. Jesuits also worked to keep traditional religious practitioners away from their church settlements. To assist in the conversion, many services were spoken in a mixture of Ojibwe, French, and Latin. A number of Ojibwe "converted" to the Catholic faith, but despite Fathers Chone, Pooter, and Fremiot's rigorous evaluation of whether these were true conversions, many held mixed religious beliefs. In 1855, the Jesuit fathers reported that at Grand Portage, they considered there to be "64 Catholics, 50 infidels, and 5 heretics."[116] Jesuit fathers looked for outward signs of religious conversion. Thus, fathers would assert the superiority of Ojibwe who used cabins versus lodges, tables and chairs versus sitting on the ground, and table salt when cooking.[117]

Other Ojibwe investigated Christianity through conversion to help them understand the power and ideas of whites. For example, chief Espagnol experimented with Christianity during 1838. He began the summer by conferring with Father Pierz at Grand Portage, but by late summer he was baptized at an Episcopal Church at Manitoulin Island. On September 30, 1838, Father Pierz baptized him a Catholic at Grand Portage.[118] However, Espagnol also was clearly guided by powerful manitous. Eight years earlier, the Spaniard had summoned all his traditional power and sanctions and shouldered the most unpleasant of traditional tasks: killing an Ojibwe man—a windigo—who had killed others. In an era before policemen, on occasion a "strong person" would be elected to kill someone who posed a danger to others. Demonstrating power to confront a windigo, Espagnol killed a man named Oom-bee-wia-bawsh near Basswood Lake.[119] With his baptisms and actions within a traditional role, it is unclear exactly what Espagnol believed and if his conversion was superficial. Or, was he turning to Christianity, any Christian faith, as a means of "gaining wealth, power, and knowledge, and [he] wanted to share in those white benefits?" He may alternately have been selectively adding elements of Christianity to his traditional religion.[120]

The syncretic nature of one nearby Ojibwe headman's beliefs is well illustrated by his exchanges with Jesuit father Specht:

One of the chiefs, M'koy [Bebamijas], told Father Hebert in my presence that "baptized white people go to heaven and are received," and that "baptized Indians go there also but are not received."

"Who told you this?" asked the Father.

"Those who have been there," he replied.

"Where are those people?" [asked the Father.]

"Out West," replied the chief.[121]

Wedding Christian and traditional beliefs, including the ability to communicate with the dead residing in the West, the Savanne River chief stunned the Jesuits. Some Ojibwe accepted both the Midewiwin and Catholicism—to the consternation of the Jesuit priests.[122]

Espagnol's successor, Joseph Peau de Chat, experienced more dictatorial Catholic authority. Jesuits were close at hand and were demanding of his behavior. While Father Pierz baptized Joseph Peau de Chat, and he called himself a Catholic chief, he skirmished with the Jesuit fathers about acceptable behavior and participating in traditional religious ceremonies. Jesuit fathers objected to his relations with a widow and threw him out of the church.[123] After making amends, he was tentatively let back in the church. Back with the widow, he was expulsed from the church again. Church leaders called him "Joseph L'Apostate" and he responded, in turn, that no Catholics should come to his lodge. Even on his deathbed, he made an uneasy compromise with the Jesuit fathers.[124] The fathers renounced Joseph's request that his body be put on a scaffold, rather than buried. The battle of wills between Joseph Peau de Chat and the Jesuit fathers was but one example of the pressure of Catholic practices, beliefs, and schedules that weighed heavily on many Fort William and Grand Portage Ojibwe.

Religious inroads impacted the social structure of North Shore Ojibwe. Once a clan-based society occupying a territory straddling the border, it became more and more organized along religious lines. Leaders hoped that by converting they could help their community and maintain their status and leadership roles. The Catholic band, initially led by Joseph Peau de Chat, was the most numerous. Illinois led the Methodist band and Attikons the traditionalists. Memashkawash led a small band of Christians at Grand Portage.[125] Doctrinal disputes between Catholic priests and Methodist ministers would be played out among the Ojibwe. Factionalism was growing with exclusionistic Christianity. The separation of Catholic, Methodist, and traditionalist Ojibwe had its parallels along the lake at L'Anse, Michigan, and Red Cliff/Bad River, Wisconsin. In some cases, the religious bands would seek to geographically separate themselves from their kinsmen of a different religion. However, selecting a "home" on one side of the international border magnified the separation between church-based bands and created new hardships.[126] For example, Catholic Indians labored heroically to have members of the church buried in consecrated grounds at the mission, even if the death occurred at Isle Royale.

Traditional Ojibwe religion continued on Minong in the 1850s and was seen by the Jesuits as "superstition" that should be extinguished. For example, to stop native ceremonies, Jesuits established a church on the former Midewiwin grounds at Grand Portage. They worked mightily to stop and ban traditional shamanistic ceremonies. At a camp at the mouth of Washington Harbor, Isle Royale, Fremiot witnessed and condemned a shaking tent ceremony. An Ojibwe grandfather—converted to Catholicism—destroyed his grandson's drum and stopped religious singing. Bits of the drum were thrown into the water.[127] For the Jesuits, Isle Royale was a place of "old scandals," which, in their way of thinking, included traditional religious activities and drinking. The Jesuits sought to extinguish a traditional belief system—for example, the belief in treating caribou souls properly so they would return to Minong, as well as ancient religious practices.[128]

To tell the story of the clash of religious faiths, we are unfortunately dependent upon Jesuit accounts, with their biases. The senior official at the Grand Portage American Fur Company fishery, Pierre Cotte, was also a Catholic layman. His effectiveness at converting North Shore Ojibwe was due in great part to his wife's healing of a sick Ojibwe man.[129] Father Franz Pierz followed up on Cotte's effort and crossed the lake and established a small mission on Isle Royale in 1838. On Minong, he proselytized among the North Shore Ojibwe fishing for the American Fur Company, but he spent little time there.[130] With the establishment of the Jesuit Mission of Immaculate Conception, Father Fremiot traveled to distant Ojibwe communities, many times by canoe. He was a regular presence at a number of locations on Isle Royale: Todd Harbor, Siskiwit Mine and Shaw's Location (in Rock Harbor), and Siskiwit Bay. He would minister to Ojibwe, Irish and Cornish miners, fishermen, "Canadians," and any converts to Catholicism. Father Fremiot even erected a cross in Siskiwit Bay.

> On my arrival, I baptized a 10 day old baby who died eight hours later. I also administered four baptisms and blessed two marriages. Then for the closing, and as a souvenir of the mission, I planted—with great solemnity—a large Cross near the little shed where I had celebrated Mass, at the very place where the steamboats land. It was agreed that this place would henceforth be called Tchibayattiko-Neyaching, Point of the Cross.[131]

Jesuits performed religious instruction as well as all rites at Isle Royale.

Not all North Shore Ojibwe converted to Christianity, or thought its coming was providential. Some Ojibwe questioned whether the presence of Jesuits meant they were healthier or not, whether they lived longer or shorter lives. Indeed, during a widespread illness at Fort William in 1850, some Ojibwe noted they were free of the disease until the Jesuits came. Other Ojibwe assumed that the mission and settling in one place had caused an epidemic. Some wondered if the untimely deaths at Fort William had come because of the presence of the priests. Some thought perhaps the Catholics died because the Black Robes often spoke of death.[132]

The Jesuits worked to have Ojibwe cease their traditional lifestyle of moving throughout the district. Jesuit fathers wanted Ojibwe to settle in their mission village, wherever located, so they could receive religious instruction year-round and be buried in consecrated ground. In one letter, Father Fremiot listed obstacles to conversion to Catholicism: (1) "nomadic life," (2) "polygamy and moral licentiousness," (3) "attachment to the Traditional Religious and Superstitious Customs of Native People," (4) the dances, and 5) "fire water." His fellow Jesuits would add that providing them religious instruction "is to attach them to their homes, is to give them the means of cultivating their lands." Jesuits and Indian agent agreed that for the deepest change to take effect, a hunting-and-gathering way of life would have to be broken.[133] Jesuit fathers and agents discouraged going to Minong.

Despite the very real pressures from priests and ministers, traditional religious activities persisted. For example in the 1920s, a priest at Grand Portage assembled a group of high-minded converts that chased a traditional religious practitioner into the woods. The priest motivated his group by saying he was going to get rid of the devil.[134]

Traditional ceremonies continued, sometimes "underground" and sometimes publicly, such as the 1901 Midewiwin ceremony noted in the Cook County newspaper. A traditional prayer ceremony was witnessed by pioneering ethnomusicologist Frances Densmore in 1905.[135] Midewiwin practitioners and kinsmen from Rainy Lake would come to Grand Portage and reinfuse religious traditions among some Ojibwe. In 1855, traditionalists from Rainy Lake came to Grand Portage for treaty payments and performed a scalp dance, to the shock of the Jesuit there.[136] Traditional doctoring, jugglery, and Midewiwin continued through the 1920s and later, but were mostly practiced covertly. "By the 1930s, those wishing to practice the old religion went to Nett or Vermillion Lakes."[137] Still, many continued to believe in the appearance of *manidoog* (manitous) at certain landmarks, such as at the Little Spirit Cedar Tree or Red Rock. Minong remained important to traditionalists, as it was home to important spirit beings.

Unexpected events could also rise up and nearly engulf Grand Portage Ojibwe. American Indian policy, beyond that of treaties, could also severely impact Portage Ojibwe. Just as they had been caught unawares by the 1842 Treaty, they were nearly swept up in a tragic downstate event. The 1862 Sioux Uprising in Minnesota, in which almost eight hundred settlers were killed, nearly had a lasting impact on North Shore Ojibwe and Minong. Two months after the "uprising" or "massacre," depending upon your point of view, an influential newspaper publisher in St. Paul proposed "Isle Royale in Lake Superior, as a penal Indian colony." Editor James Taylor, in a pamphlet entitled "The Sioux War: What Shall We Do with It?" and "The Sioux Indians: What Shall We Do with Them?" proposed putting all the Indians in Michigan, Wisconsin, and Minnesota and the "entire Sioux nation" on Isle Royale. Marooning both "Sioux" and "Chippewas"—whom he recognized as hereditary enemies—on Isle Royale was a means of getting even with them and forcing them to "quench that feud." Coming very close to advocating extermination for the Sioux "devils," Taylor proposed making Isle Royale into an insular gulag. Obviously, the anger of Taylor and many others towards the Sioux did not result in Minong becoming an Indian penal colony, but this very public debate reminds us that national Indian policy, in this case removal and the threat of extermination, could rear its head in any location and for any Indian group.[138]

Fur traders, storekeepers, and shysters all brought hard liquor to North Shore Ojibwe. What began in many instances as the gifting of liquor to cement kinship-like bonds between fur traders and Ojibwe trappers spiraled into social dislocation in many instances.[139] Drinking binges were common. As early as 1785, drinking at Grand Portage led to quarreling and the death of five Ojibwe.[140] The tragedy of heavy binge drinking continued during the first copper mining boom and McCullough's fishing operation.[141] Drinking was not confined to the Ojibwe fishermen or miners, but included everyone on the Island. The visiting Jesuit fathers were appalled at the scale of the problem.

> When all our Indians go to Isle Royale for the fishing season you will find only a few women and perhaps one man who do not drink heavily. . . . One Indian sold his pipe for a dollar and rushed to spend it for brandy. Without counting what has been sold illegally on board ship, two Americans in dealing with our Indians (at Isle Royale) within the space of two or three months,

have dispensed—would you believe it?—not less than two barrels of brandy, each containing 36 gallons.

Drinking sometimes led to fights between the various ethnic groups, as well as to harebrained actions—as happened at Siskiwit Bay.[142]

> One day, towards the end of the fishing period, two young Natives tried, as a sort of a game, to lift a half-barrel of fish up onto two barrels that had been stacked on top of each other. Another young man was watching them—he was not drunk but the drink had already gone to his head. "What are you up to?" he shouted, "You cannot set that barrel on top of the others! You are cowards. I am strong enough to lift, all by myself, more than both of you. Watch how I am going to lift this little object."
>
> No sooner said than done, he lifted the half-barrel right where he said he would, but the excessive exertion broke something or other inside his body, and there was our braggart now lying on his bed in pain and staring death in the face. He was dead within a few days, and had not been able to see a priest! He was one of those who distinguished himself all summer long by his excessive drinking.[143]

One Fort William clerk noted the strong relationship between fishing and drinking when he wrote: "Old Colin . . . is drinking part of his fish ever since he arrived."[144] Thus while fishing success was typically a guarantee against hungry times, barreled fish could also be used as currency for excesses. And at least in one instance, excessive drinking precluded fishing and resulted in a group becoming marooned on the Island for the winter. Vigorously opposed to the use of hard liquors, the Jesuits railed against the "fatal influence . . . bad words and of the manners" the Ojibwe were swept up in as part of the "American mines" at Isle Royale.

The Jesuit fathers of the Mission of Immaculate Conception fought hard to stop the trading of drink. They harassed traders, and they made conversion to Catholicism dependent on the renunciation of alcohol.[145] Some government agents also sought to stop the flow of the liquor trade to Indians, including taking the drastic step of removing individuals from treaty rolls and thus payments if caught selling whiskey.[146] Despite these attempts to suppress the flow of brandy, whiskey, and other hard alcohol, its binge use led to poverty, social stress, and occasional mayhem. Indians were drawn to places where alcohol was available, disrupting their seasonal rounds and travel to locations such as Minong.

The passage of federal legislation, the Dawes Act in 1887, heavily impacted Grand Portage Ojibwe. The act provided for individual allotments to Indians to make them farmers, and through that labor and tilling the land it was hoped Indians would quickly acculturate to American ways and give up their tribal and communal social structure. Allotments were systemized, with plat maps arriving in May 1896.[147] Normally, 160 acres were issued to a head of household, and if the property was improved and taxes paid for twenty-five years, the individual would be issued fee-simple title to the land. In 1898, there were 304 allotments on the reservation, or 24,191 acres, which is roughly half of the reservation's lands. After the trial period of twenty-five years, the land could be severed from private ownership through tax forfeit, purchase, or not getting fee-simple title. Large tracts of lands on the reservation eventually came under white ownership. The allotment idea did not work well in Grand Portage.[148] It is rocky, hardscrabble farming country. Individuals continued some of their seasonal rounds away from allotments to fish, hunt, make maple sugar, collect wild rice, and take paying jobs. There were also unintended consequences such as forcing name changes on titles. For example, Alexis Maymaushkewash's name was anglicized as Alex Posey. The Dawes Act, and other influences, shaped a more sedentary life. The message was clear: Grand Portage Ojibwe were supposed to break with their past, live in one place, and become like whites.[149] Forced assimilation isolated North Shore Ojibwe from Minong.

Some of the first cutting of white and red pine in the area began inauspiciously on the Fort William Reserve in 1871, following a questionable if not illegal agreement.[150] On the American side of the border, pine cutting commenced on the heels of allotment making. Much timber was cut on the Grand Portage Reservation. In February 1901, the Grand Portage Ojibwe were first allowed to sell timber on their allotments. By the end of the year, 16,645 cedar [railroad] ties, 4,600 cedar poles, and 1,427 feet of piling were cut and sold for a price of $8,620.[151] The Pigeon River Lumber Company operated camps on the headwaters of the Pigeon and Arrow rivers and eventually as far west as Gunflint Lake. Initially the reservation became a checkerboard of cutover lands following allotments, but before long most of the big pines were cut. The Pigeon River Lumber Company employed many Portage Ojibwe men. They excelled at keeping the river free of logjams, clearing logs from clogging rapids and narrows, and running freely down flues hugging canyon walls.[152]

The institution of schools, whether run by Jesuits or later by government teachers, had great impact on Grand Portage Ojibwe. As early as 1838, Father Pierz taught seventy-five pupils—children, adults, Ojibwe, and "French"—in Grand Portage. Throughout the early years, an evening school for Ojibwe adults was provided.[153] For a number of early years, the number of child students appears to have remained nearly constant, with forty-some attending in the 1850s. However, by the end of the century, on average, a much smaller percentage of Grand Portage youth were attending school.[154] At least two problems plagued attendance levels: (1) living on allotments meant children were a long distance from school, and (2) there was a frequent turnover in teachers that curtailed learning. Quite commonly the school was a hostile place, as many teachers did not permit speaking in the children's native tongue.[155]

The effect of operating the school at Grand Portage and at Fort William, whether run by the Jesuits or by government schoolteachers, was that both villages became magnets for settlement and transformation. Many Ojibwe moved to be close to schools, and they were harangued for leaving school to fish, hunt, or make maple sugar. Still, school attendance was often intermittent, as some families continued their traditional hunting-and-gathering lifeways. Indian agents grew frustrated with the continued "roving habits," but gradually fewer families were traveling to "the bush." Later, some Grand Portage children were sent away to distant boarding schools. School attendance—whether constant or intermittent—reinforced increasing sedentariness, and families became less likely to travel afar to places like Minong.

Sweeping changes were coming to the region that eventually impacted the hunting and gathering of Grand Portage Ojibwe. The small community of

Parkerville on the mouth of Pigeon Bay was established and became a hub of activity from 1867 to 1875. Further down the shore, Beaver Bay was established. Parkerville was the initial location where mail was exchanged between American and Canadian mail carriers. Men delivering the mail to Isle Royale would also leave from Parkerville.[156]

Mineral "rushes" swelled the number of whites arriving in Minnesota and Ontario. The Rove Lake gold rush of 1875, on the border lake, created a boomtown almost overnight. The Jesuits from the Mission of Immaculate Conception started a Catholic Indian mission at Rove Lake, with over two hundred Indians there at its zenith. The successful but relatively short-lived Silver Islet Mine, 1870–1885, brought more miners and residents to the area. Ojibwe were still able to compete for 45 out of 900 jobs at Silver Islet, but the mining work force would become less and less Native.[157] Lake Superior would eventually overwhelm the exposed small islet off Thunder Cape that mined a rich vein of silver running far underneath the lake.

Increasing vessel traffic, including the use of steam-driven propeller vessels, brought more white settlers into northwestern Lake Superior. The completion of the Canadian Pacific Railroad in 1882 made Port Arthur an important way station for Canadians traveling westward. By 1890 there were over six thousand people residing at Port Arthur.[158] The fevered hope for paying minerals in the Gunflint Lake area drove efforts to create the Gunflint Iron Range Railroad, as well as the Port Arthur Duluth and Western Railroad, to haul ore to ports. Workers streamed into the traditional territory of North Shore Ojibwe to lay track, cut ties, and bridge waters.[159] Building the Grand Marais harbor breakwater in 1879 through 1884 employed dozens of Ojibwe laborers, with many living close by at Chippewa City, east of Grand Marais. After the harbor was built, Ojibwe worked unloading lake vessels.[160] These paying jobs injected welcome dollars into a cash-starved Indian community.

Scandinavian immigrants surged into the area, especially between 1880 and 1900. Cook County's 1880 population of 65 jumped to 810 in 1900. By 1910 it had risen to 1,336. Lake County's population surged as well from 106 in 1880, to 4,654 in 1900, to 8,011 in 1910.[161] More residents meant more claimed lands and hunting competition, and traditional sugar-bush locations became others' homesteads. A new dominant population took up residence in the region, constraining traditional Ojibwe food-gathering practices.

The increase of whites and industry in the region reinvigorated an old occupation for Grand Portage men, that of guides. Ojibwe became guides and packers for miners, geologists, Ojibwe missionaries, and lumbermen. Too often, however, these were short-term jobs.[162] Still, their geographic knowledge was used to create trails, such as the Silver Mountain Trail that was grafted onto the beginning of the Grand Portage and which cuts north above the "Tunnel," across the Pigeon River, to silver mining ventures east of Whitefish Lake. The trail likely originated as a pathway to the rich wild rice beds of Whitefish Lake. On occasion, Ojibwe men served as prospectors, including Weisaw Bahgwatchinnini, who helped locate these silver resources, and whose descendants live in Grand Portage today.[163] Supplies and mail were packed over this trail, as were men seeking jobs at the mining locations.

An increase in whites eventually meant an increase in local government. At Isle Royale, two settlements grew during the second copper mining boom in the 1870s. The two villages, one in McCargoe Cove and the other at the head of Siskiwit Bay at the Island Mine townsite, were large enough that Isle Royale County was created in 1875. One of the mining captains, A. C. Davis, was elected in 1876 to the Michigan State legislature, representing a four-county district. The boom was again short-lived, and by 1880 only fifty-five people lived on Isle Royale. Isle Royale County would come to an official end in 1897 when it was absorbed by Keweenaw County, with the county seat in Eagle Harbor. Westward across the big lake, Cook County was created in 1882. A string of villages along the Lake Superior shoreline were established: Hovland, Grand Marais, Lutsen, and Tofte. Scandinavian immigrants turned to fishing and farming/homesteading in the last decades of the nineteenth century. Lands were deemed to be free for the taking, and prime real estate was homesteaded or purchased. The Grand Portage Reservation population climbed during this time, and the Indian agent permitted "an experiment" of five policemen to safeguard the reservation. In addition, three Grand Portage chiefs served as judges for minor infractions.[164]

The quiet closure of the Hudson's Bay Company's Fort William trading post in 1883 signaled more changes to come. The institution of new state fish-and-game laws—limits and seasons—curtailed traditional hunting and fishing practices. Grand Portage resident Alex LeSage had a trapping cabin in the interior of Isle Royale, and other Ojibwe trapped there as well. One Isle Royale game warden threatened and chased off Portage trappers. But the price for beaver pelts—illegal or not—was too attractive, and Indians and non-Indians trapped beaver on Isle Royale in the 1920s and 1930s. A prime beaver pelt would fetch $75 in Thunder Bay. Not allowed yet to vote, Indians could do little to change adverse hunting and fishing laws.[165] And as Isle Royale was a part of the state of Michigan, they had little recourse to complain at the distant Keweenaw County courthouse or the state capital.

The Scandinavian immigrants' success at fishing for lake trout and herring further constrained Indian fishermen's access to traditional locations.

> After that fur trading got cut off, the Indians were fishing during that time and they needed the fish and then you have your immigrant coming in. Immigrants came in, they brought turmoil and they cut each other's fish nets, shot each other out of their boats. Chased everybody off the lake. . . . My grandfather Bushman was born on Isle Royale and his family traditionally fished out there. And my great grandfather lived out there part of the year and then they'd move to Grand Portage part of the year. . . . So they just stopped fishing when the different groups came.
>
> Interviewer: Because they got forced out?
>
> Uh huh, [they] got forced out. The same thing with the wild rice gathering. They used to go for miles to go up into the lakes. Like into Canada gathering rice. . . . They were told that they had to stop their movement. They couldn't go on the water anymore, they couldn't go to these different places to gather wild rice. They were told to stay in the one community.[166]

Fishing and hunting traditions varied between the Ojibwe and the new immigrants. Immigrant fishermen often claimed a fishing territory on the lake one half mile either side of his home, whether owned or not.[167] Ojibwe had no such custom. The same clashes were repeated along the Canadian shoreline, as Ojibwe fishing practices and locations did not fit the lease system devised by the Ontario government.[168] Also during this time, big game—moose and caribou—and wolf and beaver remained rare and difficult to hunt or trap.[169] Family sugar-bush locations were sometimes broken up—at least legally—by allotment boundaries. Making a subsistence living became more difficult with more people in the region.

The anticipated and then actual increase of whites led the United States government to contemplate Indian removal to the west, beginning in the 1830s. In 1850, to compel a number of Wisconsin Ojibwe to move westward out of Wisconsin, treaty payments were withheld and distributed at a distant location at Sandy Lake, Minnesota. Many Ojibwe died in the process of traveling to and from this treaty payment location. The lateness of the treaty payment, which forced Ojibwe to forego fall food gathering, led to starvation and the death of many Ojibwe.[170] Barely a half year later, the Jesuits hoped to lure Fond du Lac Ojibwe to their Fort William Mission. The Jesuits reasoned that the more settled and grouped together the Ojibwe, the better the chance to convert them. While this last desire was based more in hope than in reality, Chief Peau de Chat of the Fort William Band felt compelled to state that he did not approve of such schemes.[171] But the prospect of moving was also being touted by a renowned Garden River/Sault Ste. Marie Ojibwe leader, Shingwaukonse. He was actively trying to convince American Ojibwe as far away as central Minnesota to move across the border to English territory near his home.[172] And at one point, the Pigeon River chief Little Englishman, along with nine other Ojibwe leaders, signed a petition asking the English authorities if his band could move to join Shingwaukonse's and other bands.[173] The Canadians, fearing a much larger Ojibwe presence at the Soo, did not encourage this relocation.[174] Nor is it clear how earnest Little Englishman was in his petition, or whether he was merely testing the waters to see what the American reaction might be.

The idea of Ojibwe removal was rekindled in 1871, when an Indian agent assumed that Grand Portage Ojibwe would be better off westward, in better agricultural lands. Acknowledging the poor agricultural prospects of

Grand Portage, he saw moving as the best way of alleviating the poverty on the reservation. Removal again hung over Grand Portage Ojibwe's future in 1887, when again it was suggested they move to White Earth because of "the sterility of their soil." The Indian agent confidently predicted, "in time they will appreciate this [move]." However, the Grand Portage Ojibwe refused the offer despite living in "abject poverty."[175]

Clinging to their reservation, and finding paying work elsewhere if at all, meant there was less reason to go to Minong. Going always was a serious enterprise. Without a major incentive to go, trips to Minong became fewer and fewer. One exception was when North Shore Ojibwe went to salvage goods—pillows, chairs, wood, and bedsprings—from the *Algoma*, wrecked off Rock Harbor. More commonly, if an Ojibwe fisher went there, he would bump into resources or locations claimed by Scandinavian immigrants, who had arrived in great numbers after 1880. Another obstacle—land ownership—made the trip to Isle Royale less inviting. Choice harbors, islands, and traditional camp areas had been purchased and were sometimes occupied.[176]

Since the calamitous treaties and boom and bust of economic opportunities (mining, railroad work, harbor construction), North Shore Ojibwe became increasingly reservation-bound. They were not always welcome in some jobs and in their old territory. Even if they continued to relocate for jobs or to pursue traditional foods, they would increasingly resort to their designated homes and allotment on the reservation or reserve. Ironically, many of the birch-bark wigwams used when traveling to Minong were set up as outbuildings to the more permanent log dwellings on the mainland.

## Languishing Use of Minong in the Twentieth Century

Enmeshed in deep poverty, and not welcome in old haunts off the reservation, fewer Ojibwe went to Minong. The traveling distances off the reservation for traditional pursuits was increasingly circumscribed in the twentieth century. Immediate pressures on the reserve, such as railroad encroachment, made it difficult for Fort William Ojibwe to access the distant parts of their traditional territory. Travel to the Island, to another country where they had no standing, was daunting. Instead, what little Native use occurred on Minong was by American Ojibwe. A few Ojibwe continued to work in the fishery, often as hired men. Willie Droulliard fished at Minong extensively. Ojibwe men Bill Howenstine, John Zimmerman, and Billie Fortune trapped on Minong during the winter of 1912.[177] Adam Roach LaPlante and his grandmother worked at the Johnson Resort in Chippewa Harbor in the 1930s. Adam Roach would accidentally drown at Wright Island.[178] Grand Portage Band members, like others of the North Shore, would occasionally travel to Isle Royale to hunt moose or perhaps trap beaver—whether legal or not. The Scott brothers from Grand Marais and Grand Portage Band members ran a pulp salvage operation at Todd Harbor in the 1940s. Their father had delivered mail to the Island by dog team, family members were born there, and he became justice of the peace at the "Cove" village in McCargoe Cove.[179]

Ironically, as real Ojibwe use of Minong was in decline, less authentic examples of an Indian past were fabricated. A rock outcrop along the Rock Harbor channel, named the "Great Indian Head," was marketed for tourists to visit.[180] And to impress the passengers on the steamship *America*, the owners of the Belle Isle Resort erected a cement teepee and had an employee dressed as an "Indian Maiden" greet incoming vessels. Indian curios were sold at a number of Island resorts in the 1930s. Even a few Ojibwe place-names were imported to, and affixed at, the Island during this time. The old Wendigo Mine Company workings at the head of Washington Harbor lent a name to the National Park Service complex now called "Windigo"—the closest major NPS facility to Grand Portage. Ironically, the known windigo-like event at Isle Royale—the ordeal of Charlie and Angelique Mott—occurred on the other end of the Isle Royale, near where park headquarters is now located. Naming a tourist destination after a dreaded Ojibwe mythic cannibalistic creature that stalks people in the winter points out how cavalier the NPS could be with Ojibwe heritage. The most visible exemplar of selectively recognizing a Native past is the set of murals painted on the NPS vessel *Ranger III* in the late 1950s. Passengers riding the *Ranger III* on the five-hour lake crossing have plenty of time to view the murals of prehistoric Native miners, working to remove nugget copper. There are no murals of historic Ojibwe.

The last Native American couple to reside on Isle Royale is also the most well-known. John (or Jack) Linklater and his wife, Helen, eventually purchased property on Birch Island, McCargoe Cove, along with a partner couple in 1926.[181] Mrs. Linklater's Ojibwe name was Tchi-ki-wis. For a number of years, the Linklaters and Hansens ran a commercial fishery from Birch Island during the summer months, and the men were game wardens in Minnesota during the winter months. A Grand Portage Ojibwe, Charlie Grandmaison, assisted the Linklaters at the fishery. They ran pound nets from their fishery, a type of fishing not commonly used by the predominantly Scandinavian fishermen. Symbolically, Birch Island is important to our story, as it is located within McCargoe Cove, the traditional portal for most Ojibwe use of Minong. The Linklaters preferred to live in one of the bark lodges, despite four log cabins perched on a small knoll. For quite a number of years prior to co-owning the fishery, John Linklater guided for the well-to-do Frank Warren and family on Isle Royale. And even while the fishery was operating, Jack guided visitors for the Rock Harbor Lodge. He was in great demand as a woodsman and as an engrossing yet reticent storyteller. As a guide, he met a number of important people and guided at least one scientific party on Isle Royale.[182] He was also an expert dog musher, and one winter as a game warden, he mushed dogs from Winton (nearly Ely) to Grand Marais through the heart of the Boundary Waters.

The Linklaters were both Ojibwe descendents with Minong roots. Tchi-ki-wis's grandmother had traveled from the North Shore to Isle Royale as a young girl. And Linklater's grandfather had also paddled across to Isle Royale.[183] Their family background encapsulates many trends in area history. Mrs. Linklater's Ojibwe family on the paternal side was originally from Sault Ste. Marie. Linklater's father was a fur trader who married a Native woman, who bore a number of children. When his mother died, his father returned to Scotland, leaving Jack and his siblings behind—a tragic custom of the fur trade. The Linklaters were the last Ojibwe family who knew how to build and use birch-bark canoes the old way. Mrs. Linklater adapted those skills and made miniature birch-bark canoes and cedar mats for the growing tourist trade.[184]

While the Linklaters were well versed in traditional ways, they did not stop there. Jack Linklater became a noted guide and photographer. In his lifetime he ventured far from a fur trade childhood to being a game warden and devoted Native conservationist.[185] He witnessed and thrived in a period of transition from Indian occupancy in the area to the dominance of white recreationalists. He was, in a word, adaptable, but also at heart a traditionalist. He and his wife preferred to speak in Anishinaabemowin, but he also spoke French as well as English. Linklater died July 8, 1933, as the park idea was being born. Tchi-ki-wis died a little more than a year later.[186] Their property was sold to the park. During the huge 1936 forest fire, Civilian Conservation Corps men used the Linklater cabins. For years the buildings were deserted, and eventually their personal property were thrown into a nearby swamp.[187] In the mid-1970s the cabins were burned to the ground in order to create wilderness. The last material remnant of an Ojibwe home on Minong was gone.

View of Isle Royale in distance from Hollow Rock, Grand Portage, Minnesota.

Fog on Lake Superior between Grand Portage and Isle Royale.

"Winter Crossing," watercolor by Carl Gawboy.

Hoarfrost on Isle Royale shoreline.

"Lac Tracy ou Superieur," map made by the Jesuit Missionaries, 1672.

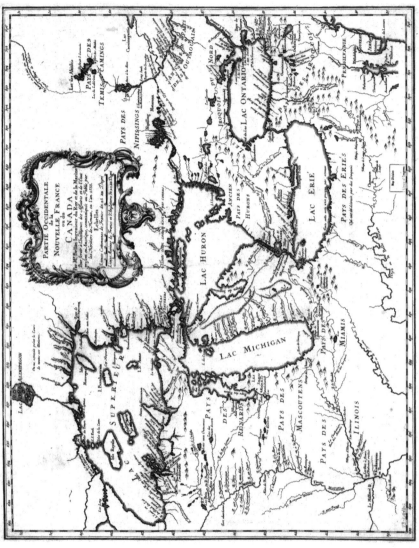

French Royale Hydrographic Engineer, Jacques Nicolas Bellin, map, 1755.

JEAN FITTS COCHRANE

View of the Sleeping Giant, or Thunder Cape, Ontario from Mt. Ojibway Lookout Tower, Isle Royale.

TRAVIS NOVITSKY

View of Isle Royale from Mt. Josephine, Grand Portage with Suzi Islands in foreground.

Siscowet trout, or fat lake trout, caught in Isle Royale waters.

"Gill-Net Fishing from Canoe," watercolor by Howard Sivertson.

"Woodland Caribou at Isle Royale shoreline," painting by Howard Sivertson.

"Spring Journey to Pigeon River Mission—1850," watercolor by Howard Sivertson.

*Recovery* cached at McCargoe Cove, Isle Royale. Painting by Howard Sivertson.

Lithograph of Little Caribou, a Grand Portage leader and a signatory of the Isle Royale Compact and 1854 Treaty. Painting by James Otto Lewis, 1836.

Whereas a difference of opinion has heretofore existed between the United States, and a portion of the Chippewa Indians of the Mississippi & Lake Superior, in relation to the cession of Isle Royale, by the treaty concluded with them on the 4th day of October 1842, at La Pointe, in the Territory of Wisconsin — Be it therefore ~~known~~ known, that the said Indians hereby declare themselves satisfied with the explanations now made by the commissioner of the United States, of the said Isle Royale having been included in the cession of that treaty, and by these presents, they ratify and confirm said cession — In consideration of which, & the regard which the President of the United States bears to his Red children of the Chippewa nation — Four hundred dollars worth of Gun Powder, & One hundred dollars worth of fresh Beef, shall be delivered to the said Indians, on their signing this compact —

In witness whereof, we hereunto set our hands, at La Pointe, this 20th day of August A. D. 1844. —

In presence of

William MacDonald
Jno Hulbert
Cyrus Mendenhall
Clement H. Beaulieu      Lac.
Chs. H. Oakes      Flambeau
J. Purdy
Jas F. Hays U.S.S. Ind agt
Wm W. Warren Intr.

Robert Stuart
United States Commissioner

( Wab ish gag gaug e      ×
( She maug un ish      ×
( Knisteno      ×
( Ud e kum ag      ×
( Now uj e wun      ×
( Medge wok gok wed      ×

19-4

First of the three-page 1844 Isle Royale Compact.

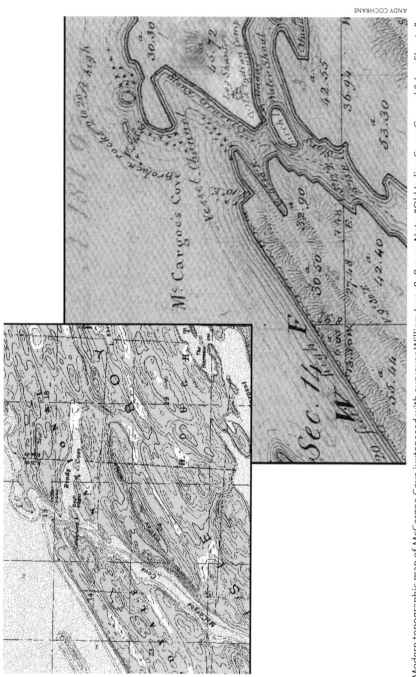

Modern topographic map of McCargoe Cove juxtaposed with surveyor William Ives 1848 map. Note: "Old Indian Camp Ground & Log Shanty."

Tchi-ki-wis and John Linklater, circa 1930, in front of their Birch Island, McCargoe Cove home.

John Linklater guiding among Lake Superior sea-stacks, Isle Royale, 1929.

# THE GOOD PLACE TODAY

· · · · · · · · · · · · · · · · · · · · · · · · · · · · · · · · · · · · · · · · · · · · · · · · · · · · · · · · · · · · · · · · ·

T he nadir of North Shore Ojibwe's relationship with Minong came
with the establishment of Isle Royale National Park. Much like before
the 1842 Treaty, there is no evidence that the Grand Portage Band was
consulted prior to the creation of the park in concept in 1931, nor
when the park was dedicated in 1946. Instead, alleviating crushing poverty
was at the forefront of Grand Portage residents' minds at the time. Despite
the park being created, initially there were few rangers on the archipelago.
Increasingly, especially in the 1960s and later, more park employees, and
more importantly the addition of seaworthy boats to get to remote Island
locations, meant that Isle Royale became less of a refuge for traditional ways
of subsistence living. Gone were the days when Portage men might shoot
a moose and sink the meat in deep water until they could bring it home to
their hungry families.[1]

The establishment of the park only created limited economic opportunities. Ironically, for Grand Portage men, emergencies or atypical situations at
Minong created the majority of jobs during the early twentieth century. The

disappearance of two North Shore fishermen in January 1918 meant that two Grand Portage men (and the missing men's relatives) were sent to search Isle Royale when "the ice is reported to be sufficiently strong for travel and no great difficulty is expected in getting to the island." Similarly in the winter of 1930, when a man was reported lost to the Coast Guard, Portage Ojibwe Willy Droulliard was deputized and told to go find him. And in 1948 "half of [Grand] Portage was over there" fighting a forest fire. Some Portage men experienced their first airplane flights as they were flown directly to fire camps on Lake Desor in the south-central portion of Isle Royale. A post-fire report concluded: "They [Grand Portage men] proved to be such excellent fire fighters, it was thought that this source of manpower should be investigated."[2] This recommendation was never pursued. Park management only turned to Grand Portage when other manpower was not readily available.

Retarding more regular economic opportunities was the fact that park headquarters was across the lake at Houghton, Michigan, and thus few Grand Portage Ojibwe could learn about park jobs. Even so, a few Ojibwe found seasonal jobs in the resort industry or National Park Service serving Isle Royale visitors. While there were few jobs on the passenger ferries, a succession of Portage men worked as deckhands on vessels taking visitors from Grand Portage to Isle Royale and back. Despite the fact that Grand Portage was seen historically as "the gateway to Isle Royale," there was only a little economic boost from that proximity. Nor was there much communication for many years between park officials and Grand Portage residents or tribal council members.

Park officials did not understand the historical links between the North Shore Ojibwe and Isle Royale. For example, in 1945 the Grand Portage tribal council turned to Isle Royale as a neighbor for help. The tribal council sought to reintroduce beaver to the reservation, noting "there is a surplus of beaver on Isle Royale." Despite urging from the acting director of the U.S. Fish and Wildlife Service to transplant Isle Royale beavers to the reservation and a problem with beavers making a number of Isle Royale boathouses and docks unserviceable, the NPS "found no legal authority" for permitting the beaver trapping operation.[3] A year later, during a break in the succession of ferry vessels serving Isle Royale, Grand Portage Band members worked to purchase two vessels to take advantage of that trade. However, as they sought loans to purchase the vessels, they were not quick enough for the park. Instead, the Sivertson family from Duluth and Isle Royale provided the ferry service that continues today.[4]

To be fair, it was not just park officials that did not understand the relationship between North Shore Ojibwe and Isle Royale. A number of long term summer residents also did not understand this link to the point; for example, one wrote in correspondence to park mangers: "They [the Grand Portage Indian Council] are not familiar with Isle Royale." Further, park service officials concluded that the Grand Portage tribal council support of continued commercial fishing at Isle Royale was illustrative of how little support there was for this idea.[5] Clearly, in the early days of park administration, park officials dismissed Grand Portage leaders' standing and views. Misunderstanding the historic relationship between North Shore Ojibwe and Isle Royale and undervaluing communications from Grand Portage set the stage for a series of events, sadly at cross-purposes, which retarded any cooperative ventures or developing relationship.

In concept, increasing visitation to Isle Royale would benefit Grand Portage Ojibwe, as tourists must find lodging, meals, vehicle parking, and supplies for the trip to the Island. On the Island, the Great Depression and the creation of the park in 1946 began a period of hotel consolidation, with the largest lodge operating in Rock Harbor on the northeast end and predominantly served by ferry vessels from Michigan. The opening and then closing of the Windigo Inn (closest to Grand Portage) after World War II limited the numbers of ferry-boat passengers who might like to stay on the Island in nice accommodations, such as those in Rock Harbor. The final closing of the Windigo Inn in 1973 led the Grand Portage Reservation Tribal Council to inquire if they could run the inn. Park officials denied this request, saying that the admittedly pleasant accommodations at the Brule and Radisson Lodge units were sited on unstable ground, leading to regular water-pipe ruptures.[6] The west end of Isle Royale became a less attractive destination for well-heeled clientele than the east end of the park because the NPS invested a comparatively small amount of money at Windigo in the decades up to the 1980s.

A post–World War II change was the rapid growth of recreational boating on Lake Superior. Also, the Minnesota North Shore was growing into a popular vacation destination area. For a number of families and groups of fishing buddies, it became a tradition to visit Isle Royale year after year. And since the Minnesota shoreline, and Grand Portage specifically, was closest to the Island among all American ports, a private marina was established in Grand Portage Bay to meet that demand. Boating numbers rose dramatically as the wonderful fishing and sense of being away from it all on the Island attracted repeat visitors. The rise of this trade—largely not economically captured by the Grand Portage band in its early days—led the band to open their own modest marina in 1971. The growing popularity of this spurred the band to propose a lodge complex with the Hilton Corporation in the early 1970s. Eventually the Radisson Corporation and the band would build a 100-room lodge in Grand Portage that opened in 1975, to serve as a get-away all-season convention center, as well as to serve Isle Royale–bound visitors.[7] The enthusiasm for tourism in general and boating in particular led the Grand Portage Band to work with the Army Corps of Engineers to propose a 250-boat marina within Grand Portage Bay. Objections by the National Park Service that it would "overwhelm" the capacity of Isle Royale and be "catastrophic" to the archipelago park defeated this proposal and any boost in economic gain by the reservation.[8] This clash, and the efforts before it, made the Isle Royale trade a feeble economic success for reservation residents.

## Reworking a Relationship and Assumptions

Running counter to the trend of disengagement and cross-purposes, the Grand Portage Band took additional actions that would culminate in a change of relationship with the National Park Service, including Isle Royale National Park. To boost tourism and financial support, the Grand Portage Band negotiated an agreement with the National Park Service to recognize "Grand Portage National Historic Site" in 1951. In 1958 they agreed to the establishment of Grand Portage National Monument, including donating some tribal lands.

The 1951 agreement and 1958 establishment of another NPS unit affirmed a greater relationship between the band and the two park units. Further, it was Isle Royale officials who often were the NPS's "face" during the historic site agreement and monument establishment.[9]

A few Grand Portage Ojibwe have gone to Isle Royale in the last few decades to fish recreationally, or sometimes for summer jobs. Those going to fish rarely identify themselves as "Indians." The Grand Portage Band now owns both marinas in the bay and, through a formal agreement, sells State of Michigan fishing licenses to customers going to Isle Royale. The rise of scuba diving on shipwrecks at Isle Royale has led a number of Isle Royale diving boats to moor at the Grand Portage marinas. Again, the Grand Portage Band is uniquely situated to intercept traffic and trade to Isle Royale.

The band's economic rise through modest casino profits has poised them for greater self-determination in their relationship with federal and state governments. The 1992 opening of the casino reinvigorated travel to Grand Portage, but primarily by Canadian gamblers with little or no interest in boat travel to Isle Royale. The Grand Portage Band's Indian Self-Governance Act agreement with the Grand Portage National Monument has led to precedent setting mutual park management, but more to the point is a rapid growth in communications and opportunities to capitalize on mutually beneficial purposes. The positive effects have spilled over into Grand Portage–Isle Royale relationships, despite some long-standing frustrations of the band.[10]

The Grand Portage tribal council and the superintendent and chief ranger of Isle Royale are now in periodic contact. Subjects discussed are marina facilities, fish stocks, exotic species, treaty rights, employment, and international-border issues. The communications are generally warm, even with disagreements. Grand Portage Ojibwe have always been interested in the abundant Isle Royale fish populations. That interest continues today. In 1985, acting through the Great Lakes Indian Fish and Wildlife Commission, the Grand Portage tribal council objected to the declaration of the four-and-a-half-mile offshore boundary around the archipelago. It was viewed as restricting potential tribal fishers, particularly the small open-boat fishing at Grand Portage.[11] Commercial fishing at Grand Portage is traditionally operated on a small scale, from skiffs, and with "relatively short lengths of gill nets (less than 2,000 feet) to fish in the near shore waters adjacent to the reservation."[12]

By 2000, the tribal council deemed fishery preservation of Isle Royale fish stocks, rather than the potential of large-scale tribal commercial fishing, as critically important. In May 2000, an attorney working for the Grand Portage Band wrote the Isle Royale superintendent pledging to help preserve and leave "substantially undisturbed" the unique fishery resources at Minong. The band felt so strongly that the letter was sent to nearby tribes, pertinent government agencies, and the Great Lakes Indian Fish and Wildlife Commission. This letter was a declaration of their unique relationship with Minong's resources—particularly its fish—and more generally a reaffirmation of the Grand Portage Ojibwe connection with Minong. The park superintendent replied to the law firm of BlueDog, Olson & Small representing Grand Portage, stressing mutual concerns about Isle Royale fish populations.[13]

A growing possibility of working together and finding subjects of mutual interest characterizes much contemporary communication between Isle Royale and the band.[14] The Grand Portage Band has recently undertaken cultural-resource research on Pigeon Point, the closest mainland point to Isle Royale. Grand Portage Ojibwe's keen interest in fish led to their pioneering restoration of native coaster brook trout in reservation streams. The band and Isle Royale now share the same goal in protecting these rare, lake-running "coasters," with remnant populations at the Island and Grand Portage. Transformation from an economically marginalized band to one with some economic clout has built a mutual awareness of the need for working together from a position of government-to-government relations, and the proposition of equal standing.

Symbols of a past alienated relationship are changing. The rock formation perched above Rock Harbor, called the "Great Indian Head," has cracked and fallen into lake waters, with little comment. The assumption that there were few, if any, Ojibwe on Minong has been dispelled by knowledge of the L'homme du Sault, Linklater, and Bahgwatchinnini (Bushman) family histories detailed herein. The concept of it being an Ojibwe homeland—a place of bungled treaties, and an island where hunters, fishers, and plant gatherers made use of and intimately knew Minong resources—contrasts with the concept of "wilderness"—and an archipelago supposedly with little human history. For a knowledgeable few, how they understand the Linklaters can tell a new Isle Royale story. Once a symbol of the last Ojibwe use of Minong, their story emphasizes a family connection to Minong. And with their annual return to the Birch Island fishery and occupation as guides, their history lends credence to the fact that returning to Minong is a traditional North Shore Ojibwe pursuit, as is fishing. Further, their history also speaks to the fact that the front door to Minong was entered through McCargoe Cove, over water or ice from the North Shore of Minnesota and Ontario. The concept of a wilderness isle must be enlarged to include it as an Ojibwe archipelago.

In one significant way, the Minong experienced by Ojibwe long ago has changed. Gone are the woodland caribou and fishable siscowet. Gone too are many of the reasons siscowet were once so desirable, when their oil was a welcome addition to a traditional diet low in fats and was useful in a number of ingenious ways. Sturgeon are rare in Island waters. The once opportunistically harvested passenger pigeons are extinct. The old sugar-maple stand remains, but no one has collected or boiled down the sap for more than a hundred years.

Not to be seen again is the fleet of North Shore Ojibwe canoes and mackinaw boats fishing Minong in the 1850s for McCullough's operation.[15] In the heyday of Ojibwe use of the Island, it was built upon the subsistence knowledge gained by families regularly resorting to Minong. An older form of social organization—clans, and in particular the Caribou and Bullhead clans—likely shaped early Ojibwe use of Minong. But we do not know the exact relationship these clan members had with Minong, or if clans had proprietary relationships with specific Minong places.

While much has changed, much of the North Shore Ojibwe relationship with Minong has endured. The geographic reality of the closeness of Grand Portage to Minong reasserts its importance in the age of increasing fuel prices (for boats, shipping fuel to the Island and the risk of transporting bulk supplies to the Island). Its closeness allows for increasing "day use" recreational fishing in which boaters fish Isle Royale waters but retreat to the mainland at the end of the day. The presence of many types of berries, beaver, snowshoe hare, and wild leeks continues from an earlier time. Also continuing today is Ojibwe reverence for the lake and important manitous. Many of these spirit beings live among the rocky shores and in the waters between the mainland and Minong. Some Grand Portage Ojibwe know of these manitous and their complexities, while others do not. But Minong remains alive in myth, and spiritually inhabited by beings important to North Shore Ojibwe. And burning brightly through time is an ever-present interest in the fish of Minong—which are highly esteemed and plentiful. Not surprisingly, many Ojibwe continue to go out on the lake, fish it, and seek to protect it.

Strong individuals populate the story of Ojibwe on Minong. Bahgwatchin-nini and his family crossed over to Minong on ice, over calm seas, and in a small boat cresting the endless succession of big swells. Some North Shore Ojibwe decided to be married there, while another was born in a canoe as it reached landfall below the Little Spirit Cedar Tree.[16] Others died in encampments or fisheries along its shores. Espagnol "worked the border" to get the best terms for North Shore Ojibwe when trading with the Hudson's Bay Company. Joseph Peau de Chat labored heroically to be recognized by U.S. Indian agents so that he and the Grand Portage delegation would have a hope of getting the best terms for the band during the Isle Royale Compact. Penassie at Fort William remembered *aadizookaan*, or sacred stories, that incorporated Minong in the landscape of Ojibwe storytelling, while all around him the reserve was changing. Linklater guided hundreds of visitors across the Island on trails no longer in existence. Surviving the death of his mother and abandonment by his father, he would go on to inspire many, including the noted conservationist author Sigurd Olson.[17] The story of Ojibwe on Minong is the story of individual strength in facing tough odds and hard situations.

The story of nearly losing Minong is part of a larger story about strong external forces coming to bear on North Shore Ojibwe. Increasing centraliza-tion into smaller and more circumscribed villages by the government, the lure of a fur trade post, the demands of Catholicism, jobs, and schools, all curtailed the traditional roving habits of North Shore Ojibwe. The creation of the international border and a growing divergence between bands because of dealing with different sovereigns initially complicated and eventually foreclosed Fort William Ojibwe use of Minong. A traditionally geographically dispersed people whose roving included Minong, they became increasingly more bound by the reservation.[18] Once a welcome work force on the Island in the first mines and fisheries, they were economically marginalized on the mainland and on Isle Royale. They had to eke out a living with jobs on the side, even dangerous ones such as delivering the winter mail to mining settlements on Minong. Or, when poor, they might continue to cross the ice to Minong to trap beaver or shoot a moose and hope not to run into a game warden. Or, Portage Ojibwe might continue to find work at the Island as deckhands, collecting pulpwood, or working seasonally for the lodges. Eventually, as on the mainland, much of Isle Royale became occupied by non-Indians during the traditional time of use—the summer months.

The three treaties and the compact that enmeshed North Shore Ojibwe and redefined their homeland—in legal terms anyway—were also part of a larger, heartbreaking process. The 1842 Copper Treaty was so hurried, and whites so greedy, that the traditional users of Minong were initially ignored. The Isle Royale portion of the 1842 Treaty and the hurry-up compact were particularly bungled and cast a shadow over the whole proceedings, particularly the legal particulars, for quite some time. The compact is marred by the geographic uncertainty of its terms and its lack of ratification. Mineral agent General Cunningham even declared that Minong was uninhabited (and thus logically not the territory of North Shore Ojibwe) while in the presence of a Grand Portage Ojibwe family. In hindsight, perhaps most telling about the Isle Royale Compact is not that it was badly bungled, but that it is virtually unknown to those interested in the Island. U.S. Indian policy was characteristically ruthless and conveniently not recollected. But the 1842 Treaty does include some reserved rights. It remains to be seen what treaty rights the traditional user group—the North Shore Ojibwe—may yet have at Minong. Or how subsequent legislation, including the creation of the park or the designation of wilderness, may affect those rights.

On the Canadian side, the Fort William Ojibwe were severed from Minong by the international border and treaty consequences. Ironically, however, they may become the closest Native American neighbor to Isle Royale. Recently the Canadian government has agreed that the reservation boundaries for the Fort

William Reserve were improperly drawn up, requiring a further land settlement. Through negotiations, the Fort William Reserve is likely to be expanded to all Crown or public lands on Welcome and Pie Islands. Thus, the Fort William First Nation will likely eventually own Pie Island, only thirteen miles away from Minong and once a way-stop for paddling to McCargoe Cove.[19] Still, their geographical proximity is unlikely to overcome the international border and re-make a contemporary connection to Minong.

Whether consciously or not, whites have sought to fully appropriate Minong. The treaty and compact gave them a legal title. But they also sought to appropriate Minong symbolically. To most convincingly do so, it had to be wiped clean of the religious beings and symbols of the Ojibwe. To many whites, belief in manitous was deemed superstitious. Cumulatively, white public discourse said that Isle Royale was a scary place for Chippewa. Angelique Mott left the Island with her life, but left it. Through corrupted windigo stories about the Motts, and the Jesuit story of stealing copper, the Island became, in effect, the "not-so-good-place." Non-Indians proclaimed that it was free of Ojibwe spirit beings—or worse, replete with Ojibwe deviltry. In essence, Minong was denuded of its deeper meaning, as Ojibwe religion was deemed spurious and foolish—remember, it talks of floating islands! And as the coup de grace, after the Ojibwe were symbolically and legally removed, resort owners and marketers started to sell an Indian past with faux Ojibwe names and handicrafts made by others.

North Shore Ojibwe had a complex relationship with Minong that was not extinguished by the dubious treaty proceedings or white "fakelore" about Ojibwe.[20] Minong was a place of utility, of highly desirable food, and of sacred beings. It was a risky place to venture to, but was deemed the good or beautiful place. It had an otherworldliness as the place Nanabushu might frequent or use for rest. Complex Ojibwe spirit beings were nearby on land, water, and in the air, and each needed to be treated gingerly. Depending upon your actions, they might act providentially or menacingly. But these manitous were on the mainland too, making Minong no different, or separate, from other Ojibwe places.

Writers on Indian and national park relationships have noted that big natural area parks often have "creation myths" that state unequivocally that these parks were uninhabited wilderness prior to their establishment.[21] These are retold and rewritten stories about the genesis of a park, and are almost always told by whites interested in a specific park. These spurious myths run counter to growing acceptance that North America was entirely inhabited prior to the arrival of whites, and certainly before the creation of park units. Indeed, one of the parks that once had this myth spun about it, Katmai in Alaska, is one of the oldest continuously inhabited locations in North America.[22]

The Isle Royale creation myth is slightly different than most others. Its creation myth is really a "pre-creation myth" that begins with prehistoric copper miners. In other words, in contrast to having a myth about uninhabited lands, Isle Royale is celebrated as being mysteriously inhabited in a distant time. Little is known about this dawn of human time on the archipelago. A great time gap is then inserted into the public discourse about the island until the arrival of whites and their technology. The synthetic myth then restarts with stories about white copper miners and fishermen. The spurious myth that Indians were fearful of Minong (or alternately Lake Superior) explains how this lacuna in human use was thought possible. Clearly there is much to explain away in the underlying premise that there was prehistoric aboriginal use, but not historic Ojibwe use. Perhaps the romance about antiquity diverts attention from more contemporary times.

The pre-creation myth deftly sidesteps the issue of prior ownership, treaties, and historic Indian use. Downplaying or ignoring these issues, these complications, makes the story go easier. If there was not any prior ownership of the Island, in any form, it makes it easier to begin the modern chapter of the story—the story many can more easily relate to with "pioneer" or white copper mining. Asserting that Ojibwe never used Isle Royale in historic times makes it born-again uninhabited lands. It shares this false "virginal" creation myth of other premier national park units, except that it has this caveat about earlier human use that was extinguished through time (and undoubtedly the rigors of crossing the lake). Isle Royale is unique in this genre of virginal creation myths in that the story says there was use, but it was light, ancient, and barely detectable to the newcomers to the archipelago. Isle Royale only becomes attractive as a potential national park years later, after the 1842 Treaty and after its economic attractiveness hits bottom, when it becomes plain that its copper deposits would not make anyone rich. It then becomes valuable for its insularity, beauty, wildlife, and for many, a faux wilderness with no human past.

North Shore Ojibwe are now more interested in shaping their future relationship with Minong than meditating on past misunderstandings. It will likely take great effort to maintain Minong as a vibrant part of their lives. To do so, they must find ways to stay economically and experientially connected. But always, as in the past, there is the physical difficulty of getting there. One way of sustaining that possibility is by operating marinas by which small boats and ferry vessels travel to the Island. Unfortunately, the rise of transportation costs has meant that fewer casual trips are taken there, effectively distancing some North Shore Ojibwe from Minong. And operating marinas provides only a modest economic tie for mainland residents. Employment on the Island, either for the NPS or the park concessionaire, could provide Portage Ojibwe with experiences on Minong that invigorate beliefs and customs regarding it.

North Shore Ojibwe's relationship with Minong is now more dependent than ever upon formal government-to-government relations between the park and the tribal council. Communications between the two parties will help define mutually beneficial actions and the degree to which the park looks across the lake to Minnesota with future plans. Only a few years ago, there was little or no government-to-government communication. In the future, Grand Portage Ojibwe might seek involvement with lodge or concessionaire operations, particularly at Windigo. The tribal government may extend its present interest in having "trust responsibilities" and treaty issues more fully articulated and addressed.[23] It is also conceivable that their successful push of Indian Self-Governance Act actions in Grand Portage could extend across the lake to Minong. And the growing natural resource capacity of the Grand Portage Band could also be exercised at the Island in future years for specific projects. The growing NPS interest in special and rare fish—coaster brook trout, and lake trout morphotypes such as "redfin" and "Rock of Ages"—in Island waters is one likely area of collaborative work.

One specific way Grand Portage may seek to affirm their connection to Minong is to contribute to having it recognized as a "sacred place"—or in government terminology, a "Traditional Cultural Property." Native American "sacred places" are sometimes nominated or deemed eligible for this National Register of Historic Places designation. Technically, TCPs are "eligible for inclusion in the National Register because of its association with cultural practices or beliefs of a living community that (a) are rooted in that community's history, and (b) are important in maintaining the continuing cultural identity of the community."[24] All or part of Minong may be eligible for the national register because of its relationship with Nanabushu, Mishipizheu, Lake Superior, and copper. In national register jargon, it would likely be eligible because of Minong's "association with important people," in this case spirits. Nearby, the Grand Portage Bay was deemed highly eligible as a TCP primarily because of its strong associations between the community and Grand Portage Island and lake spirits.[25] A nomination of Minong would have to be very inclusive, as it exists in relationship to a number of other significant places, such as the Little Spirit Cedar Tree, the "Sleeping Giant" of the Sibley Peninsula, Mt. McKay behind Thunder Bay, and Gitchi Gami—Lake Superior. Such a nomination would be remarkable because it would necessarily include a terrestrial and underwater component, if it included Mishipizheu. The dramatic underwater drop-offs on the north side of the Island and the passage into McCargoe Cove are likely places Mishipizheu might inhabit. One problem of such a nomination would be a common TCP issue, namely, delineating unmistakable boundaries.[26] Such a nomination means that boundaries must be fixed, despite there being little expression of sharp borders in traditional stories and beliefs. Prestige and outsiders' recognition of robust cultural connections might be highlighted by such a nomination. But also much could be lost through making concrete beliefs, customs, and their locations at Minong public information. To be nominated, it must be described and documented. As is customary in many native communities, keeping quiet is sometimes the best policy in protecting important, especially religious, matters.

But Minong's relationship with Grand Portage people is not being threatened at Minong. There is not a present-day developmental threat pushing Portage Ojibwe into action. If there is a threat at all, it is at Grand Portage, with the press of modern diversions and popular culture, globalization, materialistic desires, and less involvement with the natural world. Most threatening is the loss of language that is the root out of which traditional beliefs and customs grow, and in which *aadizookaan* are nestled and understood in the most profound way. Like many other Ojibwe communities in the United States, fewer Grand Portage young adults and youth know Anishinaabemowin. A Pandora's box of social and cultural ills further threaten Minong's place in Grand Portage. But Grand Portage is battling back with language instruction, a charter school built upon knowledge of traditional lifeways, recognition of elders as knowledge bearers, and the taking on of more self-government responsibilities. But a tough struggle looms to maintain their language and traditional religious beliefs, customs, and stories that still may not be easily accepted by others.

One promising event occurred during the summer of 2000 when the Grand Portage traditional drum group was invited to an official gathering in Rock Harbor. The sounds of the Ojibwe drum, long absent from Minong, were heard again. Gilbert Caribou, a lineal descendant of Little Caribou who signed the Isle Royale Compact, gave a blessing spoken in Anishinaabemowin. Building upon this, one creative way the Grand Portage Ojibwe might reconnect with Minong and combat language loss would be to hold a language-immersion "camp" at the Island, away from modern diversions.

Through time, the Ojibwe storytelling idea that was most belittled and misunderstood was Minong as a floating island. Interpreted literally, it struck most whites as so preposterous that it was used to condemn Ojibwe as superstitious. The unvoiced notion being that if Ojibwe held such fantastical notions about the Island, then surely they did not know much about it. From the proposition that Ojibwe did not know about Minong, it is an easy step to concluding they could not be its owner—"ownership" as defined by whites. And yet, turning the concept around, it becomes very useful to summarize the North Shore Ojibwe's relationship with Minong through time. Up until now, Minong has floated away from the Ojibwe in a legal, economic, and historic sense. In its depiction in eighteenth- and nineteenth-century maps, Minong has moved away from the North Shore Ojibwe. Even today's highway maps "cut and paste" Isle Royale in a convenient blank map space in Lake Superior, closer to the South Shore. Taken literally, these maps mislocate Isle Royale— essentially "floating" in Lake

Superior, rather than in its proper location. It is almost as if its real location does not matter. Its meaning to non-Indians has been shape-shifting for years until finally anchored at a great distance from its place in North Shore Ojibwe family history, regional history, and *aadizookaan*. North Shore Ojibwe have seen it historically float away further from their shores in terms of influence and connections. Certainly it floated away during the treaties, with a pittance paid for Minong to the rightful owners.

There are, however, resilient Ojibwe experiences and values connected to Minong. North Shore Ojibwe's interest in, and knowledge of, Lake Superior fish remains steady. They remain people of the lake and thus of fish. If McCargoe Cove was their portal to the Island, Siskiwit Bay was a cornucopia of siscowets, caribou, passenger pigeons, and access to sugar-maple stands. Contemporary Ojibwe remain interested in the economic potential of tourism at Minong. Also, the Island today is still the good place or good habitat for Ojibwe spirituality. Old and new beliefs have been recombined on the mainland, and their power reaches out and embraces Minong.

Minong is now starting to float back closer to the orbit of North Shore Ojibwe. The National Park Service recognizes the Grand Portage Band as an important player in the overall experience of park visitors, and as uniquely interested in management of the Island. Perhaps with Minong being a little bit closer to the North Shore, there will be greater possibilities for understanding its past and guiding it towards a bright future. Traversing the lake water has always been risky business, but that same risk and opportunity is there now to restore and sustain Minong as a special place for the Ojibwe of the North Shore as well as for visitors from afar. Greater connections between North Shore Ojibwe and Minong seem promising, with the geographic reality of the Good Place being visible from Grand Portage, and Portage Ojibwe residents determined to maintain those linkages. Visible from many Portage living rooms, it looms on the horizon of the lake. Future efforts by Grand Portage residents may yet have it float closer to home.

# NOTES
..................................................................................................

## Introduction

1. This legal, more than geographic, connection can lead to some far-fetched notions. For example, amateur archeologist and state booster Fred Dustin once wrote: "Under favorable conditions, a canoe could cross easily [between the Keweenaw and Isle Royale] between sunrise and sunset." This would mean from the Keweenaw paddling northwestward for a number of hours (maybe ten to fifteen) across a very volatile freshwater sea before you could even see Isle Royale on the horizon. Clearly this would be risky business. Fred Dustin, "An Archaeological Reconnaissance of Isle Royale," *Michigan History* 41, no. 1 (March 1957): 26.
2. Tim Cochrane, "Isle Royale: 'A Good Place to Live,'" *Michigan History* 74, no. 3 (May–June 1990): 17.
3. Hudson's Bay Company Archive (HBCA), B.231/a/18, Fort William Post Returns, July 28, 1838, Winnipeg, Manitoba.
4. Some of the letters from the Mission of Immaculate Conception had been translated and published previously, the majority of them being in French. But thousands

of pages of the mission diary had not been rediscovered, transcribed, translated, or more importantly consulted for many, many years. This wonderfully rich vein of historical documentation begins when the mission was first located on Pigeon River in the summer of 1848. A year later, the mission and the three Jesuit fathers moved to a new location along the Kaministiquia River in what is now Thunder Bay. A small group of Jesuit fathers and scholars have translated some of French originals. Grand Portage National Monument has copies of these translations.

5. The late Father William Maurice's genealogical work is widely consulted by Ojibwe descendants. There have been four copies hand-made. Father Maurice's historical collection contains this genealogy and translations of many years of the Mission of Immaculate Conception Diary and Letters, St. Anne's Church, Fort William Reserve, Ontario.

6. HBCA, B.231/a/15 and 16, Fort William Post Returns, August 13, 1835, and August 2, 1836.

7. Theodore Catton, *Inhabited Wilderness: Indians, Eskimos, and National Parks* (Albuquerque: University of New Mexico Press, 1997); Robert H. Keller and Michael F. Turek, *American Indians and National Parks* (Tucson: University of Arizona Press, 1998); Mark David Spence, *Dispossessing the Wilderness: Indian Removal and the Making of the National Parks* (New York: Oxford University Press, 1999); and Philip Burnham, *Indian Country, God's Country: Native Americans and the National Parks* (Washington, D.C.: Island Press, 2000).

8. At the time of this writing, the Grand Portage Band of Minnesota Chippewa and the Grand Portage National Monument have the longest-running Indian Self-Governance Act agreement in the NPS that includes sharing of management decision making, finances, and staff.

9. Peter Nabokov and Lawrence Loendorf, *Restoring a Presence: American Indians and Yellowstone National Park* (Norman: University of Oklahoma Press, 2004). Yellowstone historian Lee Whittlesey also noted this phenomenon: "While Indians appear not to have feared Yellowstone geyser regions, we know that many tribes revered them. Revere and fear are two different things." Like Isle Royale, the geyser country was considered by Indians to be sacred, not scary. Lee H. Whittlesey, "Native Americans, the Earliest Interpreters: What Is Known about Their Legends and Stories of Yellowstone National Park and the Complexities of Interpreting

Them," *George Wright Forum* 19, no. 3 (2002): 50.

10. Douglas Houghton, "Dr. Houghton's Remarks at the Canal Meeting," 28th Cong., 1st sess., Sen. Exec. Doc., 1843, serial no. 434, p. 21.

11. Whitefish normally spawn in the fall. When they are concentrated in or near spawning grounds, it makes for the most productive fishing. The small whitefish concentrated in the river shoal may not have been spawning, but nonetheless they were there in high numbers and thus became a target for Ojibwe (and fur trade) fishermen. HBCA, B.231/a/19, "Thermometrical Journal Kept at Hudson's Bay Company Trading Establishment Fort William in the Lake Superior District for Outfit 1839," June 21 and 26, and July 3, 1839.

12. Billy Blackwell et al., *A History of Kitchi Onimgaming: Grand Portage and Its People* (Cass Lake: Minnesota Chippewa Tribe, 1982), 18; and Justine Kerfoot, *Gunflint: Reflections on the Trail* (Duluth, Minn.: Pfeifer-Hamilton, 1991), 42.

13. HBCA, B.231/a/11, Fort William Post Returns, June 12–19, 1831; Mission of Immaculate Conception Diary, August 8, 1855, and October 1, 1866.

14. Alexander Henry the elder, *Travels and Adventures in Canada and the Indian Territories between the Years 1760 and 1776* (New York: I. Riley, 1809), 241.

15. There were 196 "Fort William" Ojibwe counted in 1829; 820 at Nipigon in 1805; and 455 at Rainy Lake in 1823. M. Duncan Cameron, "A Sketch of the Customs, Manners and Way of Living of the Natives in the Barren Country about Nipigon, 1804–1805," in *Les Bourgeois de la Compagnie du Nord-Ouest*, edited by L. R. Masson (New York: Antiquarian Press, 1960), 246; HBCA, B.231/e/6, "Report for Fort William District, 1828–1829"; HBCA, B.105/e/2, John McLoughlin, "Rainy Lake District Report for 1822 & 1823"; HBCA, J. MacKenzie to W. B. Robinson, June 10, 1850, and "Diary of W. B. Robinson," September 7, 1850, Public Archives of Ontario, Toronto, Ontario. The "Robinson Treaty" was concluded in 1850 at Sault Ste. Marie, and a number of Ft. William/Grand Portage chiefs were signatories.

16. James G. E. Smith, "Leadership among the Southwestern Ojibwa," *Publications in Ethnology*, no. 7 (Ottawa, Ont.: National Museum of Man, 1973), 16ff. Smith writes: "The authority of the chief was limited, and coercive power completely lacking, in an egalitarian society in which decisions were traditionally reached by consensus."

17. Personal communication with Ojibwe elder Ellen Olson, March 14, 2007, Grand

Portage; and "Census Population of Lake Nipigon, June 1, 1850," record group 10, vol. 9501, pp. 154–59, reel C-7167, National Archives of Canada, Ottawa, Ontario. Recognition of this strong relationship is illustrated by a recent hosting of forty or more elders from Nipigon and Thunder Bay at Grand Portage. *Moccasin [Grand Portage] Telegraph*, November 1997, 13.

18. William Jones Field Notebook, American Philosophical Society, Philadelphia, Pennsylvania. Jones recorded these clans—and spellings—from Chief Penassie at the Fort William Reserve in 1904 or 1905. Penassie was born in 1828 in the Nipigon area and died at Fort William Reserve in 1910. *Daily Times [Fort William] Journal*, March 26, 1910. See also "Nipigon Ojibwe totems," 1852, Father Specht papers, microfilm 871, reel 11, Archives of Ontario, Toronto, Ontario; "Notice of Intent to Repatriate Cultural Items from Grand Portage, Minnesota in the Possession of the Minnesota Historical Society, St. Paul, Minnesota," *Federal Register* 65, no. 184 (September 21, 2000): 57209; and Carolyn Gilman, *Grand Portage Story* (St. Paul: Minnesota Historical Society Press, 1992), 110.

19. For Caribou clan use, I am dependent upon personal communication with Ellen Olson, August 23, 2002, Grand Portage; and for the Fish clan use, see the 1853 entry for P. Addikonse, Fort William Mission Marriage Records, compiled by Father William Maurice, St. Anne's Catholic Church, Fort William Reserve.

20. Jesuit father Francis Nelligan came to the same conclusion, stating, "We must note here that all the Ojibwas of Grand Portage, Pigeon River, and Fort William are closely related, and belonged to the same band." Father Francis Nelligan, S.J., "History of the Diocese of Fort William," unpublished manuscript circa 1950. A copy of the unpublished history is held at Grand Portage National Monument.

21. When asked by the Canadian-English treaty negotiator about receiving treaty payments from the American government (and by implication how he could receive treaty payment from both sides), Peau de Chat replied, "The English land is also my land." "Chief Peau du Chat's Report on His Interrogation by Visiting Indian Agents," in Elizabeth Arthur, *Thunder Bay District, 1821–1892* (Toronto: Champlain Society, 1973), 17.

A primary way I realized that the Fort William and Grand Portage Ojibwe were once one group was by charting traditional-use territories by using the Hudson's Bay Company's clerk's notes about a number of Ojibwe men in the

1820s and 1830s. Ojibwe hunters and trappers—"L'homme de Sault," "La Bete," "Medishean," "Espagnol," "Scandagance," "Pacutchininies"—all made extensive use of lands on both sides of the border. Their movements greatly overlapped, and they would on occasion travel and camp together. There was no identifiable division such as a border in plotting out the movements of these men and their families.

22. Personal communication with Gilbert Caribou, March 1, 2007, and A. A., March 8, 2007, Grand Portage; Jones Notebooks, American Philosophical Society; Daniel G. Cude; "Identifying the Ojibway of North Lake Superior and the Boundary Water Region, 1650–1750," in *Papers of the Algonquian Conference, 32nd Conference*, edited by John D. Nichols (Winnipeg: University of Manitoba, 2001), 96; and Henry Sibley, "Report no. 13," Commissioner of Indian Affairs, Annual Report 1850, 31st Cong. 2nd sess., House Exec. Doc., 1850–1851, serial no. 595, pp. 53 and 59.

23. "Statement Made by the Indians, [1864]," edited by John D. Nichols (London, Ont.: Centre for Research and Teaching of Canadian Native Languages, 1988). The original petition is held at the State Historical Society of Wisconsin, Madison, Wisconsin.

24. For example, the 1798 agreement to lease land to the North West Co., on the Kaministiquia River, by Grand Portage chiefs is evidence of sovereignty. National Archives of Canada, Indian Affairs, record group 11, vol. 266, pp. 163,151–54, "Conveyance of Land at Fort William from the Indians to the North West Company (1798)"; and Thomas L. McKenney and J. Hall, *The Indian Tribes of North America* (Edinburgh: John Grant Co., 1933), 344–45. Apparently because of strong kinship ties, a Bois Forte chief, Kepechkotowe, asserted in 1856 that he was the true chief of the Grand Portage Band. His claims were not recognized. Mission of Immaculate Conception Diary, Fort William, Ontario, Canada, July 26, 1856.

25. HBCA, B.231/e/1, John Haldane, "Report on the State of the Country, Indians in Lake Superior Department, 1824." Haldane writes: "There is one principal Chief to whom the others in a great measure look up—the only name he goes by, even with the Indians is 'Espagnol.' Other traders called him 'the Spaniard.'" See Bela Chapman, Journal or "Log for Traveling," April 11, 1824; and "Lists of Indians

and Their Debts," Henry Sibley Papers, Minnesota Historical Society, St. Paul, Minnesota. Both HBC and American Fur Company entries illustrate Espagnol's prominence, as they frequently provide much greater "gratis" goods to Espagnol than other leaders and hunters.

26. Personal communication with Ellen Olson, March 14, 2007. About 1905, J. B. Penassie said, "The Fort William Ojibways only recently did away with the old clan organization. Children used to get their names from the clan of the father." Jones, Field Notebook, American Philosophical Society.

27. Ibid.

28. William W. Warren, *History of the Ojibway People* (St. Paul: Minnesota Historical Society Press, 1984), 83 ff.


## Chapter 1. Knowing Minong

1. When searching for an overdue survey party who had perhaps diverted to Isle Royale, Ojibwe climbed to the highlands of Wauswaugoning Bay for the best vantage point. "The Canada Pacific Party Conjectured Lost," *Duluth Minnesotan*, February 10, 1872.

2. Isle Royale has a number of alternative names and spellings. Officially, today, it is known as Isle Royale, although often it is spelled Isle Royal. A regional slang name for Isle Royale is "the Island," pronounced by many "the A-land." It is sometimes referred to as an archipelago—which it clearly is, with over four hundred satellite islands around the main island.

   The Ojibwe or Anishinabe word for Isle Royale is "Minong," pronounced "Mee-Nong." The most common English spelling is Minong with an "o." However, one reliable rendering of "Minong" was with a "u"—"Minung"—by linguist William Jones in his "Ojibwa Texts," edited by Truman Michelson, *Publications of the American Ethnological Society*, vol. 7, pt. 1 (1917), 428; and vol. 7, pt. 2 (1919), 191. Jones's informant, John B. Penassie of the Fort William Reserve, told him two stories that name Minung. Grand Portage elder John Flatte once wrote out "Mi Nong" as the correct rendition for the Island, including his indication about how to pronounce it correctly. John Flatte Diary, "Names of Places around Grand

Portage," 1975, copy held at Grand Portage National Monument. But I wanted to stay fairly close to the standard orthography, hence I am using "Minong" in this book.

3. Morris T. Longstreth, *The Lake Superior Country* (New York: Century, 1924), 315; and "There is Only One Magic Isle Royale," *Mining (Houghton, Michigan) Gazette*, June 27, 1937.

4. Hudson's Bay Company official Colin Robertson wrote about a noteworthy traverse of Black Bay:

> I reached the Big Point, but the swell was by no means high, still my Iroquois seemed reluctant to attempt the traverse; when I imprudently ordered them a glass of spirits, the whoop was immediately given and in a moment the canoe was in the water. All went well, until we came to the opening of the bay on the right where a very heavy sea was running, here we began to ship water, when the guide ordered the steersman to be changed, and the bowsman removed to the second bar of the canoe which lightened the canoe by the head. . . . The silence that prevailed when one of those heavy swells was seen rolling upon us was truly appalling.

E. E. Rich, ed., *Colin Robertson's Correspondence Book, September 1817 to September 1822* (London: Champlain Society, 1939), 55–56; Arthur T. Adams, ed., *The Explorations of Pierre Esprit Radisson* (Minneapolis: Ross and Haines, 1961), 124; and Johann Georg Kohl, *Kitchi-Gami: Life among the Lake Superior Ojibway* (St. Paul: Minnesota Historical Society Press, 1985), 181.

5. "Father Dominic Du Ranquet: A Sketch of His Life and Labors (1813–1900)," *The Woodstock Letters* 30, no. 2 (1901): 184.

6. Father Fremiot letter, June 28, 1849, in *Letters from the New Canada Mission, 1843–1852*, pt. 2, edited by Lorenzo Cadieux, translated by William Lonc and George Topp (privately published, 2001), 103, copy held at Grand Portage National Monument.

7. William Jones Field Notebooks, undated, unattributed, but he is likely talking with Fort William Reserve Ojibwe elder John B. Penassie, American Philosophical Society, Philadelphia, Pennsylvania.

8. "Lake Superior Lakewide Management Plan 2000," Environmental Protection Agency, 2000, ch. 6, pp. 22–24.

9. Personal communication with Nancy Lienke, June 2002, and Ellen Olson, January 30, 2003, Grand Portage, Minnesota. A rare newspaper article noted Ojibwe use of the Island: "The Indians in bygone days did reach Isle Royale in canoes from Minnesota and Ontario, but they knew that the trip was dangerous." Dietrich Lange, "Camper Calls Isle Royale Miniature Continent," *Duluth News Tribune*, November 24, 1935.

10. Personal communication with Ellen Olson, Grand Portage, Minnesota, August 23, 2002; and accounts of crossings in Cadieux, *Letters from the New Canada Mission*, 103, 168, 321. David Thompson Journals, August 22, 1823, microfilm reel 4, series 1, bound vol. 22, p. 5572, Ontario Provincial Archive, Toronto, Ontario.

11. Henry Sibley, "Report no. 13," Annual Reports of the Commissioner of Indian Affairs, 31st Cong., 2nd sess., House Exec. Doc. (1850–51), serial no. 595, p. 53.

12. Mission of Immaculate Conception Diary, July 12, 1854, Fort William, Ontario. The original diary is held at St. Regis College, Toronto, Ontario, and a copy is located in Grand Portage National Monument. A number of "savages" worked on the steam boat *Cage*, serving Isle Royale at this time. A. Myers, "Transcript of a Journey to Siskowit Mine in 1851," Historical Society of Pennsylvania, Philadelphia, Pennsylvania.

13. "Report on La Pointe Agency," 1891, Annual Report of the Commissioner of Indian Affairs, 470.

14. Interview with elder Richard Anderson, October 16, 1988, Grand Portage, Minnesota, Minnesota Historical Society, St. Paul, Minnesota.

15. "Mishipizheu" has been spelled many different ways. One older variant is "Missibiz." Personal communication with A. A., December 30, 1998, Grand Marais, and November 20, 1988, Grand Portage, Minnesota; and Silvester John Brito, "The Witch Tree Complex," *Wisconsin Academy of Sciences, Arts, and Letters* 70 (1982): 61–67.

There is also a significant biological relationship between Manido Gee-zhi-gance and Isle Royale, Suzie Islands, and Lake Superior. If not for the protection of Isle Royale and the Suzi Islands, heavy seas—especially northeasters—would pound Manido Gee-zhi-gance, whose base is approximately only ten feet above the water.

16. E. James, ed., *A Narrative of the Captivity and Adventures of John Tanner during*

*Thirty Year Residence among the Indians* (Minneapolis: Ross and Haines, 1956), 25.

17. "Centennial Notes," *Michigan History Magazine* 19 (1935): 455. A newspaper account noted: "Historians wonder, too, why recent Indians were in awe of the island and only journeyed there after dances, appeals to the spirit and ceremonies on the Canadian shore." George Pritchard, "Mystic Lore Shrouds Isle," *Duluth News Tribune*, December 29, 1936.

18. Frances Densmore, *Chippewa Customs* (Minneapolis: Ross and Haines, 1970), 80ff.

19. "Great Lakes Ice Cover, 2003," and "Average Ice Duration, 2004," Great Lakes Environmental Research Laboratory, National Oceanic and Atmospheric Administration, Ann Arbor, Michigan.

20. The *Duluth Minnesotan*, January 9, 1875; and William P. Scott, "Reminiscences of Isle Royale," *Michigan History Magazine* 9, no. 3 (1925): 403.

21. Mission of Immaculate Conception Diary, March 5, 1849.

22. *Duluth Weekly Tribune*, March 24, 1876; The *Duluth Minnesotan*, March 13, 1875; A. C. Davis, "Report to the Directors," Minong Mining Company, December 1, 1876, Bentley Historical Library, Ann Arbor, Michigan; Death notices for James Jones and Meichael [*sic*] Walsh, February 26, 1876, and Thomas Labee and John Skelton, December [no day], 1876, Michigan Department of Community Health, East Lansing, Michigan; Keith Denis, "The Winter Mail to Pigeon River, *Thunder Bay Historical Museum Society* 1 (1973): 16; and Mission of Immaculate Conception Diary, February 18, 1854, and February 27, 1857.

23. "Father Du Ranquet," *The Woodstock Letters*, 183–84.

24. Lawrence J. Burpee, ed., *Journals and Letters of Pierre Gaultier de Varennes De La Verendrye and His Sons* (Toronto: The Champlain Society, 1927), 52.

25. Ramsay Crooks to Lyman Warren, February 28, 1837, American Fur Company Papers (AFC Papers), New York Historical Society, New York. Euro-American knowledge of the Island and the international border was so meager in 1837 that American Fur Company officials wondered if it was an American or British possession.

26. Ben East, "Winter Sky Roads to Isle Royale," *National Geographic* 60, no. 3 (December 1931): 769 and 772; and interview with Willie Droulliard, tape-recorded

by Nancy Lienke, 1961, Grand Portage, Minnesota. Willie Droulliard did not locate the missing man, Iver Anderson, who had left the Island beforehand with illegal furs and rowed a borrowed boat from Washington Harbor to Port Arthur to sell his furs.

27. Personal communication with Ellen Olson, April 10, 2003, Grand Portage, Minnesota; and Chrysostom Verwyst, "Geographic Names in Wisconsin, Minnesota, and Michigan, Having a Chippewa Origin," in *Collections of the State Historical Society of Wisconsin*, vol. 12, edited by Reuben Gold Thwaites (Madison: Democrat Printing Co., 1892), 393.

28. William Ratigan, *The Adventures of Captain McCargo* (New York: Random House, 1956). On page 55 the author wrote, "Minong . . . christened with the Indian name for Isle Royale, as if she were hurrying to claim her own land—the good place to get copper."

29. Alfred C. Lane, "Geological Report on Isle Royale Michigan," *Geological Survey of Michigan 6* (Lansing: Robert Smith Printing, 1900), 4 and 36.

30. N. King Huber, "Glacial and Postglacial History of Isle Royale National Park, Michigan," *Geological Survey Professional Paper 754-A*, 1973, no pagination.

31. Adams, *Pierre Esprit Radisson*; Lawrence J. Burpee, ed., *Journals and Letters of Pierre Gaultier de Varennes de la Verendrye and His Sons* (Toronto: The Champlain Society, 1927); Antoine Denis Raudot, letter 48 in "Memoir Concerning the Different Indian Nations of North America," *The Indians of the Western Great Lakes, 1615–1760*, edited by W. Vernon Kinietz (Ann Arbor: University of Michigan Press, 1940), 375. Is the spelling "Minoncq" simply a typing error, or does it have some accuracy? John Parker, ed., *The Journals of Jonathan Carver and Related Documents, 1766–1770* (St. Paul: Minnesota Historical Society Press, 1976); and *The Falcon: A Narrative of the Captivity & Adventures of John Tanner*, with an introduction by Louise Erdrich (New York: Penguin Books, 1994). There are many other Lake Superior authors that have skipped mention of Minong. Indeed, skipping any mention is the norm; naming it is the exception.

32. Despite extensive efforts, I have only found one instance in which fur traders called Isle Royale "Minong." This is particularly curious as the HBC clerks regularly reported about Ojibwe going to Isle Royale, but used other, non-Native names for it.

The exception to the rule of not identifying "Minong" comes from the retired fur baron William McGillivray in a letter to British authorities concerning the not-yet-agreed-upon international border. In 1824, McGillivray named Isle Royale "or Isle Minos, as it is generally called." Later, he wrote, "Isle Royale (longer known under the appellation of isle Menon)." While his spelling is poor, and the first allusion to the Greek island of Minos takes us afar, McGillivray is clearly trying to render "Minong." William McGillivray letter to Honorable John Hale, September 4, 1824, in 25th Cong., 2d sess., House Exec. Doc. no. 451, pp. 34 and 73, "Boundary between the United States and Great Britain."

33. Henry Schoolcraft, *Algic Researches: Indian Tales and Legends* (Baltimore: Clarfield Co., 1992), original in 1839. In 1831, while on an exploration trip, Schoolcraft eyed Minong from the heights of the Keweenaw Peninsula. Describing this moment, he calls the archipelago "Isle Royale." *Personal Memories of a Residence of Thirty Years with the Indian Tribes of the American Frontier: With Brief Notices of Passing Events, Facts, and Opinions, A.D. 1812 to A.D. 1842* (Philadelphia: Lippincott, Grambo and Co., 1851), 357; and "Minosha, or the Magician of the Lakes," container 74, reel 58, Library of Congress, Washington, D.C. A printed version of this story does not mention Isle Royale; Henry Schoolcraft, *Schoolcraft's Ojibwe Lodge Stories*, edited by Philip P. Mason (East Lansing: Michigan State University Press, 1997), 64–71. William Warren, *History of the Ojibway People* (St. Paul: Minnesota Historical Society Press, 1984).

34. Personal communication with Ojibwe linguists David Pentland, January 27, 2003, and John Nichols, March 12, 2003.

35. Personal communication with Ellen Olson, April 10, 2003, Kalvin Ottertail, June 23, 2004, and Gilbert Caribou, Secretary-Treasurer, Grand Portage Tribal Council, August 19, 2002, all in Grand Portage, Minnesota.

36. Personal communication with Ellen Olson, August 23, 2002, and April 10, 2003; and personal communication with Gilbert Caribou, August 19, 2002, and July 2, 2004, and Kalvin Ottertail, June 23, 2004. Kalvin noted that if it was badly corrupted from its original spoken word, with an "m" replacing a "g," it could possibly have been *Gini sina ang*, or "can provide shelter to"—or in context, among those who knew of Isle Royale, it would mean an island that can provide shelter.

37. Personal communication with John Nichols, January 31, 2003; and Alan H. Hartley,

"The Expansion of Ojibway and French Place-Names into the Lake Superior Region in the Seventeenth Century," *Names* 28, no. 1 (March 1980): 60. Alan Hartley's discussion of the possible interpretations of Minong is concise and accurate.

38. Grand Portage spiritual leader Alex Posey, as reported by foster-daughter Ellen Olson, personal communication, August 23, 2002; and "Chief" John Flatte to Nancy Lienke, July 12, 1963, in Nancy Lienke's notes, Grand Portage, Minnesota.

39. Charles Jackson, "Report on the Geological and Mineralogical Survey," 31st Cong., 1st sess., Sen. Exec. Doc. (1849), 379.

40. Personal communication with Gilbert Caribou, August 19, 2002, and with Kalvin Ottertail, March 7, 2005.

41. Arthur Juntunen, *Duluth News Tribune*, May 17, 1936.

42. Durward L. Allen, *Wolves of Minong* (Boston: Houghton Mifflin Company, 1979). Dr. Allen's use of "Minong" in his book title, which details the celebrated long-term study of wolves and moose on Isle Royale, ensured a more widespread knowledge of the obscure word for Isle Royale. Virgil J. Vogel, *Indian Names on Wisconsin's Map* (Madison: University of Wisconsin Press, 1991), 162; and Vogel, *Indian Names in Michigan* (Ann Arbor: University of Michigan Press, 1986), 136. Vogel mentions alternative meanings for "Minong," including "a good high place" or "blueberry place." See also website nps.gov/nature/animals for this interpretation.

43. Verwyst, "Geographic Names in Wisconsin, Minnesota, and Michigan," 393; Vogel, *Indian Names in Michigan*, 136; Walter Romig, *Michigan Place Names: The History of the Founding and the Naming of More Than Five Thousand Past and Present Michigan Communities* (Grosse Pointe, Mich.: privately printed, 1973), 288–89; and website www.geocities.com/Heartland/Plains/3454/counties.

44. Personal communication with Kalvin Ottertail, July 20, 2005; Gay Page, "Legendary Lore of Lake Superior," *Thunder Bay Historical Museum Report* 7 (1916): 25; and *Marquette Mining Journal*, March 15, 1932.

45. Jean Claude Allouez was a gifted linguist. He reportedly spoke six different Ojibwe dialects. This skill lends some credence to their recording of the word "Minong." Cornelius J. Jaenen, ed., *The French Regime in the Upper Country of Canada in the Seventeenth Century* (Toronto: Champlain Society, 1996), 72.

46. Charles Jackson, "Report on the Geological and Mineralogical Survey," 31st Cong.,

1st sess., Sen. Exec. Doc. 1 (1849); and F. W. Foster and J. D. Whitney, "Report on the Geology and Topography of a Portion of Lake Superior Land District in the State of Michigan," 31st Cong., 1st sess., House Exec. Doc. 69, serial 578, map printed following p. 224.

47. Francis Parkman, *La Salle and the Discovery of the Great West, Part Third* (Boston: Little, Brown and Company, 1869). The timing of Parkman's work is important as it precedes the second and largest era of copper mining on Isle Royale and thus is influential in reminding eastern mining-company investors of the name Minong. A. P. Swineford, *History and Review of the Mineral Resources of Lake Superior* (Marquette, Mich.: The Mining Journal, 1876). Swineford's book was influential in keeping the word Minong current, as it was reprinted many times in the late 1800s.

48. G. Malcolm Lewis, "Metrics, Geometries, Signs, and Language: Sources of Cartographic Miscommunication between Native and Euro-American Cultures in North America," *Cartographica* 30 (1993): 99 and 101.

49. "Sketch of the Current River Route to the Great Dog Lake," appendix to vol. 16 of the *Journals of the Legislative Assembly of the Province of Canada* (Toronto: G. Desbarats & T. Cary, 1858), no pagination.

50. G. Malcolm Lewis, "First Nations Mapmaking in the Great Lakes Region in Intercultural Contexts: A Historical Review," in *Mapping in Michigan and the Great Lakes Region*, edited by David I. Macleod (East Lansing: Michigan State University Press, 2007), 43.

51. "Map Made by the Jesuit Missionaries in the Years 1670 & 1671 and published at Paris 1672," in *Jesuit Relations and Allied Documents*, vol. 55, edited by Reuben Gold Thwaites (Cleveland: Burrows, 1899), facing p. 94.

52. Ibid., 12.

53. The size and shape of the southwestern islands of the Jesuit map made no sense to me until one fall day, looking at the Island from Pincushion Mountain above Grand Marais, I realized what they saw more than three hundred years earlier. Many topographical features can be seen from the North Shore, but some, like the lowlands, "disappear" below the watery horizon because of the curve of the earth. From a distance, then, ridges visually appear as islands, especially Feldtmann Ridge in southwestern Isle Royale.

54. Thomas B. Costain, *The White and the Gold: The French Regime in Canada* (Toronto: Doubleday Canada, 1954), 276–77.

55. "Enumeration of the Indian Tribes Connected with the Government of Canada; the Warriors and Armorial bearings of each Nation, 1736," *Documents Relative to the Colonial History of the State of New York* (Albany: Weed, Parson & Co., 1853–1887), Paris Documents 8, p. 1054. Members of the Fish clan continue to live in the area today, in both Grand Portage and Fort William.

56. Conrad E. Heidenreich, "The Fictitious Islands of Lake Superior," *Inland Seas* 43, no. 3 (Fall 1987): 170–74; and Robert W. Karrow, "Lake Superior's Mythic Isles: A Cautionary Tale for Users of Old Maps," *Michigan History* 69, no. 1 (January–February 1985): 28–29.

57. Rev. Henry Scadding, "Canadian Local History," *Canadian Journal of Science, Literature, and History* 14, no. 5 (July 1875): 666.

58. Heidenreich, "The Fictitious Islands," 174; and Louis C. Karpinski, "Michigan and the Great Lakes upon the Map, 1636–1802, *Michigan History Magazine* 29, no. 3 (July–September 1945): 302.

59. "Joint Report upon the Survey and Demarcation of the Boundary between the United States and Canada from the Northwestern most Point of Lake of the Woods to Lake Superior" (Washington: U.S. Printing Office, 1931), 208–9.

60. "A Map of Lewis and Clark's Track across the Western Portion of North America from the Mississippi to the Pacific Ocean, by order of the Executive of the United States in 1804, 5 & 6. Copied by Samuel Lewis from the Original Drawing of Wm Clark," copy at the Minnesota Historical Society, St. Paul, Minnesota.

61. Jean Morrison, *Fort William in the Canadian Fur Trade* (Toronto: Natural Heritage/ Natural History, 2001), 116–18.

62. David Thompson made a later map of Lake Superior for the British Boundary Survey that was printed in 1824 after he "circumnavigated" its perimeter. Thompson's rough and distorted rendition of Isle Royale on this map suggests he never went there, nor was he able to incorporate others' knowledge of it.

63. Hudson's Bay Company Archives (HBCA), B-231/a/10, 12, 14, and 15, Fort William Post Returns, August 7 and 9, 1830, September 12, 1832, July 11, 1834, August 11, 1835, Winnipeg, Manitoba; and AFC Papers, Lyman Warren to Ramsay Crooks, October 16, 1834. See also AFC factor William Aitken's letter to William Crooks,

November 4, 1836, AFC Papers. Aitken wrote: "Million Island is thought to have even better fishing than the North Shore."

64. AFC Papers, Ramsay Crooks to Wildes & Co., London, February 28, 1835 and June 9, 1835, and Ramsay Crooks to [Captain] Benjamin Stanard, Cleveland, Ohio, June 3, 1843.

65. Major Joseph Delafield, *An Unfortified Boundary* (New York: privately printed, 1943), 398 and 403.

66. James Ferguson letters to Peter B. Porter, September 23, 1822, from Arrow Lake, Ontario, and October 14, 1822 from Fort William, in Peter B. Porter Papers, Buffalo and Erie Historical Society, Buffalo, New York; and William Bird, "Reminiscences of the Boundary Survey," *Publications of the Buffalo Historical Society* 4 (1896): 5.

67. National Archives, record group 76, series 33, pt. 2, map filed October 23, 1826, College Park, Maryland.

68. Fort William Post Returns for July 27 and 28, 1824, Thunder Bay Historical Museum Society, Thunder Bay, Ontario.

69. AFC Papers, Ramsay Crooks to William Brewster, December 21, 1836, and Lyman Warren to Ramsay Crooks, October 16, 1834.

70. Captain Robert McCargo worked for the American Fur Company in 1834 and 1835. If they had been able to continue his employment, he could have greatly assisted the establishment of their fish stations at Isle Royale. The 1845 map, more accurately called "Map of the Part of the Mineral Lands Adjacent to Lake Superior Ceded to the United States by the Treaty of 1842," is in U.S. 29th Cong., spec. sess., Senate 175, no. 461. John Stockton was in charge of the production of the map and voyaged to Isle Royale.

71. Mission of Immaculate Conception Diary, July 29, 1857, May 24, 1859, August 24, 1869; and HBCA, B.231/a/11, 12, and 16, Fort William Post Returns, February 2, 1832, November 1, 1832, and August 6, 1836.

## Chapter 2. Minong Narratives

1. William Jones, "Ojibwa Texts," edited by Truman Michelson, *Publications of the American Ethnological Society*, vol. 7, pt. 1 (1917), 399–407. There are many recorded

examples of this flood—sometime called "earth-diver"—myth. However, a North Shore Ojibwe, Chief John Penassie of Fort William, Ontario, told this version circa 1904. Alexander Henry, *Travels and Adventures in Canada and the Indian Territories, Between the Years 1760 and 1776* (New York: Riley, 1809), 213.

2. Walter J. Hoffman, "The Midewiwin or 'Grand Medicine Society' of the Ojibwa," *Bureau of Ethnology, Seventh Annual Report, 1885–1886* (Washington, D.C.: General Printing Office, 1891), 166; Gay Page, "Legendary Lore of Lake Superior," *Thunder Bay Historical Society* 7 (1916): 25; and William Jones, "Ojibwa Texts," pt. 1 (1917), 483–501. Mishosha, an evil magician, lives on an "enchanted island" and takes and kills his victims on other islands. Henry Rowe Schoolcraft, *Algic Researches: Indian Tales and Legends*, vol. 2 (Baltimore: Clearfield Co., 1992), 91–104. This work was originally published in 1839.

3. Ojibwe linguists John Nichols and Earl Nyholm state that "aadizookaan" would translate as legend and myth. John D. Nichols and Earl Nyholm, *A Concise Dictionary of Minnesota Ojibwe* (Minneapolis: University of Minnesota Press, 1995), 206 and 216.

4. Nanabushu is spelled many ways because of differences in recorders' skills and differences in Ojibwe dialects. I am adopting the spelling of William Jones, a gifted anthropologist, who recorded stories in the area.

5. Sister Bernard Coleman, Ellen Frogner, Estelle Eich, *Ojibwa Myths and Legends* (Minneapolis: Ross and Haines, 1962), 4 and 65; *Ojibwa Narratives of Charles and Charlotte Kawbawgam and Jacques LePique, 1893–1895*, edited by Arthur P. Bourgeois (Detroit: Wayne State University Press, 1994), 13; and Basil Johnston, *The Manitous: The Spiritual World of the Ojibway* (New York: Harper Collins, 1995), 171.

6. Nichols and Nyholm, *A Concise Dictionary*, 259; and A. Irving Hallowell, *The Ojibwa of Berens River, Manitoba,* edited by Jennifer S. H. Brown (New York: Harcourt Brace, 1992), 65.

7. Theresa S. Smith, *The Island of the Anishnaabeg: Thunderers and Water Monsters in the Traditional Ojibwe Life-World* (Moscow, Idaho: University of Idaho Press, 1995), 22–23.

8. Johann G. Kohl, *Kitchi-Gami: Wanderings Round Lake Superior* (Minneapolis: Ross and Haines, 1956), 88.

9. George Copway or Kah-ge-gah-bowh, *The Traditional History and Characteristic Sketches of the Ojibway Nation* (Toronto: Coles, 1972), 95. The original was published in 1850. John Boatman, *My Elders Taught Me: Aspects of Western Great Lakes American Indian Philosophy* (New York: University Press of America, 1992), 13.

10. Charles Lanman, *A Summer in the Wilderness* (New York: Appleton, 1847), 134.

11. R. G. Thwaites, ed., *The Jesuit Relations and Allied Documents: Travels and Explorations of the Jesuit Missionaries in New France, 1610–1791* (Cleveland, Ohio: The Burrow Brothers, 1900), 54:153–57. We must be careful to recognize Jesuit biases implicit in this written version, particularly toward Ojibwe deities. Being watchful for these biases does not make this version invalid, or distorted beyond careful use. Though it is beyond the scope of this chapter, Euro-American interpretation of Ojibwe storytelling often ignores the possibility that Ojibwe use artistic and creative allusions, metaphors, symbolism, and highlighting to contrast elements in their myths, much as Euro-Americans do.

    This story is repeated in every century, including works by: Antoine Denis Raudot, "Memoir Concerning the Different Indian Nations of North America," in *Indians of the Western Great Lakes*, edited by W. Vernon Kinietz (Ann Arbor: University of Michigan Press, 1972), 375–76; Charles Jackson, "Geological and Mineralogical Survey," 31st Cong., 1st sess., Sen. Exec. Doc. 1 (1849), 378–79; Morris T. Longstreth, *The Lake Superior Country* (New York: Century Co., 1924), 315; Isle Royale summer resident Charles Parker Connolly's unpublished novel "A Feather in His Cap," and Ben Cheynoweth's unpublished history of Isle Royale, "Here's Isle Royale," both maintained at Michigan Technological University Archives, Houghton, Michigan; and even as poetry in Louise Leighton, "The Legend of Copper Stones," *The Great Carrying Place* (New York: Harbinger House, 1944), 41–42.

12. Michael Angel, *Preserving the Sacred: Historical Perspectives on the Ojibwa Midewiwin* (Winnipeg: University of Manitoba Press, 2002), 64–65.

13. Grace Rajnovich, *Reading Rock Art* (Toronto: Natural Heritage, 1994), 102–6; Jennifer S. H. Brown and Robert Brightman, *"The Orders of the Dreamed": George Nelson on Cree and Northern Ojibwa Religion and Myth, 1823* (St. Paul: Minnesota Historical Society Press, 1988), 108–9; Ojibwe artist Norval Morrisseau website: www.kstrom.

net/isk/art/morriss; Smith, *The Island of the Anishnaabeg*, 95–125; Christopher Vecsey, *Traditional Ojibwa Religion and Its Historical Changes* (Philadelphia: The American Philosophical Society, 1983), 74.

Fond du Lac Ojibwe headman Mang'osid stated that Mishipizheu had a copper tail. Further, he had a piece of that tail, which prevented him from having bad dreams and getting sick. Edmund F. Ely Journal, February 8, 1837, St. Louis County Historical Society, Duluth, Minnesota.

A story told by Ojibwe elder Pete Martin in 1942 made graphic the connection between Mishipizheu and copper. Two young women paddling across a lake encountered Mishipizheu in "a hole of clear water." In a fight with Mishipizheu, one girl struck the underwater manitou's tail with her canoe paddle while saying, "Thunder is striking you." A part of the tail was cut off and dropped in the canoe. It was copper, and then was used for luck and good fortune in hunting and fishing, particularly for Mang'osid in hunting bear. Note in this case, as well as others, that something very positive (copper) comes from a threatening encounter with Mishipizheu. Victor Barnouw, *Wisconsin Chippewa Myths & Tales and Their Relation to Chippewa Life* (Madison: University of Wisconsin Press, 1977), 132–33; and Edmund Ely Journal, February 8, 1837.

14. *Fort William Daily Times Journal*, March 26, 1910; William Jones, "Ojibwa Texts," vol. 7, pt. 1 (1917), xvi–xvii; Henry Milner Rideout, *William Jones: Indian, Cowboy, American Scholar, and Anthropologist in the Field* (New York: Stokes Co., 1912), 97–98, 109–10; and W. S. Piper, *The Eagle of Thunder Cape* (Thunder Bay, Ont.: Thunder Bay Historical Museum Society, 2001), 53. Piper's book was originally published in 1924. William Jones died prematurely, and fellow linguist Truman Michelson completed his work. It is unknown which of the two, Michelson or Jones, translated these texts into such a stiff Victorian style.

15. Toad Woman is "another name for Mother Earth, or the grandmother of Nanabushu." Jones, "Ojibwa Texts," pt. 1, p. 431. Jones notes that Toad Woman is inherently both good and bad, exhibiting a range in character. Jones, Field Notebooks, undated, American Philosophical Society, Philadelphia, Pennsylvania.

16. William Jones, "Ojibwa Texts," pt. 1, pp. 429–33. Jones writes about Nanabushu's involvement in Ojibwe places with the following footnote on page 432: "In various places in the Ojibwa country may be observed a rock, island, or high land looking

like a human being either reclining or seated, when seen from the distance, and is generally called Nanabushu."

Grand Portage elder Wilfred Montefrand told another version of this story, except that it takes place in what is now Duluth rather than at Isle Royale and Michipicoten. "*A Long Time Ago Is Just Like Today*, edited by David Martinson (Duluth, Minn.: Duluth Indian Education Advisory Committee, 1976), 10.

Does this legend contain an ecological message? Does it express alarm, conveyed symbolically, about the extirpation of beaver at Isle Royale because of the folly of Nanabushu's greediness? What makes this contemplation more credible is that beaver were extirpated, or nearly so, from Isle Royale during Penassie's adult life and were rare on the Island during the time that this story was recorded, in the first years of the twentieth century. For more on the rarity of beavers during this time, see William P. Scott, "Reminiscences of Isle Royale," *Michigan History Magazine* 9, no. 3 (1925): 408.

17. American Fur Company Papers (AFC Papers), Lyman Warren to Ramsay Crooks, 16 October 1834, New York Historical Society, New York.

18. Gay Page, "Legendary Lore of Lake Superior," *Thunder Bay Historical Society* 7 (1916): 25. This obscure written version is a primary source for Dorothy M. Reid, *Tales of Nanabozho* (Toronto: Oxford University Press, 1963), 107–10.

19. William Jones, "Ojibwa Tales from the North Shore of Lake Superior," *Journal of American Folklore* 29 (1916): 384.

20. Dewey Albinson, "A Grand Portage Story," unpublished manuscript, 1963, Minnesota Historical Society, St. Paul, Minnesota; and Silvester John Brito, "The Witch Tree Complex," *Transactions of the Wisconsin Academy* 70 (1982): 63.

21. Piper, *The Eagle of Thunder Cape*, 10, 64, 95, 109; Coleman, Frogner, Eich, *Ojibwa Myths and Legends*, 102–3; Richard Dorson, *Bloodstoppers and Bearwalkers: Folk Tales of Immigrants, Lumberjacks and Indians* (Cambridge, Mass.: Harvard University Press, 1952), 55–56; Brown and Brightman, "*The Orders of the Dreamed*," 112.

22. Frances Densmore, *How Indians Use Wild Plants* (New York: Dover, 1974), 384–85.

23. Ibid., and Mille Lacs Ojibwe elder Maude Kegg told a traditional tale about a similar "floating island" in *What My Grandmother Told Me*, translated by John D. Nichols (St. Paul: Minnesota Historical Society Press, 1983), 68.

24. H. O. Whittemore, "Radio Address," March 15, 1932, in the *Detroit News*, Isle Royale Collection, Bentley Library, Ann Arbor, Michigan. Similar comments are found in "Isle Royale Is Described by State Game Warden in Radio Address from WBEO," *Marquette Mining Journal*, March 15, 1932. There are numerous other instances where non-Ojibwe focus on the fantastic nature of this assertion of Minong being a floating island. See A. A. Webster, "Minong—the Floating Island," *American Forests* (August 1932): 439.

25. Gerald Vizenor, *Anishinabe Aadizookaan* (Minneapolis: Nodin Press, 1970), no pagination.

26. *Duluth Minnesotan*, May 10 and September 25, 1875; and Anon., *Sixth Report of the Bureau of Mines, 1896* (Toronto: Legislative Assembly of Ontario, 1897), 109. An account of a floating island in Massachusetts was a recently featured piece in the *New York Times*, November 6, 2005. The novelty and nuisance of the floating island remained key features of this article.

27. Kohl, *Kitchi-Gami*, 188. Articles also noted that on occasions observers would see what appeared to be Isle Royale floating upside down in the air. "There Is Only One Magic Isle Royale," *The [Marquette] Mining Gazette*, June 27, 1937; Page, "Legendary Lore of Lake Superior," 25.

28. Jackson, "Geological and Mineralogical Survey," 12; Mr. John Johnston, "An Account of Lake Superior: 1792–1807," in *Les Bourgeois de la Compagnie du Nord-Ouest*, edited by L. R. Masson (New York: Antiquarian Press, 1960), 162–63; and "Scenery of Lake Superior—Isle Royale," *Canadian Agriculturist* 3, no. 4 (April 1851): 94.

29. Charles T. Jackson, "Mirage on Lake Superior," in *The Annual of Scientific Discovery, Or, Year-book of Facts in Science and Art*, edited by David Ames Wells et al. (New York: Gould and Lincoln, 1850), 151. "Superior" or arctic mirages are nicely explained in "Readers Want to Know," *Seiche* (May 2007): 5.

30. Page, "Legendary Lore of Lake Superior," 25. This version of the "great diver myth" is very similar to many other Ojibwe versions. It is different in its localization of the story, especially at Isle Royale. Some versions of this Ojibwe myth provide a specific location in which it occurred; others do not.

31. For two versions of this current story, see "The Legend of the Sleeping Giant" and "The Sleeping Giant."

32. Piper, *The Eagle of Thunder Cape*, 10.

33. Mishipizheu is sometimes described as a giant sturgeon or is associated with sturgeon, although it is unclear if Schoolcraft meant the allusion to be part of this story. Kinietz, *The Indians of the Western Great Lakes*, 286.

34. The original version of this story appears in Henry R. Schoolcraft's *Algic Researches* (New York: Harper, 1830), 2:91–104, and is republished in *Schoolcraft's Ojibwe Lodge Stories*, edited by Philip P. Mason (East Lansing, Michigan State University Press, 1997), 64–71. The manuscript version of "Mishosha or the Magician of the Lakes" appears in the Henry Rowe Schoolcraft Papers, Library of Congress, container 73, reel 58. A later rendition that reinterprets the story is contained in Loren R. Graham, *A Face in the Rock: The Tale of a Grand Island Chippewa* (Washington, D.C.: Island Press, 1995), 18.

35. Ruth Landes, quoted in Angel, *Preserving the Sacred*, 145.

36. Charles Jackson, "Geological and Mineralogical Survey," 428–29. The crew was becoming desperate enough that they contemplated crossing the lake in a small boat, against the advice of the few resident copper miners.

37. Personal communication with Ellen Olson, January 30, 2003, Grand Portage. Kohl mentions that French voyageurs told a windigo story set on Isle Royale. It is quite likely this is a reference to Charlie and Angelique Mott's struggle and that the date was inverted from 1845 to 1854 when put into print. Kohl, *Kitchi-Gami*, 356.

38. Timothy Cochrane, Introduction to "Charlie & Angelique Mott," in *Borealis: An Isle Royale Potpourri*, edited by David Harmon (Houghton: Isle Royale Natural History Association, 1992), 79. For many years, visitors to the Island could read a small pamphlet about Charlie and Angelique Mott sold by the Isle Royale Natural History Association. The pamphlet was only one of over eleven different versions of this story. All the versions I have found are written, and it is unclear whether this story ever existed in oral tradition. A similar altered version of a windigo story centered on the Passage Island, Isle Royale, lighthouse keeper in the 1880s. The Charlie and Angelique Mott story was related primarily through written versus oral expression.

39. Brown and Brightman, "*The Orders of the Dreamed*," 163–71. See also Brightman, "The Windigo in the Material World," *Ethnohistory* 35, no. 4 (Fall 1988): 337–79.

40. "Charlie and Angelique Mott," Isle Royale Natural History Association, n.d. Other seminal versions of the Mott legend include R. P. Nevin, "Who Fared and

How Fared in the Hut on Isle Royale," *Lake Superior Journal,* July 3, 1850; George Duffield, "Angelique," *Detroit Tribune,* February 7, 1876; Anon., "Through an Icy Hell," *Magazine of Michigan* (May 1929): 6, 7, 22, and 24; Dennis Glen Cooper, "The Tragedy of Mott Island," *Inland Seas* 3, no. 1 (January 1947): 17–20; and most recently Karl Bohnak, *So Cold a Sky: Upper Michigan Weather Stories* (Nagaunee, Mich.: Cold Sky Publisher, 2006), 56–61.

The Mott legend contains a number of elements that resonate in both Ojibwe and "white" culture, including the civilizing and saving nature of fire, the tragic nature of greed and groundless trust. These elements are critical to the story's meaning, but are beyond our scope here.

41. Personal communication with Ellen Olson, January 30, 2003, Grand Portage, Minnesota.

42. James Ferguson letter to General Peter Porter, September 23, 1822, Peter Porter Papers, Buffalo and Erie Historical Society, Buffalo, New York, and William Ives notes, September 20 and 28, 1847, and June 6 and July 18, 1848 and "Land Survey and Plats of Isle Royale, Michigan," General Land Office, copy of the survey held by Isle Royale National Park, Houghton, Michigan.

43. Ellen Olson, January 30, 2003.

44. Thwaites, *The Jesuit Relations and Allied Documents,* 50:265 and 267.

45. Kohl, *Kitchi-Gami,* 60.

46. Piper, *The Eagle of Thunder Cape,* 109.

47. William Warren, *History of the Ojibway People* (St. Paul: Minnesota Historical Society Press, 1984), 89, 98–99.

48. Edmund Ely Journal, February 8, 1837. Interestingly, both Mongazoid (or Loon's Foot) and the chief interviewed by Warren who had copper in their possession were of the Loon Clan. It is not known if the Loon Clan, versus some other clan, had a particularly unique association with copper.

49. Kohl, *Kitchi Gami,* 61–64.

50. Father Fremiot letter, May 11, 1850, in *Letters from the New Canada Mission, 1843–1853,* edited by Lorenzo Cadieux, translated by William Lonc and George Topp (privately printed, 2001), 166; Ellen Olson, January 30, 2003; Walpole Roland, *Algoma West* (Toronto: Warwick & Sons, 1887), 52 and 91–92. Roland details the role of local Ojibwe Weisaw Bahgwatchinnini in finding veins of

silver near Whitefish Lake, Ontario (west-southwest of Thunder Bay). At nearby Silver Island off Thunder Cape in the early 1870s, there were forty-five Ojibwe working at the silver mine and living together in a "small Indian ghetto." Thomas W. Dunk, "Indian Participation in the Industrial Economy on the North Shore of Lake Superior, 1869–1940," *Thunder Bay Historical Museum Society Papers and Records* 15 (1987): 7.

51. Personal communication with Kenneth Johnson, October 1988, Duluth, Minnesota. Ken said he heard the story from his father, Milford, that the Indians who visited Isle Royale died because of cooking with copper rocks. They died because the heated copper rocks poisoned their food, and thus other Indians became afraid of Minong. This explanation stems from Father Dablon, *Jesuit Relations*, 54:157.

52. Susan Martin, *Wonderful Power: The Story of Ancient Copper Working in the Lake Superior Basin* (Detroit: Wayne State University Press, 1999), 180. Dr. Martin states: "Native copper was worked and used until the introduction of European metals in the seventeenth century."

53. "Isle Royale," *Bulletin of the Michigan Department of Conservation*, undated but circa early 1950s, Isle Royale National Park Archives, Houghton, Michigan.

54. Thwaites, *Jesuit Relations*, 54:159–61.

55. Ibid.

56. A. P. Swineford, *Mineral Resources of Lake Superior* (Marquette: The Mining Journal, 1876), 9.

57. General Walter Cunningham to James Madison Porter, Secretary of War, October 2, 1843, in 28th Cong., 1st sess., Exec. Doc. (1843), serial no. 438, p. 286.

58. Mrs. Bessie Phillips, Michigan WPA manuscript, Isle Royale National Park Archives, Houghton, Michigan.

59. Personal communication with Ellen Olson, August 23, 2002; Tony LeSage, quoted by Larry Oakes, "Sacred Roots," *Minneapolis Star Tribune*, October 9, 1994; Norval Morrisseau website: www.kstrom.net/isk/art/morriss/morbio; Mission of Immaculate Conception Diary, July 22, 1857; Nancy Woolworth, "The Grand Portage Mission: 1731–1965," *Minnesota History* (Winter 1965): 305; and Kohl, *Kitchi-Gami*, 422.

I do not mean to imply here that traditional religious thought was extinguished. There is ample evidence it was not. For example, the same rituals to propitiate the "spirits" of the lake for a safe crossing that John Tanner and his Ojibwe travelers made in the 1790s continue today. Illustrating the continuation of traditional Ojibwe religious thought and the blending of it with Christian beliefs is beyond the task of this work.

60. Prominent examples of this interpretation of Ojibwe storytelling include Morris T. Longstreth, *The Lake Superior Country* (New York: Century Co., 1924), 315; "Centennial Notes," *Michigan History Magazine* 19 (1935): 454; Benjamin Cheynoweth, "Here's Isle Royale," unpublished manuscript, Michigan Technological University Archive, Houghton, Michigan.

61. Personal communication with Stan Sivertson, October 14, 1988, Duluth, Minnesota. Stan, a folk historian of Isle Royale and lifelong commercial fisherman, remarked that he often wondered why Indians were not using Isle Royale much in his lifetime (during much of the twentieth century), as they obviously had been using it before.

62. "Who Worked Isle Royale Mines?" *Duluth News Tribune*, February 19, 1939.

63. Personal communication with Ellen Olson, August 23, 2002, Grand Portage, Minnesota.

64. A classic example of this is in the "flagship" publication of Isle Royale National Park, available for many years. Napier Shelton's *The Life of Isle Royale* (Washington: National Park Service, 1975), 22, says this about Ojibwe use of the Island: "By the 1840s, when white miners came to Isle Royale, the only Indian encampments were one on Sugar Mountain, where they tapped maples for the sap, and a seasonal fishery." This statement, almost daring in its time in mentioning some Indian presence, in retrospect clearly minimizes the connections North Shore Ojibwe had with Minong.

65. Interview with Mrs. Ellen Hanson, Floodwood, Minnesota, November 11, 1988.

66. H. O. Whittemore, "Isle Royale as a National Park," radio broadcast, undated but during the 1930s or early '40s, *Detroit News*, Isle Royale Collection, Bentley Library, Ann Arbor, Michigan.

67. Kohl, *Kitchi-Gami*, 60. The example is from the South Shore and applied to Isle Royale, since there is no indication that Ojibwe reverence for copper was different from the South to North shores of Lake Superior.

## Chapter 3. On Minong

1. Mission of Immaculate Conception Diary, August 14, 1854, St. Regis College, Toronto, Ontario. A copy of the diary is held at Grand Portage National Monument, Grand Portage, Minnesota.

2. Horace M. Albright testified in favor of the establishment of Isle Royale as a national park, in part because of its archeological remains, especially those around McCargoe Cove. Horace M. Albright, National Park Service Director, February 25, 1931, *Congressional Record*, U.S. Senate, March 3, 1931.

3. Henry Gillman, "Ancient Works at Isle Royale, Michigan," *Appleton's Journal* 10 (August 9, 1873): 173–75; and William P. F. Ferguson, "The Franklin Isle Royale Expedition," *Michigan History* 8 (1924): 450–68.

4. Personal communication with Dr. Caven Clark, June 2002; and Clark, "Archeological Survey and Testing Isle Royale National Park, 1987–1990 Seasons," edited by F. A. Calabrese, Midwest Archeological Center Occasional Studies in Anthropology no. 32 (1995), 3 and 167ff.

5. David Arthurs, "Lake Superior Surveys, 1978–1989," North Central Region Conservation Archaeology Report, Ontario Ministry of Citizenship, Culture and Recreation, Thunder Bay, 244, 240, and 51; Susan Martin, *Wonderful Power: The Story of Ancient Copper Working in the Lake Superior Basin* (Detroit: Wayne State University Press, 1999), 178; Clark, "Archeological Survey," 21–22; Clark, "Group Composition and the Role of Unique Raw Materials in the Terminal Woodland Substage of the Lake Superior Basin," Ph.D. dissertation, Michigan State University, 1991, 70, 175–76, and 209; and Terrance J. Martin, "Prehistoric Animal Exploitation on Isle Royale," in Clark, "Archeological Survey," 210.

6. Tyler J. Bastian, "Archeological Survey of Isle Royale National Park, Michigan, 1960–1962," University of Michigan Museum of Anthropology, Ann Arbor, Michigan, p. 376. One ring is dated as circa 1650–1750 and is made of brass with a glass inset with a grasped-hands motif. Clark, "Archeological Survey," 56. Tinkling cones are small metallic cones strung together and used as jewelry and to make a jingle noise while dancing.

   Archeologically, the line between prehistoric and historic periods on Isle Royale is not as distinct as the words suggest. Some artifacts, such as pottery, thought to be prehistoric could be historic. There has not been exacting-enough research to make these distinctions clear. Personal communication with archeologists Dr. Caven Clark, June 2002, Phoenix, Arizona, and Dr. Guy Gibbon, July 2002, Grand Marais; and Clark, "Archeological Survey," 167.

7. Clark, "Archeological Survey," 167; and Judith Ann Hauser, "Jesuit Rings from Fort Michilimackinac and Other European Contact Sites," Mackinac Island State Park Commission, Archeological Report no. 5 (1982), 1 and 39. A similar ring was found on Lake Nipigon, though it was dated to be from some time in the 1670s or 1680s, when the first Jesuits entered this geographical area. David Arthurs, "An 'IHS': Finger Ring from Lake Nipigon," *Arch Notes: Newsletter of the Ontario Archaeological Society*" (May–June 1983), 20. Another Jesuit ring, thought be from the 1725–1750 period, was found at Grand Portage. Anon., "Chippewas Get New Community Hall," *Duluth News Herald*, August 25, 1939.

8. "McCargoe" is spelled two different ways in this document. McCargoe Cove, with an "e," is the official spelling for this well-sheltered inlet. "McCargo" without an "e" is the spelling of Captain Robert McCargo, for whom the cove is named.

    McCargoe Cove was called "Pike Bay," or Gnoozhekaaning in Ojibwe. "Father Dominic Du Ranquet: A Sketch of His Life and Labors, 1813–1900," *Woodstock Letters* 30, no. 2 (1901): 183–84. Unfortunately, comparatively few Ojibwe place-names have survived, including Chippewa Harbor, Siskiwit (Bay, Lake, Mine, River, Falls, Swamp), Sheshab (Duck) Lake, Ojibway Lake, Lake Ahmik (beaver). Most Ojibwe place-names appear to have been lost, such as "Pakomonaning Bay" in northeastern Isle Royale. An authentic, but largely unknown Ojibwe name for Washington Harbor is Osagaadeng, or "place where the beaver comes out of his lodge." Rev. Chrysostom Verwyst, "A Glossary of Chippewa Indian Names of Rivers, Lake and Villages," *Acta et Dicta* 4, no 2 (1916): 273 and Mission of Immaculate Conception Diary, July 4, 1854. Beaver Island in Washington Harbor appears to have been derived from Ojibwe. William Ives, "Isle Royale Survey," July 18, 1848, General Land Office, copy held at Isle Royale National Park Archives.

9. Clark, "Archeological Survey," 169.

10. Hudson's Bay Company Archive (HBCA), B.231/a/11, Fort William Post Returns, June 2 and August 2, 1831.

11. North Shore Ojibwe would begin to move to the wild rice district as early as August

6th. Mission of Immaculate Conception Diary, August 6, 1855. However, compared with their kinsmen at Rainy Lake who had ample wild rice and maize to harvest, North Shore Ojibwe had scant wild rice resources. For more on the importance of wild rice in the Rainy Lake district, see *Sixteen Years in the Indian Country: The Journal of Daniel Williams Harmon*, edited by W. Kaye Lamb (Toronto: Macmillan Co., 1957), 91–92.

12. Clark, "Archeological Survey," 3, 171, 172, 180; and Clark, "Group Composition," 115–16. We know that the Grand Portage people attempted to grow maize, but in one recorded instance in 1803 the garden plot, called "Vieu Desert," was abandoned. Laura Peers and Theresa Schenk, eds., *My First Years in the Fur Trade: The Journals of 1802–1803 [of] George Nelson* (St. Paul: Minnesota Historical Society Press, 2002), 98. Maize was an important crop for the Grand Portage kinsmen at Rainy Lake. Leo G. Waisberg and Tim E. Holzkammn, "'A Tendency to Discourage Them from Cultivating': Ojibwe Agriculture and Indian Administration in Northwestern Ontario," *Ethnohistory* 40, no. 2 (1993): 175–211.

13. Caven Clark and Timothy Cochrane, "Haytown: A Nineteenth Century Copper Mining Site on Isle Royale's North Shore," *Michigan Archaeologist* 44, no. 2 (June 1998): 74. Also, in 1849 one Jesuit father observed at treaty negotiations: "Joseph, La Peau de Chat, was seated in the first line. He was dressed like the whites, as were all our Natives." Father Fremiot letter, October 18, 1849, edited by Lorenzo Cadieux, translated by William Lonc, S.J. and George Topp, S.J., in *Letters from the New Canada Mission, 1843–1852* (Hamilton, Ont.: privately printed, 2001), 129.

14. Mission of Immaculate Conception Diary, June 21, 1850.

15. Mission of Immaculate Conception Diary, October 27, 1854. This "integration" with the outside world was short-lived. By 1857 the mines were closed, sites abandoned, and few if any Euro-Americans remained. Accordingly, our documentary sources of what happened from 1857 until the next copper era in the 1870s are largely silent during this time.

16. Henry R. Schoolcraft, "Annual Report of the Commissioner of Indian Affairs," 25th Cong., 3d sess., 1839, House Doc. no. 2, serial no. 344. Though he was a respected and experienced Indian agent, Henry Schoolcraft never traveled to northwestern Lake Superior. However, his brother-in-law, George Johnston, did work for the

American Fur Company at Grand Marais during the winter of 1824–1825 and likely learned something about Minong during this time. Henry R. Schoolcraft Papers, Manuscript Division, Library of Congress, Washington, D.C.

17. Schoolcraft, quoted by D. P. Bushnell, Commissioner of Indian Affairs, Annual Report for 1841–42, p. 106, microfilm 1599, Minnesota Historical Society (MHS), St. Paul, Minnesota.

18. "Annual Report for 1840," U.S. Commissioner of Indian Affairs, 27th Cong., 2nd sess., House Doc. no. 2, serial no. 401, p. 354.

19. General Walter Cunningham to Hon. James Madison Porter, Secretary of War, (reporting what Alfred Brunson said), October 2, 1843, 28th Cong., 1st sess., 1843, Exec. Doc., serial no. 438, p. 286.

20. "Father Ranquet," *Woodstock Letters* 30, no. 2 (1901): 183–84; and from the Mission of Immaculate Conception Diary, July 2, 1854. For example, the Chawanibitang family hiked from Siskiwit Mine in Rock Harbor to Todd Harbor.

21. Fort William Post Returns, June 7, 1824, Thunder Bay Historical Museum Society (TBHMS), Thunder Bay, Ontario; R. N. "A Summer's Ramble on the North-West Shore of Lake Superior," *The Anglo-American Magazine* 6, no. 3 (March 1855): 279; and HBCA, B.231/a/14, Fort William Post Returns, July 24, 1834; and Mission of Immaculate Conception Diary, June 8 and 22, 1853, and September 22, 1854.

22. William Gibbard, "Report on the Fisheries of Lakes Huron and Superior," December 31, 1861, *Sessional Papers*, vol. 3, 1st Session of the Seventh Parliament, Province of Canada, 1862, no pagination.

23. W. S. Piper, *The Eagle of Thunder Cape* (Thunder Bay, Ont.: Thunder Bay Historical Museum Society, 2001), 25–26; and Johann Georg Kohl, *Kitchi-Gami: Life among the Lake Superior Ojibway* (St. Paul: Minnesota Historical Society Press, 1985), 24. See Mrs. Henry Conary, "Early Life on Isle Royale," *Daily [Houghton, Michigan] Mining Gazette*, June 21, 1939. For an example of Ojibwe getting fish from a small stream, see Mission of Immaculate Conception Diary, June 21, 1853, and October 4, 1854; HBCA, B.231/a/13, Fort William Post Returns, July 23, 1833; and personal communication with Ellen Olson, January 30, 2003, Grand Portage.

Fort William Ojibwe John B. Penassie described the use of fish traps. A box-shaped trap was used for fishing for speckled trout and suckers in streams. He also indirectly affirmed the use of weirs in the area when he told the *aadizookaan*

"Nanabushu and the Fish Trap." Nanabushu's fish trap is a great success, but he is tricked into feeding his catch to clever animals. William Jones, *Ojibwa Texts*, edited by Truman Michelson, *Publications of the American Ethnological Society*, vol. 7, pt. 1 (Leyden: Brill, 1917), 437ff; and Jones, Field Notebooks, American Philosophical Society, Philadelphia, Pennsylvania.

24. More than one third of all references to Ojibwe on Minong pertain to fishing. This historic subsistence-fishing strategy mirrors that of the late prehistoric period detailed by Charles E. Cleland, "Analysis of the Fauna of the Indian Point Site on Isle Royale in Lake Superior," *Michigan Archaeologist* 14, nos. 3–4 (1968): 143–46; and Terrance J. Martin, "Prehistoric Animal Exploitation on Isle Royale," in Clark, "Archeological Survey and Testing," 210 and 213.

25. Personal communication with Ellen Olson, August 23, 2002, Grand Portage; and Sister M. Inez Hilger, "Chippewa Hunting and Fishing Customs," *Minnesota Conservationist* 35 (1936): 3.

26. TBHMS, September 6, 1825; HBCA, B.231/a/7, Fort William Post Returns, March 27, 1828; Gibbard, "Fisheries of Lake Huron and Superior," 1862.

27. For wintertime use of hooks and lines, see HBCA, B.231/a/15 and 17, Fort William Post Records, December 29, 1835 and February 17, 1837; and Sharon Moen, "Ice Cover Lacking on Lake," *Seiche* (April 2006): 2.

28. James Meeker, Joan E. Elias, and John A. Heim, *Plants Used by the Great Lakes Ojibwa* (Odanah, Wisc.: Great Lakes Fish and Wildlife Commission, 1993), 235.

29. For example, the 1797 inventory of goods at Grand Portage includes 13 pounds of net thread, "seal twine," 20 bunches of sturgeon twine, and 3500 cod hooks. "Inventory at Grand Portage," [North West Company] June 1797, Toronto Public Library, Toronto, Ontario. Ojibwe women and sometimes freemen were regularly employed by the HBC to "knit nets" from twine. HBCA, B.231/a/8, Fort William Post Returns, August 27, 1828; and B.231/e/1, "Report on the State of the Country and Indians in Lake Superior District, 1824."

30. Erhard Rostlund, "Freshwater Fish and Fishing in Native North America," *University of California Publications in Geography* 9 (1952), 168–69; and Kohl, *Kitchi-Gami*, 31. Nettles appear to be a favored fish cord among many Ojibwe, but are only occasionally found in disturbed soil in the Kaministiquia River floodplain and

Grand Portage area. Piper, *The Eagle of Thunder Cape*, 24 and 76. Nettles are much more common inland. Fort William Ojibwe Penassie clearly preferred linden (basswood) bark twine in his narratives. Jones, *Ojibwe Texts*, 375, 379, 401, 403, and 405. Even if present on Isle Royale, nettles would likely have been sparingly used, as nettles were harvested for fiber after a hard frost in the fall—that is, after most Ojibwe had left Minong—after the stinging capacity of the plant is greatly reduced. Personal communication with Karen Daniels Petersen, December 27, 2003, West St. Paul, Minnesota; and Carrie A. Lyford, *Ojibwa Crafts* (Washington, D.C.: Bureau of Indian Affairs, 1953), 44–45.

31. HBCA, B.231/a/19, "Thermometrical Journal Kept at the Hudson's Bay Company Trading Establishment Fort William in the Lake Superior District for 1839," September 19, October 7 and 18, 1839.

32. George Copway, *The Traditional History and Characteristic Sketches of the Ojibway Nation* (London: Gilpin, 1850), 41. "Siscowet" was initially spelled a bewildering number of ways. I am adopting the most common spelling of the fish in the nineteenth century, or "siscowet." Siskiwit becomes the proper scientific spelling for the fish in the twentieth century. Since we are largely talking about a nineteenth-century phenomenon, I have chosen the historic spelling.

33. Personal communication with Ellen Olson, February 17, 2006, Grand Portage; and David Gidmark, *Building a Birchbark Canoe* (Mechanicsburg, Penn.: Stackpole Books, 1994), 24. Bear grease traditionally used in canoe "gum" was not available on Minong, because bears did not live on the Island.

34. Seth A. Moore and Charles R. Bronte, "Delineation of Sympatric Morphotypes of Lake Trout in Lake Superior," *Transactions of the American Fisheries Society* 130 (2001): 1237; Michael J. Wilberg, Michael J. Hansen, and Charles R. Bronte, "Historic and Modern Abundance of Wild Lean Lake Trout in Michigan Waters of Lake Superior: Implications for Restoration Goals," *North American Journal of Fisheries Management* 23 (2003): 100; and personal communication with Charles Bronte, New Franken, Wisconsin, March 29, 2006.

35. One hundred eighty feet was the deepest the American Fur Company was able to fish. Most nets were set in much shallower water—15 to 20 fathoms, or 90 to 120 feet. An earlier reference for the Huron Indians suggests that nets were occasionally set in 30 fathoms of water, or 180 feet. American Fur Company Papers

(AFC Papers), Lyman Warren to Ramsay Crooks, February 10, 1835, New York Historical Society, New York, New York; W. Vernon Kinietz, *The Indians of the Western Great Lakes, 1615–1760* (Ann Arbor: University of Michigan Press, 1940), 29; and Kohl, *Kitchi-Gami*, 31.

36. Dr. John McLoughlin, "The Indians from Fort William to Lake of the Woods," ca. 1807, Minnesota Historical Society (MHS), St. Paul, Minnesota; and Gabriel Franchere to Ramsay Crooks, September 26, 1837, American Fur Company Letters, Bayliss Library, Sault Ste. Marie, Michigan.

37. American Fur Company Papers, (AFC Papers), Ramsay Crooks to Stephen Halsey, September 6, 1839, New York Historical Society, New York. Siscowet sold for $7.50 per barrel, compared with $6.00 for trout and $6.50 for whitefish. Because siscowet were valuable, American Fur Company management tried to have them barreled separately. AFC Papers, Gabriel Franchere to Ramsay Crooks, September 29, 1835.

38. Ironically the *Siskawit* would go aground at Siskiwit Bay in 1840. AFC Papers, James Scott to Charles Borup, October 6, 1840.

39. Gabriel Franchere, "G. Francheres Journal of his Voyage in the 'Brewster' with Mr. Scott to Grand Portage, Ile [*sic*] Royale & the Ance in August 1839," Gabriel Franchere Papers, Minnesota Historical Society, St. Paul, Minnesota.

40. William Ives, "Isle Royale Survey," 1847, and "Discussion," *The Canadian Agriculturist and Journal of the Board of Agriculture of Upper Canada* 9, no. 5 (May 1858): 116. Surveyor Ives noted a year later that siscowet were also caught at Washington Harbor.

41. Father Fremiot letter, September 27, 1850, *Letters from the New Canada Missions*, 187–88. McCullough offered $2 per barrel of fish, but $9 per barrel for rendered oil. He recommended that if Ojibwe fishers ran out of salt for barreling fish, they should instead produce oil. Mission of Immaculate Conception Diary, June 22, 1853, and July [no date], 1854.

42. Early advertisements in a Sault Ste. Marie, Michigan, newspaper read "Siskawit, 50 barrels siskawit, 50 half barrels, from Isle Royale, Lake Superior," and "Siskiwit: Just Received from Isle Royale and for sale at the Mineral Warehouse, a few barrels of Siskawit," *Lake Superior News and Miners' Journal*, May 22 and November 11, 1850. Complicating assessing the importance of siscowet in this early period is that

many writers did not distinguish between "lean" trout and siscowet.

43. AFC Letters, Gabriel Franchere to Ramsay Crooks, September 26, 1837, Bayliss Library, Sault Ste. Marie; AFC Papers, R. Crooks to Stephen A. Halsey, August 19, 1839; Charles Borup to Ramsay Crooks, December 24, 1839; Douglas Houghton Field Notes and Observations, July 29 and August 4, 1840, Bentley Historical Library, University of Michigan, Ann Arbor; William Ives, July 15, 1847, "Survey Notes," Isle Royale National Park Archive; R. N. "A Summer's Ramble on the North-West Shore of Lake Superior," 279; Mission of Immaculate Conception Diary, July 23, 1850, and August 14, 16, 18, 1854; Father Fremiot wrote about Siskiwit Bay: "The fish that the Sauteaux [Canadian name for Ojibwe] call Siskawet are extraordinarily abundant there." Fremiot letter in *Letters from the New Canada Mission*, 188.

44. Personal communication with Gene Skadberg, Grand Marais, Minnesota, April 3, 2006; and Charles R. Bronte, "Evidence of Spring Spawning Lake Trout in Lake Superior," *Journal of Great Lakes Research* 19 (1993): 625 and 627. Personal communication with Charles Bronte, February 16, 2006, who mentioned during research that he caught two spawning siscowet females at the mouth of Siskiwit Bay in August. Perhaps these females are a remnant of a once larger population of early-spawning siscowet in Siskiwit Bay. This hypothetical fish population of early and shallow-spawning siscowet—which are exceptions to the rule—were less numerous and thus more fragile to impacts.

A small population of siscowets are particularly vulnerable to overfishing. "The apparent sensitivity of historical populations of siscowet to overfishing is related to their slow growth, low production to biomass (P/B) ratio, later age at maturity, and lower fecundity compared to lean lake trout from Lake Superior." Charles R. Bronte and Shawn P. Sitar, "Harvest and Relative Abundance of Siscowet Lake Trout in Michigan Waters of Lake Superior, 1929–61" (in press, 2008), 12; a copy of this article is held at Grand Portage National Monument.

45. The first recognized name for what are now Paul Islands was "Siskowit Islands." Pioneering surveyor William Ives's map noted the "Siskowit Islands," and particularly the "South Island valuable for fishing purposes." Ives, Isle Royale Survey, Isle Royale National Park Archive.

46. Hugh H. McCullough, December 1, 1851, certificate 772, Sault Ste. Marie General

Land Office, GLO Records, www.glorecords.blm.gov/patentsearch. McCullough appears to have purchased a site that was used by the AFC in the late 1830s. Gabriel Franchere, "Journal," 1839, MHS.

47. Maurice E. Stansby, "Development of Fish Oil Industry in the United States," *Journal of the American Oil Chemists' Society* 55 (February 1978): 238; and William Hutchinson Rowe, *The Maritime History of Maine* (New York: Norton, 1948), 284.

48. McCullough came from Newark, New Jersey, to become a mining agent on Isle Royale. He later became a trader, as well as postmaster at Grand Portage. R. B. McLean, "Reminiscences of Early Days at the Head of the Lakes," in J. Wesley White, compiler, "Historical Sketches of the Quetico-Superior," 2:7–8 (May 1967); and Mission of Immaculate Conception Diary, August 18 and October 7, 1854. In the fall of 1854, the Grand Portage Ojibwe, in essence, allowed McCullough to have exclusive trading privileges with them.

   McCullough purchased boilers to render the fat from siscowets to sell as oil. The boilers appear to have been used when there was a shortage of salt. According to Grand Portage resident Henry LeSage, the oil was used as a base for paint used on iron. Mission of Immaculate Conception Diary, August 1854. Elliot Davis letter (Grand Portage Superintendent) to Isle Royale Superintendent, January 25, 1962, Isle Royale Archives; and personal communication with Roy Oberg, October 15, 1988. Roy learned much about the siscowet rendering operation from Steve Johnson, whose family fished out of Wright Island during much of the twentieth century.

49. The multiple and early use (1836) of the name Siskiwit also suggests some presence of this fish species. It is the most common place-name on Isle Royale, used to denote the main bay, two islands, the largest lake, a couple of small rivers, campground, falls, a "mount," mine, and the largest swamp.

50. HBCA, B.231/a/19, "Thermometrical Journal," June 21 and 29, 1839; B.231/a/8–11, 13, Fort William Post Returns, September 9, 1828, October 16 and 22, 1829; October 16, 1830; October 17 and 21, 1831; September 26, 1833; Fort William Records, June 29, 1839, microfilm M19, MHS; Fort William Records, TBHMS, July 24, 1824. Whitefish more typically live and spawn in Lake Superior, making this river-running variety very precious for North Shore Ojibwe and Fort William residents.

51. J. L Goodier asserts that herring were not harvested for the Fort William post—a remarkable oversight given such a plentiful resource. Herring were not harvested much, but they were caught and used as bait. HBCA, Fort William Post Returns, B.231/a/16, June 29 and July 9, 1835. J. L. Goodier, "The Nineteenth-Century Fisheries of the Hudson's Bay Company Trading Posts on Lake Superior: A Biogeographical Study," *Canadian Geographer* 28, no. 4 (1984): 351.

52. Personal communication with Milford Johnson Jr., May 5, 2006, Grand Marais, Minnesota.

53. Edwin James, ed., *A Narrative of the Captivity and Adventures of John Tanner*, 24–26. And personal communication with A. A., Grand Portage, Minnesota, November 1988.

54. Personal communication with Grand Portage tribal chairman Norman Deschampe, Grand Portage, March 2, 2006; and Rick Anderson, Grand Portage, February 23, 2006. Norman told of his father inadvertently catching a sturgeon in his net that was so strong it pulled his boat and net for quite some distance. Grand Portage residents could see the shadows of sturgeon spawning or warming themselves in Wauswaugoning Bay from the heights of Mt. Josephine.

55. William Raff, *Pioneers in the Wilderness: Minnesota's Cook County, Grand Marais, and the Gunflint in the Nineteenth Century* (Grand Marais, Minn.: Cook County Historical Society, 1981), 28.

56. Loren R. Graham, *A Face in the Rock* (Washington, D.C.: Island Press, 1995), 18.

57. Father N. Fremiot to Rev. Micard, February 2, 1851, in *Letters from the New Canada Mission*, p. 275.

58. The Fort William post experienced a shortage in coarse salt for brining in June 1831. HBCA, B.231/a/11, Fort William Post Returns, June 26 and 29, 1831.

59. Exactly when salting fish was introduced into the area is unknown. However, the North West Company, Hudson's Bay Company, and the American Fur Company relied heavily on salted fish for their winter food in this area. See, for example, William McGillivray's orders to Kenneth MacKenzie, National Archives of Canada, MG 19, B1, vol. 1, North West Company Letterbook, August 16, 1800; Fort William Post, TBHMS, November 4, 1824; HBCA, B.231/a/9 and 14, Fort William Post Returns, September 1, 1829, and October 16, 1834; HBCA,

B.231/a/3, Point Meuron [Thunder Bay] Returns, September 20 and 21, 1819. During the 1850s, families would "salt down from 2 to 12, 15, 16, 20, and even 25 barrels of fish." Father Fremiot letter, February 2, 1851, *Letters from the New Canada Missions*, 275.

60. By the late 1820s a trader would write, "Moose [were] literally extinct [in the region] and carribou were numerous [but] few now are seen." HBCA, B.231/e/1, "Report on the State of the Country and Indians in Lake Superior District, 1824."

61. Clerk Mailloux traded for "38 does and cariboux, dressed" at Kamanistiquia in 1806. Elliot Coues, ed., *The Manuscript Journals of Alexander Henry and of David Thompson* (Minneapolis: Ross & Haines, 1965), 284. At least for some time, the HBC assigned a "country produce value" to "Reindeer Skins" in the 1820s. HBCA, B.135/k/1, Moose Factory Minutes, "Council at Michipicotten, May 21, 1827." This same record notes that 218 "Orignals" [French for moose] skins were traded. Hence a few moose were still available for the hunt in 1806.

62. Jean Fitts Cochrane, "Woodland Caribou Restoration at Isle Royale National Park: A Feasibility Study" (Isle Royale National Park, 1996), 74; and "Report of the North Central Caribou Corporation, 1988–1994" (Duluth, Minn.: privately printed, 1994), 29–31. Isle Royale National Park has a copy of this report.

63. William Jones, "Ojibwa Texts," edited by Truman Michelson, *Publications of the American Ethnological Society*, vol. 7, pt. 2 (1919), 593 and 595.

64. Francis Densmore, "Uses of Plants by the Chippewa Indians," *45th Annual Report of the Bureau of American Ethnology* (Washington, D.C.: U. S. Government Printing Office, 1928), 322. HBCA, B.231/a/14, Fort William Post Returns, March 29, 1834. Medishean was one Ojibwe who overwintered at Isle Royale.

65. HBCA, B.231/a/16, Fort William Post Returns, August 2, 1836.

66. Caribou were of such an interest to the HBC clerk at Fort William that he noted Indian accounts on August 10th: "Rein Deer rutting season commences about this place." And later, on September 2nd, he noted, rutting season "terminates by Indian accounts." HBCA, B.231/a/19, "Thermometrical Journal," August 10 and September 2, 1839.

67. Charles T. Jackson, 32nd Cong., 1st sess., Sen. Exec. Doc. no. 112, serial no. 622, p. 234.

68. HBCA, B.231/a/13, Fort William Post Returns, May 23, 1833; and Fort William

Post Returns, TBHMS, July 24, 1824.

69. Jones, Field Notebooks, American Philosophical Society.

70. Alexander Henry, *Travels and Adventures in Canada and the Indian Territories, Between the Years 1760 and 1776* (New York: I. Riley, 1809), 130.

71. "Returns of Fort William 8th July 1816," Public Archives of Canada (microfilm copy at MHS, reel M19); and HBCA, B.231/e/6, William R. MacKenzie Sr., "Report for the Fort William District, 1828–29." "Extirpated" in this statement means in a large-scale commercial sense. Beavers were still to be found and trapped; for example, L'homme du Sault and party trapped twenty-nine beavers in 1839, and another Ojibwe trapped thirteen in 1839 on the mainland. HBCA, B.231/a/19, Fort William, March 3 and May 6, 1839. However, beavers were rare on the mainland up until at least the 1850s. Father Fremiot letter, February 2, 1851, *Letters from the New Canada Missions*, 277.

72. Exactly when beaver were locally trapped out is unknown. Isle Royale land surveyor William Ives noted only old and abandoned beaver dams in 1847. Mission of Immaculate Conception Diary, November 9, 1852, and October 24, 1853; and Laurits W. Krefting, "Beaver of Isle Royale," *Naturalist* 14, no. 2 (Summer 1963): 2–11. William Scott, the doctor at Wendigo Mine in Washington Harbor, found only abandoned beaver houses in the early 1890s. William P. Scott, "Reminiscences of Isle Royale," *Michigan History Magazine* 9, no. 3 (1925): 403.

73. Personal communication with Ellen Olson, January 30, 2003, Grand Portage.

74. Father Fremiot letter of April 16, 1849, in *Letters from the New Canada Mission*, 98. Fremiot noted that the major sugar bush was about a half-day journey from their mission on the Pigeon River, but some went farther away.

75. Father Fremiot letter of February 2, 1851, in *Letters from the New Canada Mission*, 280. Personal communication with Roy Oberg, October 1988, Grand Marais. Roy noted that in the twentieth century, few Grand Portage Ojibwe would go to Isle Royale for the sole purpose of making maple sugar, as there was ample sugar bush in back of Grand Portage. HBCA, B.231/a/9, Fort William Post Returns, March 21, 1830.

76. William Ives, "Isle Royale Survey Notes," General Land Office, June 6, 1848. A copy of his survey is held at the Isle Royale National Park Archives.

77. "Mr. [George] Dickenson's Report," in "Report on the Geological and Mineralogical

Survey of the Mineral Lands of the United States in the State of Michigan," 505, and Mr. [James] McIntyre's Report," 508, edited by Charles T. Jackson, 31st Cong., 1st sess., Sen. Exec. Doc. no. 1 (1849).

78. Fred Dustin, "An Archaeological Reconnaissance of Isle Royale, Michigan," *Michigan History* 41, no. 1 (March 1957): 22. Dustin was an amateur archeologist with a long-term interest in Isle Royale.

If there was an aboriginal trail from Washington Harbor to the sugar-maple stand, it suggests a more direct route from Grand Portage to the sugar bush than the more common route from the Thunder Bay area to McCargoe Cove and then dispersing throughout the Island. The antiquity of the trail is not known, nor is the frequency of its early use.

79. William Jeffery, "Early Life at Island Mine," *Daily [Houghton, Michigan] Mining Gazette,* June 21, 1939; and Mrs. Henry Conary in the same publication. M. M. Shea, "Early Life at the Minong Mine," in Lawrence Rakestraw, "Post-Columbian History of Isle Royale: Part I, Mining," unpublished manuscript, Isle Royale National Park, Houghton, Michigan; Sarah Barr Christian, *Winter on Isle Royale: A Narrative of Life on Isle Royale during the Years 1874 and 1875* (privately printed, 1932), 32ff., a copy of this small book is available at the Minnesota Historical Society, St. Paul.

80. One observer of the tradition of maple-sugaring at the nearby Bois Forte reservation claimed that the right to a sugar bush descended from mother to female child. If this was true and a similar custom was followed on Minong, then it is interesting to speculate that North Shore Ojibwe women might have some aboriginal claims to the sugar-maple area. Albert Reagan, "Plants Used by the Bois Fort Chippewa (Ojibwa) Indians of Minnesota," *Wisconsin Archeologist* 7, no. 4 (July 1925): 233.

81. Ellen Olson interview by Carolyn Gilman, November 1, 1989, MHS. Isle Royale institution Captain Roy Oberg once met a former Civilian Conservation Corps "boy" who found a large kettle for boiling sugar sap in this same grove. The sugar-maple kettles and supplies were often stored on site and left there for the next year. Personal communication with Roy Oberg, October 15, 1988.

82. HBCA, B.135/k/1, "Minutes of the Moose [Factory] Council," 1837 and 1854.

83. HBCA, B.231/a/13–14, Fort William Post Returns, April 18, 1834, and May 6, 1835.

84. Thomas Clark, "The Physical Geography, Meteorology, and Botany of the Northeastern District of Minnesota," *Report of the State Geologist* (St. Paul: Frederick Driscoll, 1865), 77.

85. Dennis Glen Cooper, "The Tragedy of Mott Island: The Story of Angelique and Charlie Mott," *Inland Seas* (January 1947): 17–20; and "Charlie and Angelique Mott," in *Borealis: An Isle Royale Potpourri,* ed. David Harmon (Houghton: Isle Royale Natural History Association, 1992), 79–84. The reliance on snaring rabbits and threat of starvation is repeated in an apocryphal legend of the Passage Island lighthouse keeper's wife and children. W. H. Law, *Among the Lighthouses of the Great Lakes* (Detroit: privately printed, 1908), 14; and Charles K. Hyde, *The Northern Lights: Lighthouses of the Upper Great Lakes* (Lansing: Two Peninsula Press, 1986), 61. The lighthouse keeper in this case was likely Richard Singleton, who died in an accident in Port Arthur when getting supplies. The stories are incorrect on two essential points: his wife (his third) was not an Ojibwe woman, nor was the family left there over winter.

86. HBCA, B.231/a/15, Fort William Post Returns, November 21, 1835, and February 23, 1836.

87. HBCA, B.231/e/1, John Haldane, "Ft. William Report for 1824." Use of rabbits (on the mainland) is also mentioned in the November 24, 30, and December 2, 8, 9, 1824, entries at the Fort William Post Returns, TBHMS. Often the clerk's "woman" was a major producer of rabbits; hence, one enterprising woman snared thirty rabbits in December 16, 1843, and sixty more on January 5th. Fort William Post Returns, December 16, 1843, and January 5, 1844, microfilm M19, MHS.

88. M. M. Shea, "Early Life at the Minong Mine," Isle Royale Archives.

89. HBCA, B.231/a/10, Fort William Post Returns, January 26, 1831.

90. Father Fremiot letter, February 2, 1851, *Letters from the New Canada Missions,* 280; and HBCA, M. Mackenzie (from Ft. William) to Sir George Simpson, December 27, 1850. Mackenzie wrote: "Rabbits and lynx have almost disappeared in this quarter, & I fear there will be much starvation among the Indians this year."

91. HBCA, B.162/e/1, Donald McIntosh, "1828 Pic District Report."

92. William Jeffrey, "Early Life at Island Mine, 1873 and 1874"; and HBCA, B.231/a/8, Fort William Post Returns, September 29 and 30, 1828. One Jesuit father noted "an abundance of wild pigeons" on Isle Royale on July 19, 1854. Mission of Immaculate

Conception Diary, July 19, 1854.

93. James, *Adventures of John Tanner*, 25.

94. Cornelius G. Shaw Diary, August 3, 1847, Michigan Historical Collections, Bentley Historical Library, Ann Arbor, Michigan. Mission of Immaculate Conception Diary, July 19, 1853. The "wild leek" appears to be *Allium schoenoprasum var. sibericum*, which is still present on Isle Royale but is fairly rare and deemed threatened in Minnesota. Gary B. Walton, "Rare Plant Species of Grand Portage National Monument," draft, 1999, 15–17; 2003, NPSpecies list for Isle Royale, Isle Royale National Park; Nancy A. Johnson, "Suzie Island: Minnesota's Arctic Outpost," *Minnesota Monthly* (June 1984): 20; and Thomas Clark, "The Physical Geography," 78.

95. Allison D. Slavick and Robert A. Janke, *The Flora of Isle Royale National Park, Michigan* (Houghton: Michigan Technological University, 1985), 21–22; and Densmore, *How Indians Use Wild Plants*, 294 and 298.

96. Ellen Olson, Grand Marais, Minnesota, October 16, 1988.

97. William Jeffrey, "Early Life at Island Mine, 1873 and 1874."

98. Interview with Mrs. Ellen Hanson, Floodwood, Minnesota, November 11, 1988 and Paula Sundet, "Anishinabe Mat and Bag Weaving," master's thesis, Vermont College, 2002, 106–9. A number of Mrs. Linklater's creations are displayed at the National Park Service, Grand Portage Heritage Center.

99. James, *Adventures of John Tanner*, 24–26.

100. Caven Clark, "A Dog Burial from Isle Royale, Lake Superior: An Example of Household Ritual Sacrifice in the Terminal Woodland Period," *Midcontinental Journal of Archaeology* 15, no. 2 (1990): 265–78. A dog sacrifice might be for other purposes, such as one held on July 24, 1855, in Grand Portage when the Grand Portage and Bois Forte bands were awaiting treaty payments. Mission of Immaculate Conception Diary, July 24, 1855.

101. Statement by John Linklater in "Centennial Notes," *Michigan History Magazine* 19 (1935): 455; and Silvester John Brito, "The Witch Tree Complex," *Wisconsin Academy of Sciences, Arts and Letters* 70 (1982): 62–63.

102. Kohl, *Kitchi-Gami*, 38–39; and Norval Morriseau, *Legends of My People, the Great Ojibway* (Toronto: McGraw-Hill, 1965), 27.

103. Much of our information about aboriginal religious activities stems from Jesuit

accounts, obviously very biased against traditional Ojibwe religious beliefs. The goal of this section is to not provide an overview of the rich Ojibwe religious traditions or the Jesuit attempts to halt them. Instead, my principal point is to establish that religious ceremonies were performed on Minong as they would be in any place of importance.

104. Mission of Immaculate Conception Diary, June 1853.

105. William Warren, *History of the Ojibway People* (St. Paul: Minnesota Historical Society Press, 1984), 65–66; personal communication with Gilbert Caribou, July 2, 2004, Grand Portage, Minnesota; and Christopher Vecsey, *Traditional Ojibwa Religion* (Philadelphia: American Philosophical Society, 1983), 179.

106. HBCA, B.231/a/11, Fort William Post Returns, June 12–19, 1831. There is little recorded information about when North Shore Ojibwe held Midewiwin ceremonies. Three documented dates—June 12–19, 1831; August 8, 1855; and the first week of October 1866—do not illustrate a pattern of when the rites were held. Mission of Immaculate Conception Diary, August 7–8, 1855, and October 3, 1866.

107. Bruce M. White, "A Skilled Game of Exchange: Ojibway Fur Trade Protocol," *Minnesota History* 50 (Summer 1987): 231; and Lara Peers, *The Ojibwa of Western Canada, 1780 to 1870* (St. Paul: Minnesota Historical Society Press, 1994), 34.

108. James Croil, *Steam Navigation and Its Relation to the Commerce of Canada and the United States* (Toronto: William Briggs, 1898), 256; James Cooke Mills, *Our Inland Seas: Their Shipping and Commerce for Three Centuries* (Chicago: A. C. McClurg, 1910), 72–73; G. A. Cuthbertson, "Fur Traders on Fresh Water: An Account of the Northwest Company's Sailing Ships on the Great Lakes," *The Beaver* (December 1934): 29; and Grace Lee Nute, *Lake Superior* (Indianapolis: Bobbs-Merrill, 1944), 119. The *Duluth Minnesotan* April 13, 1872 account of the caching of the *Recovery* at "McCargers Cove" [*sic*] is garbled, and its facts about why the vessel was cached incorrect. However, it does demonstrate the story was in oral tradition at Pigeon River, with its likely source being a North Shore Ojibwe. Who remembered and told the story strongly infers Ojibwe knowledge of hiding the *Recovery* and thus protecting it.

109. Jean Morrison, "Fur Trade Families: Then & Now," 1993, Friends of Grand Portage Meeting, St. Paul; and Shirley Taitt Metz, "Taitt Ancestry" unpublished family tree, Grand Portage National Monument. The extended family genealogy

is fascinating, but beyond the scope of our interests. Nancy McKay McCargo's father, Alexander McKay, was one of the Northwesters who accompanied MacKenzie across the continent to the Pacific Ocean, eleven years before Lewis and Clark. By some accounts, Mt. McKay in Thunder Bay was named after Nancy's father. Nancy McKay McCargo's maternal grandfather, Jean Etienne Wadens, was one of two men likely killed by the infamous Peter Pond. Wadens died at Lac La Rouge in March 1782. Other relatives of Nancy McKay include trader William Morrison, who worked at Fond du Lac and quite possibly at Grand Portage.

110. Metal was extremely valuable and useful in this period; hence it was much sought after by Ojibwe. It was highly prized for utilitarian and trade purposes. For example, the HBC regularly burned bateaux to recover nails, or broke up old boats, and in one instance sent laborers to Point Meuron to recover "iron" where an old building was burned. Fort William Post Returns, July 8 and 16, 1825, TBHMS; and HBCA, B.231/a/12, Fort William Post Returns, August 17, 1832.

111. The best available evidence of the North Shore Ojibwe British sympathies during the 1812 War was their tradition of traveling to Manitoulin Island to receive British presents. Lise Hansen, "The Anishinabek Land Claim and the Participation of the Indian People Living on the North Shore of Lake Superior in the Robinson Superior Treaty, 1850," Ontario Ministry of Natural Resources, November 22, 1985, 20; and Carolyn Gilman, *The Grand Portage Story* (St. Paul: Minnesota Historical Society Press, 1992), 99–100; and Gilman, "Grand Portage Ojibway Indians Give British Medals to Historical Society," *Minnesota History* 43 (Spring 1980): 26–32. North Shore Ojibwe received presents of King George medals and the British flag that are important objects of patrimony in Grand Portage today.

112. There is an obvious bias to the Fort William HBC journal entries; namely, they were much more prone to record Ojibwe travelers who went from Ft. William elsewhere or returned to Ft. William from an American location. They were not able to record Ojibwe leaving Grand Portage directly for Minong, unless they traveled through Ft. William. Further, during the period between 1833 and 1846, there was a secret agreement between the Hudson's Bay Company and the American Fur Company that precluded the latter from trading for furs in Grand Portage and along the border. Hence, during this period Fort William continued

to be an important economic hub for North Shore Ojibwe, with the exception being when the AFC began its commercial fishing operations at Grand Portage and Isle Royale in the late 1830s. Nute, *Lake Superior*, 48.

113. HBCA, B.231/a/6, Fort William Post Returns, June 31, 1826, and May 15, 1827. There is an oral tradition of "Nipigon Indians" from near Armstrong, Ontario, having commonly resorted to Minong in addition to those North Shore Ojibwe (who eventually became the Fort William and Grand Portage bands). Personal communication with Marcie McIntyre, September 2001, Grand Portage, Minnesota. Another example of movement at the time is explained in the trader's statement: "The Saulteaux of Fond du Lac [Duluth area] invariably come to Lac la Pluie in a sugar year for the purpose of trading blankets and clothes." HBCA, B.105/e/4, "Lac la Pluie Report for 1824–25."

114. "Father [Nicholas] Fremiot's Report to His Superior in New York, October 18, 1849," in Elizabeth Arthur, *Thunder Bay District, 1821–1892* (Toronto: Champlain Society, 1973), 14.

115. HBCA, B.231/e/1, John Haldane, "Report on the State of the Country & Indians in the Lake Superior Department."

116. HBCA, B.105/a/15, September 17 and October 3, 1830, "Lac La Pluie Journal of Daily Occurancing [*sic*] Commenscing June 1st, 1830." In another instance, an Indian named Wolf who was from Fort William returned there after living at Rainy Lake for six years. HBCA, B.231/a/8, Fort William Post Returns, December 29, 1828.

117. HBCA, B.231/a/14 and 15, Fort William Post Returns, July 12, 1834, February 23, 1835, and June 23, 1835.

118. HBCA, B.231/a/17 and 8, Fort William Post Returns, May 27, 1838, and June 20, 1828.

119. Genealogical information on the Illinois/L'homme du Sault/Singleton family line is drawn from a number of sources. Particularly helpful have been the marriage and death records kept at the Mission of Immaculate Conception, Fort William, and organized and made understandable by Father William Maurice, St. Anne's Church, Fort William Reserve, Ontario. Also helpful are the Fort William Post Returns, HBCA; 1871 and 1881 "family census" records from Ontario Genealogical Society records housed at the Thunder Bay Museum; and Richard Singleton's

obituary, "Terrible Accident: The Oldest Pioneer of the North Shore Run Over by a Train and Killed," *Thunder Bay Sentinel*, May 26, 1883. Just as this history demonstrates, North Shore Ojibwe had a number of names in Ojibwe, French, or English. This variability in names and also spellings of names makes tracking their history difficult but interesting detective work. Mission of Immaculate Conception Diary, June 22 and October 5, 1853.

One weak link in this family genealogy is the possible confusion over a "Jacob Amadjiwegabow," who might be an alternative name for L'homme du Sault. If so, a Jacob Amadjiwegabow did not die at Isle Royale; instead he was still alive on January 2, 1852, when he (and others) signed a petition to the Governor of Canada.

120. Arthur, *Thunder Bay District*, 199.

121. Mission of Immaculate Conception Diary, November 2, 1857.

122. 1871 Canadian Census, St Ignace Township, West Algoma. Singleton's latter two wives were non-Ojibwe, and through time his children all converted (from Catholic) to his religion, Church of England.

123. His unexpected and tragic death was surprisingly quickly noted. A Letter Book of the Light House Board noted his death on May 23, 1883. And a month later, the Light House Board noted "assistance to keeper's family." Record group 26, Light House Board Letters, National Archives, Washington, D.C.

It is quite possible, perhaps even likely, that Singleton worked at Isle Royale during the 1870s copper mining boom, but to date there is no record of his whereabouts at that time.

124. Personal communication with Ellen Olson, January 30, 2003, Grand Portage. The last name is spelled a variety of ways in published and unpublished documents ranging from Bahgwatchenennee, to Buhkwujjenenne, to Bouquachininni, to even Pakwajininni. I have standardized the name here as Bahgwatchinnini. When Grand Portage Ojibwe had to sign land allotment papers, the Ojibwe name was prohibited, and the family adopted the last name of Bushman.

125. HBCA, B.231/a/10 and 12, Fort William Post Returns, February 26, 1831, and November 1, 1832.

126. Fort William Post Returns, TBHMS, March 4 and May 1, 1824; HBCA, B.231/a/8, April 22, 1829; AFC Papers, "List of Employees at Isle Royale for 1838 and 1839,

Northern Outfit." He was paid $120 for his labors in 1838 and was given a raise to $150 for 1839.

127. Mission of Immaculate Conception Diary, June 22 and October 5, 1853, and July 9, 1868; genealogical records of Father William Maurice, St. Anne's Church, Fort William Reserve; Ellen Olson interview, November 2, 1989; and Keith Denis, "Oliver Daunais—The 'Silver King,'" *Thunder Bay Historical Museum Society Papers and Records* 2 (1979): 13.

128. Walpole Roland, *Algoma West: Its Mines, Scenery and Industrial Resources* (Toronto: Warwick & Sons, 1887), 52, 91–92, and 99; and Mission of Immaculate Conception Diary, July 29, 1857, and May 24, 1859.

129. Ellen Olson, October 16, 1988, Grand Marais; Obituary for Mike Flatte, *Cook County News Herald*, 7 April 1983; personal communication with Nancy Lienke, June 11, 2002, Grand Portage; Mission of Immaculate Conception Marriage Records, compiled by Father William Maurice, St. Anne's Catholic Church, Fort William Reserve, Ontario.

130. "Enumeration of the Indian Tribes Connected with the Government of Canada: The Warriors and Armorial Bearings of Each Nation, 1736," *Documents Relative to the Colonial History of the State of New York* (Albany: Weed, Parsons & Company, 1853–87), 1054.

131. Delafield, *An Unfortified Border*, 404; Ruth Landes, *Ojibwa Sociology* (New York: AMS Press, 1969), 37; R. W. Dunning, *Social and Economic Change among the Northern Ojibwa* (Toronto: University of Toronto Press, 1959), 79–83.

132. Charles A. Bishop, "The Question of Ojibwa Clans," *Actes du vingtième congrés des Algonquinistes*, edited by William Cowan (Ottawa: Carlton University, 1989), 56; Harold Hickerson, "The Southwestern Chippewa: An Ethnohistorical Study," *American Anthropological Association* 64, no. 3, pt. 2 (June 1962), 83; and Landes, *Ojibwa Sociology*, 97–98.

133. Ellen Olson, October 16, 1988, Grand Marais.

134. Personal communication with Norman Deschampe, June 20, 2002, Grand Portage; Ellen Olson, November 1, 1989, Grand Marais, Minnesota; J. B. Penassie in Jones Notebooks, American Philosophical Society.

135. Personal communication with Warner Wirta, March 27, 2006, Duluth, Minnesota.

136. AFC Papers, Ramsay Crooks to John Holliday, June 26, 1837.

137. AFC Papers, Ramsay Crooks to Lyman Warren, February 28, 1837, and Crooks to William Brewster, September 8, 1836.

138. AFC Letters, Gabriel Franchere to Ramsay Crooks, September 26, 1837, Bayliss Library, Sault Ste. Marie, Michigan. Charles Chaboillez was once a highly trusted employee, but a drinking and temper problem stained his reputation. He may have been sent to Isle Royale to "dry out," but still he was in charge of this relatively large workforce of Ojibwe working on a per-barrel basis.

139. Ibid.

140. HBCA, B.231/a/17, Fort William Post Returns, August 22, 1837; and Iraneus Frederic Baraga, "Baptismal Records, 1835–1887, Kept at LaPointe and Bayfield, Indian Missions," transcribed by John L. Schade, *Lost in Canada? Canadian-American Journal of History & Genealogy* 17, no. 3 (Summer 1994): 111, 114, 115, 118, and 18, no 2 (Fall 1995): 75.

141. "G. Franchere Journal of his Voyage in the 'Brewster' with Mr. Scott to Grand Portage, Ile [*sic*] Royale & Ance in August 1839," Gabriel Franchere Papers, MHS, St. Paul.

142. HBCA, B.231/a/18, Fort William Post Returns, May 27, 1839.

143. AFC Papers, "Isle Royale Outfit for 1838 and 1839," Northern Outfit.

144. AFC Papers, "Grand Portage Outfit for 1837, 1838, and 1839," Northern Outfit.

145. AFC Papers, Ramsay Crooks to George Simpson, October 7, 1837.

146. AFC Papers, James Scott to C. Borup, October 6, 1840, and Borup to R. Crooks, December 24, 1839. The *Siskawit* was salvaged and operated until 1849, but the AFC operation on Isle Royale was over.

147. At least two families, the LeGardes and Naganob families, came to Grand Portage this way, according to Alan Woolworth, personal communication, September 17, 2002, St. Paul, Minnesota. Alan recalled information told to him by Paul LeGarde, who worked with Alan for many years in archeological investigations.

148. Lawrence Rakestraw, "Historic Mining on Isle Royale," *Borealis: An Isle Royale Potpourri*, ed. David Harmon, 71. Rakestraw notes the miners were Cornish, Americans, Germans, or Irish.

149. Mission of Immaculate Conception Diary, October 5, 1853.

150. Robert Root Jr., *Time by Moments Slips Away: The 1848 Journal of Ruth Douglas*

(Detroit: Wayne State University Press, 1998), 74.

151. Mission of Immaculate Conception Diary, September 3, 1848. Ed Holte, a longtime resident of Isle Royale, also stated in an oral history interview about the Minong Mine in the 1870s: "They were quite a few Indians working for the mining company." In particular Jack Scott, married to a part-Ojibwe woman, worked at one of the mines, and one of their children was born there. Oral history interview with Ed and Ingeborg Holte, by Lawrence Rakestraw, September 10, 1965, Isle Royale National Park. Ernie Olson, a nephew of Benjamin Scott, believes Benjamin was born at Island Mine, not McCargoe Cove. Personal communication with elder Ernie Olson, January 30, 2003, Grand Portage.

152. Father Nicolas Fremiot letter, June 21, 1850, in *Letters from the New Canada Mission*, 166–67.

153. Mrs. Jane Masters, "Recollections of an Old Copper Country Resident," *Daily [Houghton, Michigan] Mining Gazette*, March 17, 1913.

154. Mrs. Henry Conary, "Early Life on Isle Royale," *Daily Mining Gazette*, June 21, 1939. The Ojibwe phrase is slightly corrupted in the original, but clearly is a rendition of *bozhoo neeji*. Jones, Field Notebooks, American Philosophical Society.

155. William Jeffery, "Early Life at Island Mine," *Daily Mining Gazette*, 21 June 1939.

156. M. Shea, "Early Life at the Island Mine."

157. Sarah Barr Christian, *Winter on Isle Royale*, 32.

158. Mrs. Conary, "Early Life on Isle Royale"; and Bessie Phillips interview by Edmond Little, WPA Manuscript, ca. 1930s, in the Isle Royale National Park Archive.

159. Mission of Immaculate Conception Diary, July 13, 1854; and Clark, "Archeological Survey and Testing," 53, 70, and 80.

160. Lieutenant Mallery, U.S. Lake Survey, June 20, 1868, Cheynoweth Collection, Michigan Technological University Archive, Houghton, Michigan.

161. G. R. Fox, "The Ancient Copper Workings of Isle Royale," *Wisconsin Archeologist* 10, no. 2 (1911): 100; Mission of Immaculate Conception Diary, October 8, 1855; and William Jeffery, "Early Life at Island Mine."

162. Historic records spell McCullough's name in a confusing variety of ways. The correct way is Hugh H. McCullough, as written by himself in land-patent documents at Isle Royale. Also confusing is that he was concurrently associated with the Isle Royale and Pittsburg Company mining operation at Todd Harbor, and with fishing

operations. In a few sources, the mining superintendent and agent is spelled James T. McCulloch, or sometimes spelled "Doctor MacKulagh." Land Patent no. 772 and 809, December 1, 1851, General Land Office, Sault Ste. Marie, Michigan; Father Fremiot letter, June 28, 1849, in *Letters from the New Canada Mission*, 105; Root, *Time by Moments Slips Away*, 42 and 72; Alfred Lane, "Isle Royale," vol. 6, pt. 1, *Geological Survey of Michigan* (Lansing: Robert Smith, 1898), 5; *Lake Superior News and Miners' Journal*, August 8, 1846, May 13 and October 28, 1848, and May 31, 1849. McCullough's Lake Superior fishing operation ran from 1848–1863, but his fishing operations ceased on Isle Royale in 1857. Matti Kaups, "North Shore Commercial Fishing, 1849–1870," *Minnesota History* 46 (Summer 1978): 52.

Further complicating matters, there were two men—Hugh H. McCullough and Hugh H. McCulloch—who are sometimes confused or conflated into one. The other man, Hugh H. McCulloch, was an Indiana financier, but had an interest in the American Fur Company fishing operations on Lake Superior and later became a land speculator in Duluth. McCulloch is most known for becoming the U.S. Secretary of the Treasury twice. Grace Lee Nute, "Calendar of the American Fur Company's Papers" *Annual Report of the American Historical Association* (Washington, D.C.: U.S. Government Printing Office, 1945), 2:1848; "Lakeside a Family Community from the Start," *Duluth News Tribune*, November 11 and 20, 1988; and "McCulloch, Hugh," *American National Biography* (New York: Oxford University Press, 1999), 948–50.

163.  General Land Office Records, nos. 772 and 809, December 1, 1851, and no. 2160, June 9, 1855; and Raff, *Pioneers in the Wilderness*, 6. Interestingly, McCullough bought the Fish or Belle Island property in 1855 after his purchases in Siskiwit Bay (on the main Island, just inside Hay Bay, or section 18, and a set of islands (Paul and Siskiwit Islands) on the outside of Siskiwit Bay. Purchasing these outer and exposed islands when he could have chosen almost any others is suggestive of optimal fishing grounds nearby. He never purchased property at the site of his reputed siscowet rendering plant at Wright Island, but could have if he wanted to. It was not purchased until 1854 by a Barnard Hoopes and George Trotter, General Land Office, no. 1421, February 10, 1854.

164.  Mission of Immaculate Conception Diary, November 9, 1852, and November 1, 1850.

165. Mission of Immaculate Conception Diary, January 23, 1851.

166. Mission of Immaculate Conception Diary, June 27, 1854.

167. Two very different censuses in 1855 and 1856 assert that there were over 350 North Shore Ojibwe. The Jesuit fathers estimated there were 349 North Shore Ojibwe in 1855 (119 at Grand Portage and 230 at Fort William). A census taken by Hudson's Bay Company in 1856 asserted there were 350 Ojibwe at Fort William and 50 at Pigeon River. Hence, if all the North Shore Ojibwe were at Isle Royale, upwards of 300 people were there for the fishing season. Mission of Immaculate Conception Diary, August 16, 1855; and Census of Canada, 1856–1871 (Ottawa, 1876), 4: lxxiv–lxxix.

168. Mission of Immaculate Conception Diary, July 23, 1850.

169. Mission of Immaculate Conception Diary, June [no specific day], 1853.

170. Marie Wickop death record, September 25, 1850; Pierre Ishkwikijikweshkang and Susanne Ogabewinjog marriage record, September 15, 1853; and Syntique Wenanickang birth record, September 12, 1850, Fort William Reserve, St. Anne's Church.

171. For example, Susan Memashkawash [misspelled Wemaskawash] (born 1855) and Alexander Benjamin Scott (born 1879) were likely born on Isle Royale (see the 1880 U.S. Census), and William Bagnatchinins was born in 1854 at Isle Royale, Marriage Records, St. Anne's Church, Fort William Reserve, Ontario.

172. McLean, "Reminiscences of Early Days," 7.

173. Jerome Mushkat, "Mineral and Timber Prospects in Upper Michigan: The Diary of John V. L. Pruyn," *Inland Seas* 30, no. 2 (Summer 1974): 88. The lighthouse keeper was likely Richard Singleton and his Ojibwe wife and children.

174. Fred Dustin, "A Summary of the Archaeology of Isle Royale, Michigan," *Papers of the Michigan Academy of Science, Arts and Letters* 16 (1931): 5; and Elmer O. C. Krause, Map of Isle Royale, 1939, Isle Royale National Park Archive. This map, replete with many spurious Isle Royale stories, says: "Old Indians row in 50 foot canoes from the North Shore (Minnesota) to Isle Royale in one day, rest overnight then continue to the Michigan mainland."

175. For example, members of the LeSage, perhaps Sherrer, Boyer (becomes a Scott) and LaPlante families, well known in Grand Portage, came from Sault Ste. Marie. Personal communications with Tony LeSage, October 16, 1988, Norman

Deschampe, November 15, 2002, and Alan Woolworth, November 13, 2002; and Janet Chute, *The Legacy of Shingwaukonse: A Century of Native Leadership* (Toronto: University of Toronto Press, 1998). Chute identifies one influence that encouraged many Sault Ste. Marie/Garden River Ojibwe men to wander westward in search of work in the late 1870s. The exodus of Ojibwe men was a consequence of the 1879 [Canadian] 'Conservative' government's policy of economic tariffs to protect Canadian businesses from American competition; lumbering slumped, which forced many sawmills to close down. The sawmill workforce, Sault Ste. Marie and Garden River Ojibwe, lost their jobs, and many moved west to find employment. A number of these men ended up marrying Grand Portage women, or bringing their families and settling in Grand Portage.

176. Arthur T. Adams, ed., *The Explorations of Pierre Esprit Radisson* (Minneapolis: Ross and Haines, 1961), 124; and Nute, *Lake Superior*, 22.

177. Loon's Foot quoted in "The Ancient Miners of Lake Superior," by Charles Whittlesey, in Roy W. Drier and Octave Josephy De Temple, *Prehistoric Copper Mining in the Lake Superior Region* (Calumet, Michigan: privately printed, 1961), 48.

178. Chute, *Shingwaukonse*, 100 and 278; Warren, *History of the Ojibway People*, 89 and 96; Kohl, *Kitchi-Gami*, 150–53; and Edmund Ely Journal, June 9, 1837.

179. Clark, "Archeological Testing of Isle Royale," 11–12; and Clark, "Late Prehistoric Cultural Affiliation Study, Grand Portage National Monument," November 1999, Cultural Resources Report no. 111, Archeological Consulting Services, figure 9.

180. George Johnston Journal, September 22, 1824, to March 1, 1825, in Henry R. Schoolcraft Papers, Library of Congress, Washington, D.C.

181. "Scientists Conduct First Large-Scale Study of Lake Superior," press release, National Science Foundation, October 24, 1997.

182. National Archives, Alfred Brunson to J. D. Doty, November 20, 1843, Letters Received by the Office of Indian Affairs, 1824–1881, reel 388, La Pointe Agency. This Office of Indian Affairs reference that North Shore Ojibwe were the traditional users of Minong contrasts with a newspaper account that Bad River and Red Cliff Ojibwe "may yet own" Isle Royale because of a faulty treaty. *Duluth News Tribune*, August 27, 1971.

183. Personal communication with Donald Auger, June 26, 2002, Thunder Bay, Ontario.

184. It is reported that Jack Linklater introduced wild rice to a number of Boundary Water lakes. He did not, evidently, do the same at Isle Royale. Sister Noemi Weygant, *John (Jack) Linklater: Legendary Indian Game Warden* (Duluth, Minn.: Priory Books, 1987), 9. On the other hand, Island fisherman historian Stanley Sivertson recalled a "rumor" that Linklater planted Red Lake whitefish at the mouth of McCargoe Cove. The scientific conclusion that there are two populations of whitefish at Isle Royale, being slightly different in size, gives some plausibility that Linklater introduced a different kind of whitefish to Island waters. Interview with Stanley Sivertson by Tim Cochrane, April 4, 1980, Duluth, Minnesota, Northeast Minnesota Historical Center, Duluth; and Ann M. Koziol, "Dynamics of Lightly Exploited Populations of the Lake Whitefish, Isle Royale Vicinity, Lake Superior," Fisheries Research Report no. 1911, Michigan Department of Natural Resources (1982), vii.

Wild chives were being domesticated at Grand Portage during this period and are found on Isle Royale, but whether they where brought there is an open question. North Shore Ojibwe could have brought other plants and perhaps animals, such as snowshoe hare, to the Island. Personal communication with Dr. Rolf Peterson, Isle Royale, May 3, 2007.

## Chapter 4. Removed from Minong

1. S. J. Dawson, "Memorandum in Reference to the Indians on the Line of Route between Lake Superior and the Red River Settlement," December 19, 1870, National Archives of Canada, MG11, C.O. 42, vol. 698, p. 135; W. Kaye Lamb, ed., *The Journals and Letters of Sir Alexander Mackenzie* (Cambridge: Cambridge University Press, 1970), 103; and William W. Warren, *History of the Ojibway People* (St. Paul: Minnesota Historical Society Press, 1984), 259–62. Warren estimated approximately 1,500 to 2,000 Ojibwe died in Northern Minnesota from this smallpox epidemic.

2. For example, a mysterious eight-day illness whose symptoms included violent headaches with bleeding nose and ears killed a number of Ojibwe at Fort William in 1834. Hudson's Bay Company Archive (HBCA), B.231/a/15, Fort William Post

Returns, December 28, 1834, through early January 1835. Father du Ranquet to Father Bapst, Thunder Bay Station, September 24, 1871; and *Woodstock Letters* 1 (1872): 25.

3. "Conveyance of Land at Fort William from the Indians to the North West Company (1798)," Indian Affairs, RG 10, vol. 266, pp. 163,028–378, Public Archives of Canada, Ottawa, Canada. The Canadian government would eventually determine that the lease was illegitimate, concluding that the Northwesters did not have the legal right to complete this land deal.

4. HBCA, B.231/e/5, "Fort William District Report for 1828"; and Father Fremiot to Rev. Micard, February 2, 1851, in *Letters from the New Canada Mission*, edited by Lorenzo Cadieux, translated by William Lonc and George Topp (Hamilton, Ontario: privately printed, 2001), 277.

5. Charles A. Bishop, "Northern Algonquins, 1760–1821," in *Aboriginal Ontario: Historical Perspectives on the First Nations*, edited by Edward S. Rogers and Donald B. Smith (Toronto: Dundern Press, 1994), 302.

6. J. B. Penassie, Fort William, c. 1904, in William Jones Notebooks, American Philosophical Society, Philadelphia, Pennsylvania.

7. American Fur Company Papers (AFC Papers), "Goods Given on Credit to the Indians of Grand Portage at La Pointe, August 1844," Northern Outfit, New York Historical Society, New York, New York.

8. Edward D. Neill, "The Development of Trade on Lake Superior and Its Tributaries during the French Regime," *Macalester College Contributions* 4 (1890): 112; and Pierre Margry, ed., *Découvertes et établissements de Français dans l'ouest et le sud de l'Amérique Septentrionale, 1615–1754* (Paris: D. Jouast, 1876–86), 508–9.

9. The Portage Ojibwe sympathies towards the British are not very surprising when you consider that a Fort William detachment of North West Company personnel were sent to Michilimackinac. In other words, they were most involved with British subjects, not the land-hungry Yankees. Jean Morrison, *Superior Rendezvous Place* (Toronto: Natural Heritage, 2001), 73.

10. Michael Angel, *Preserving the Sacred: Historical Perspectives on the Ojibwa Midewiwin* (Winnipeg: University of Manitoba Press, 2002), 123.

11. Henry C. Gilbert letter to George W. Manypenny, Office of Indian Affairs, National Archives 75, microfilm, October 10, 1855. See also Commission of Indian Affairs,

Annual Reports 1839–40, 201; 1871, 600; 1891, 470. AFC Papers, J. Suppantsihitsck [J. Peau de Chat] to R. Crooks, April 30, 1840.

12. An economic downturn and poor sales doomed the enterprise. Grace Lee Nute, "The American Fur Company's Fishing Enterprises on Lake Superior," *Mississippi Valley Historical Review* 12, no. 4 (March 1926): 496.

13. AFC Papers, Ramsay Crooks to General Charles Gratiot, New York, December 20, 1834, and Charles Borup to Crooks, La Pointe, June 18, 1842.

14. We have very few records of any use of Isle Royale by Ojibwe or whites in the 1860s and 1880s, making it difficult to state exactly what the use was during this time. Small-scale subsistence and commercial fishing likely persisted during this time. For example, Wishgob and his family were on the Island during the 1866 summer. Also, U.S. naval surveyors noted that "Six canoes and a mackinaw [boat] loaded with Indians and families came up the harbor today and encamped opposite us." A year later, the same surveyors ran into "fishermen from Pigeon River." "Journal of Lieut. Green, 1867," July 28, 1867, and "Journal of Lieut. Mallory, 1868," June 20, 1868, U.S. Naval Survey, Chynoweth Collection, Copper Country Archives, Michigan Technological University, Houghton, Michigan; and Mission of Immaculate Conception Diary, Fort William, October 3, 1866, copy at Grand Portage National Monument, Grand Portage, Minnesota.

Another piece of evidence of waning use of Isle Royale is that the Jesuit proselytizing trips to Isle Royale subsided in the 1860s and later, with the exception of a few trips during the second mining boom. The Mission of Immaculate Conception Jesuits were traveling far and wide in the region, but not often to Isle Royale during the last four decades of the nineteenth century.

15. Henry Schoolcraft, *Personal Memories of a Residence of Thirty Years with the Indian Tribes on the American Frontier* (Philadelphia: Lippincott, Grambo & Co., 1851), 243. A "delegation of Old Grand Portage Chippewa attended the Fond du Lac Treaty."

16. Janet E. Chute, *The Legacy of Shingwaukonse: A Century of Native Leadership* (Toronto: University of Toronto Press, 1998), 67–68; "1840 Annual Report of the Acting Superintendent of Indian Affairs for Michigan," September 24, 1840, p. 4; and Frances Paul Prucha, *American Indian Treaties* (Berkeley: University of California Press, 1994), 185.

17. AFC Papers, Charles Borup to the "Gentleman in Charge" [at Fort William], October 1, 1840.

18. AFC Papers, William Aitkin to Ramsay Crooks, December 25, 1834, and George Simpson to William Aitken, July 10, 1837.

19. HBCA, B.231/a/16, Fort William Post Returns, August 27, 29, 30 and September 23 and October 10, 1836. After some wrangling, it was agreed that AFC employees could not trade furs with Grand Portage Ojibwe, but they were allowed to trap themselves. AFC Papers, George Simpson to Ramsay Crooks, London, November 15, 1837. Fur trade scholar Nute opined that this agreement was likely illegal in both countries. Nute, "The American Fur Company's Fishing Enterprises," 489.

20. John Swanton to Peter [Pierre] Cotte, February 13, 1839, microfilm M19, Minnesota Historical Society (MHS), St. Paul, Minnesota. The original records are held at the Public Archives of Canada.

21. HBCA, B.231/a/1, Fort William Post Returns, November 30, 1831; and John Swanton to John D. Cameron, December 16, 1838, microfilm M19, MHS.

22. George Simpson, *Narrative of a Journey Round the World during the Years 1841 and 1842* (London: Henry Colburn, 1847), 34–35.

23. David J. Krause, *The Making of a Mining District: Keweenaw Native Copper, 1500–1870* (Detroit: Wayne State University Press, 1992), 132ff.

24. Sister Mary Aquinas Norton, *Catholic Missionary Activities in the Northwest, 1818–1864* (Washington, D.C.: Catholic University of America, 1930), 67.

25. Lise C. Hansen, "The Anishinabek Land Claim and the Participation of the Indian People Living on the North Shore of Lake Superior in the Robinson Superior Treaty, 1850," 1985, Ontario Native Affairs Secretariat, Toronto, Ontario, 20–21; and Father Francis Nelligan, "History of the Diocese of Fort William," no pagination, n.d., p. 23. A copy is held at the Grand Portage National Monument.

26. Journal of Mr. Henry Blatchford in the letter of L. H. Wheeler to David Greene, May 3, 1843, American Board of Commissioners of Foreign Missions, Minnesota Historical Society, St. Paul.

27. Henry R. Schoolcraft's fears about treaty making in 1827 foreshadow what Portage Ojibwe would experience concerning negotiations for Isle Royale.

The cession of lands from Indians, should invariably be made by a map drawn by them & appended to the original treaty. Countries are sometimes bartered by a wave of the hand. A bad or careless interpreter, who in explaining a written treaty, points his finger wrong in defining a boundary, leads a tribe to suppose they have not ceded, accessory to this wave of the hand. Millions of acres are thus, sometimes, put in dispute. Treaties are made to explain treaties, & purchases to cover purchases. All resulting from a bad interpreter, or the want of a ms. or sketch map.

Philip P. Mason, ed., *Schoolcraft's Ojibwa Lodge Stories: Life on the Lake Superior Frontier* (East Lansing: Michigan State University, 1997), 59.

28. L. H. Wheeler, May 3, 1843, MHS.
29. The concern over "halfbreed" payment was significant enough initially that Stuart wondered aloud in a letter to T. Hartley Crawford that he feared a lack of payment might result in an insurrection. Robert Stuart to Crawford, February 28, 1843, Letters Received by the Office of Indian Affairs, microfilm reel 388, La Pointe Agency, 1840–1843, National Archives, Washington, D.C.
30. Personal communication with archivist Keith Kerr, August 11, 2005, National Archives, Washington, D.C. A similar search at the Library of Congress also did not yield a treaty map.
31. Robert Stuart to T. Hartley Crawford, Detroit, November 19, 1842, La Pointe Agency; and Stuart, "Sketch of Opening Speech at Council, October 2nd, 1842."
   Stuart wrote about a map to Commissioner of Indian Affairs Crawford:

Enclosed herewith, are two diagrams of the country treated for &c:—that one wrapping paper, was made by a Half Breed at La Pointe, and is the more accurate of the two—with the boundary of the Treaty, is also traced on it, the boundary of the country reserved as the common property and home of the Indians party to the treaty.

At least the maps Stuart enclosed to Commissioner Crawford appear to be related to his speech of September 29th, 1842, in which he included an important phrase dropped from the formal treaty. He said in the September 1842 "Sketch" that the treaty area began at the Chocolate River "running across the Lake to the British line, and up that line to the Grand Portage, or Pigeon River, thence along the Lake Shore" to Fond du Lac. Stuart, "Sketch," and Stuart to Crawford, November 19, 1842, in Ronald N. Satz, "Chippewa Treaty Rights: The Reserved Rights of

Wisconsin's Chippewa Indians in Historical Perspective," *Wisconsin Academy of Sciences, Arts and Letters* 79, no. 1 (1991): 164.

32. Stuart, "Sketch"; and L. H. Wheeler, May 3, 1843, MHS. In a letter from Indian agent Alfred Brunson to J. D. Doty, Brunson provides testimony from a number of Ojibwe leaders (Balsom of Fond du Lac, Black Bird and Buffalo of La Pointe, and Peter Marksman of Keweenaw) at the treaty who all denied that Isle Royale/Minong was mentioned by name, nor had they sold it. Brunson to Doty, November 20, 1843, La Pointe Agency, National Archives.

33. There was a low level of geographic uncertainty about the American–British Canadian border that was only formally resolved in the same summer of 1842. The Webster-Ashburton Treaty was signed in August 9, 1842, with both countries agreeing upon a mutual border. One location where there had been disagreement was the border west of Isle Royale. At one point, the British argued for a more southerly border beginning roughly where Duluth is located; the Americans countered with a proposed border beginning where Thunder Bay is located. Eventually the Pigeon River route was agreed upon in the treaty. William Lass, *Minnesota's Boundary with Canada* (St. Paul: Minnesota Historical Society Press, 1980), 69. It is unlikely that Stuart, en route to the Indian treaty negotiations, learned of the results of the British-American border negotiations. Hence, Stuart was set to conclude a treaty with area Ojibwe in a region where the United States and Britain had not formally decided on a border.

34. Hole in the Day, quoted in L. H. Wheeler letter, May 3, 1843, MHS. Much of the letter is in the handwriting of Henry Blatchford, one of the two treaty interpreters.

35. Charles J. Kappler, ed. and comp., *Indian Affairs: Law and Treaties* (Washington, D.C.: Government Printing Office, 1904), 2:542.

36. Stuart to Crawford, Commissioner of Indian Affairs, March 29, 1844, La Pointe Agency.

37. It would have been difficult for Stuart to have a "reasonably accurate " map for the 1842 treaty. For example, an 1844 map, "Sketch of the Public Surveys in Michigan," does not include Isle Royale. Few 1842 maps showed Isle Royale in its proper geographic location—the only exception being the British maps derived from Lieutenant Bayfield's charts from the late 1820s. These were hard to come

by in the United States, and they do not provide the detail on lands of the South Shore that were the primary lands under discussion during the treaty. In short, it is unlikely an accurate map of the treaty area, especially including Isle Royale, was used, as they generally were not available at that time. Stuart's statement that the maps were "two diagrams of the country treated for &c:—that on wrapping paper, was made by a Half Breed at La Pointe, and is the more accurate of the two" illustrates the geographic shortcomings of the treaty. Stuart to Crawford, Commissioner of Indian Affairs, November 19, 1842, La Pointe Agency.

38. There is an important legal question regarding the large aggregate of Ojibwe groups treating for lands that some in the west, for example, did not traditionally use. The legal question is: Can a treaty create a use right not exercised before the treaty? In other words, do the various bands subsumed under "one [Chippewa] nation" in the 1842 Treaty and 1844 Isle Royale Compact have equal access to all areas of the treaty? Or, more pointedly, do signatory Chippewa bands with no tradition of use of Minong have the same rights as the Grand Portage Band that has an extensive history with Minong? Or, as appears customary now, would bands without that history always defer to those who do?

39. Brunson to J. D. Doty, August 29, 1843, La Pointe Agency.

40. A much later Indian Claims Case Commission report assigned the ratification date as March 28, 1843. *The Minnesota Chippewa Tribe et al. v. The United States of America*, docket no. 18-S, January 14, 1976, for Royce Area 261 of the 1842 Treaty, p. 147.

41. James Madison Porter, Secretary of War to General Walter Cunningham, April 13, 1843, in Lawrence Trever Fadner, ed., *Fort Wilkins 1844 and the U.S. Mineral Land Agency, 1843* (New York: Vantage Press, 1966), 156; and Commissioner Crawford to Stuart, March 30, 1843, in Fadner, *Fort Wilkins 1844*, 159.

42. Cunningham was on the Island in July and early September, 1843. General Cunningham to Secretary of War Porter, October 2, 1843, La Pointe Agency.

43. "Articles of Association of the Isle Royale and Ohio Mining Company," Cincinnati, 1846, n.p. Wisconsin Historical Society Archives, Madison, Wisconsin.

44. Lieut. Col. G. Talcott to Secretary of War Porter, October 16, 1843, in Fadner, *Fort Wilkins 1844*, 167.

45. Brunson to Doty, November 20, 1843, La Pointe Agency. Brunson was first informed

that the Grand Portage Band claimed the Island from Reverend Frederic Baraga in August 1843.

46. Brunson to Doty, August 29, 1843, La Pointe Agency.

47. "Petition" of the Grand Portage Chiefs, at La Pointe, September 14, 1843, La Pointe Agency.

48. Brunson to Doty, November 20, 1843, La Pointe Agency.

49. "Petition" of the Grand Portage Chiefs, at La Pointe, September 14, 1843, La Pointe Agency.

50. Proposal included in a letter from Joseph Samatchiniash (alternate name for Joseph Peau de Chat), Alex Udtekonse (Attikons), and Joseph Shaganashins to Alfred Brunson, September 19, 1843, La Pointe Agency. William W. Warren served as interpreter to this proposal.

51. Ibid.

52. General Cunningham to Secretary of War Porter, October 6, 1843, La Pointe Agency.

53. Brunson to General Cunningham, September 27, 1843, La Pointe Agency.

54. General Cunningham's argument is internally inconsistent, as he stated there "were no Indians living upon it" and then added that "an old exiled Indian, with his three sons came in a canoe to see me." And Cunningham only visited Rock Harbor, one part of Isle Royale. Clearly other Ojibwe could have been on the Island in addition to the family he met, yet he maintained, "there were no Indians living upon it." Ibid.

55. Secretary of War Porter to Doty, October 24, 1843, La Pointe Agency.

56. Brunson to Doty, November 20 and 30, 1843, La Pointe Agency.

57. John Hurlbert, La Pointe subagent, to Stuart, January 19, 1844, La Pointe Agency.

58. Commissioner Crawford to Secretary of War Porter, October 20, 1843, and Stuart to Commissioner Crawford, November 24, 1843, La Pointe Agency.

59. Stuart to Commissioner Crawford, April 11, 1844, La Pointe Agency.

60. Hurlburt to Stuart, January 19, 1844, La Pointe Agency. Six days later, Hurlburt wrote again to Stuart with a strategy for resolving the problem; namely, that Stuart go directly to Grand Portage in the spring and "offering them. . . . As much for their land as the rest get per ratio—This will be a mere trifle." Hurlburt

also reported that the Grand Portage chief said at the fall treaty payment that he was not an American. Instead, Chief Peau de Chat, Elias Atikons, and Joseph Shaganashins stated that they were "Grand Portage Chiefs," asserting they were American. Hurlbert to Stuart, January 25, 1844; Stuart to Commissioner Crawford, March 29, 1844; and Joseph La Pot [*sic*] de Chat to Brunson, September 14, 1843, La Pointe Agency.

61. Stuart to Commissioner Crawford, March 29, 1844, La Pointe Agency. In this letter, Stuart also repeated the misinformation about the Grand Portage chief, saying "they were not American."

62. After the secret agreement expired, the HBC established a post on the British side of Pigeon River to continue to lure Indians to travel and trade "northward." From 1852 to 1858, the HBC maintained a post on the Canadian side of Pigeon River. HBCA, B/135/k/1, "Minutes of a Temporary Council for the Southern Department held at Michipicoten." The Pigeon River post was also listed in the 1852, 1854, 1855, and 1857 "Minutes."

63. Robert Stuart was an important player in the AFC operations. Still, there is no evidence yet discovered that Robert Stuart was informed of this secret agreement. Stuart left the AFC in June 1834, one year after the agreement began. Most AFC employees did not know of its existence. Donald W. Woelker, "Robert Stuart: A Man Who Meant Business," *Michigan History Magazine* (September–October 1990): 12–18.

Those AFC employees who knew of the agreement likely included William Aitkin, Ramsay Crooks, William Brewster, Gabriel Franchere. Only Franchere, normally stationed at Sault Ste. Marie, had the dubious distinction of knowing of the agreement, having traveled to Isle Royale and observed the Portage Ojibwe fishermen there, and also having been a witness to the 1842 treaty. A few other AFC men, such as James Scott and Charles Borup, also knew much about Grand Portage and Isle Royale and witnessed the treaty. AFC Papers, Ramsay Crooks to William Aitkin, Sandy Lake, March 6, 1835; Crooks to William Brewster, Detroit, March 6, 1835; Crooks to Gabriel Franchere, Sault Ste. Marie, March 9, 1835; George Simpson to Aitkin, September 8, 1836; Simpson to Crooks, September 15, 1836; and "G. Francheres Journal of His Voyage in the 'Brewster' with Mr. Scott to Grand Portage, Ile [*sic*] Royale & the Ance in August 1839,"

Gabriel Franchere Papers, MHS.

64. But was Joseph Peau de Chat a "British Indian"? In hindsight, and using sources available today to track his movements, the answer is equivocal. Using the HBC Fort William clerk's records, we can track his movements when he is a recognized leader in his thirties. Of course, using this source builds in a number of biases, but even flawed, it provides us with some useful information. Joseph Peau de Chat would often winter along the border, particularly at Arrow and Whitefish Lakes (in Canada but close to the border). His families' traditional sugar bush appears to be in the sugar-maple belt above Fort William. He was born circa 1809 or 1810, after the North West Company post had moved from Grand Portage to Fort William. One the other hand, he was first baptized in Grand Portage by Father Pierz on July 8, 1838, and would frequent it through time. What can be said is that he would resort to both sides of the border, being predisposed to being on the side that had the greatest trade opportunities and a Catholic priest. When the priests were in Grand Portage, he was more likely to be there. After they moved to Fort William, he was more often there. HBCA records, B.231/a/7–16, Fort William Post Returns, 1827–1836; F. Francis Pierz Papers, "Baptismal & Marriage Register," Minnesota Historical Society.

The recorded movements of other leaders such as Attikons and the Spaniard suggest a more southerly home territory than Peau de Chat's. For example, during 1831 the Spaniard spent considerable time near Grand Marais—at his family's sugar bush and fall trout fishing. HBCA, B.231/a/10–11, Fort William Post Returns, March 21 and September 12, 1831. However, all shared a tremendous amount of geographic overlap along the border, especially the use of the area between Arrow and Whitefish Lakes, Fort William, and Grand Portage.

65. Commissioner of Indian Affairs, Annual Report, 1842–43, 98.

66. For example, there are records of a U.S. Indian agent licensing a trader for Grand Portage for the years of 1823, 1824, 1831, 1840, 1841, 1843, as well as the commercial fishing operation from 1837–1841. In addition, in 1825 and 1839 the U.S. Indian agent completed a census for Grand Portage. There were more traders—perhaps unlicensed—at Grand Portage and nearby. The Fort William Post records show that there were American traders in the area in 1828, 1830, 1833, 1834, 1835. For their part, the HBC clerks at Fort William viewed Grand Portage as American

soil, and many of the Ojibwe who traded at Fort William as "American Indians."
HBCA, B.231/a/4–15, Fort William Post Returns, records for years 1824, 1825, 1827,
1828, 1833–35; 22nd Cong, 2nd sess., Sen. Doc. 90, p. 50; AFC Letters, John R.
Livingston to James Ord, September 11, 1839, Bayliss Library, Sault Ste. Marie;
26th Cong., 1st sess., Public Docs., Senate, serial no. 354, doc. 1 (1840), 488; "1825
Census," in Schoolcraft Papers, Library of Congress, Washington, D.C.. Other
licenses had been issued in La Pointe. D. P. Bushnell, Indian agent, National
Archives, Office of Indian Affairs, reel 388, 1840–43; and 22nd Cong., 2nd sess.,
Sen. Doc. 90, p. 150.

67. Commissioner of Indian Affairs, Annual Report, 1841–42, 106. This report was
made after Stuart had taken office as superintendent and was filed by his subagent
D. P. Bushnell. Stuart must have read and approved this report, as his subagent
disputes Schoolcraft's claim of Chippewa living on Isle Royale.

68. Joseph Delafield Papers, June 1823, in Delafield Family Papers, Princeton University
Library, Princeton, New Jersey.

69. Stuart to General Peter Porter, August 3, 1822, and James Ferguson to General
Peter Porter, July 13 and October 11, 1822, Peter Porter Papers, Buffalo and Erie
County Historical Society, Buffalo, New York. In the latter two letters, Ferguson,
a U.S. surveyor and newcomer to the area, explicitly stated he "consulted" and
"communicated" with Stuart about logistics and border-related news. Working
along the border lake country in 1822–1824, members of the United States Border
Survey frequently went eastward to their homes, and during these travels they
would have had multiple chances to talk with Stuart at Mackinac about their
conclusions. Indeed, Stuart's job as a senior American Fur Company agent was
to intercept such strategic information and use it to the company's advantage.

70. Pierre Cotte arrived in Grand Portage in 1836 and was at Grand Portage as late as
July 30, 1841. Sister Norton, *Missionary Activity*, 60; and AFC Papers, "Register
of Men Employed by the American Fur Company's Northern Outfit," July 30,
1841.

Cyrus Mendenhall is the same individual who would "stake" Charlie and
Angelique Mott on Isle Royale (discussed in chapter 2). It took three and a
half months to haul the fifty-five-foot *Algonquin* over the St. Mary's Portage in
1840 to Lake Superior. The *Algonquin* sailed throughout Lake Superior. In 1843,

Mendenhall's company received a license to trade at Grand Portage. Licenses, 1843, La Pointe Agency. For more on the *Algonquin*, owned by Samuel Richardson and Cyrus Mendenhall, see Ralph D. William, *The Honorable Peter White* (Cleveland: Penton, 1907) 112–13; and AFC Papers, John R. Livingston to R. Crooks, March 18, 1840.

George Bonga was an AFC employee at Grand Marais in 1823–24, and George Johnston was the clerk at Grand Marais in 1824–25. Bonga and Johnston undoubtedly learned of Portage Ojibwe's use of Minong during their time among them. Bela Chapman, "Log for Traveling," 1823–24, Sibley Papers, MHS; and George Johnston, "Journal," 1824–1825, Schoolcraft Papers, Library of Congress, Washington, D.C.

71. HBCA, B.231/e/9, Donald McIntosh, "Report of Fort William Trade & Indians, 1833/34"; and B.231/e/6, "Report for Fort William District, 1828/29." The North West Company was trading at Fond du Lac as late as 1817. Hence Portage Ojibwe would have had no choice but to trade with the British up until this time, or travel to trade in the traditional territory of the Fond du Lac Ojibwe.

72. Fort William clerk John Swanton to Hector McKenzie, November 26, 1844, microfilm M19, MHS. The Fort William clerk frequently recorded Rivet's whereabouts, as he was a good trapper and often did small jobs for the HBC. Iraneus Frederic Baraga, "Baptismal Records, 1835–1887, Kept at LaPointe and Bayfield Indian Missions," transcribed by John L. Schade, *Lost in Canada? Canadian-American Journal of History and Genealogy* 17, no. 3 (Summer 1994): 115, and 17, no. 4 (Winter 1994): 118.

73. Stuart to Commissioner Crawford, September 21, 1844, La Pointe Agency.

74. Joseph Peau de Chat was very sick in January, 1844, and many thought he might not live. HBCA, Fort William Post Returns, January 1844, microfilm M19, MHS.

It is unclear why twelve chiefs did not have marks following their names on the original compact. It is quite possible that because of the haste in concluding this compact that a number of chiefs had already left, did not attend, or chose not to mark their names. In addition to the missing marks, the original document is not clean of writing errors, which are corrected in ink.

75. The American Fur Company provided blankets, blue cloth, printed cotton, moose and deer skins, soap, fishing line and hooks, knives, gunflints, and pound candy

on credit to the Grand Portage Indians at La Pointe. Their desire was that these goods on credit would help convince the Grand Portage Ojibwe to not trade with the Cleveland Company. AFC Papers, "Statement of Sundry Goods Given on Credit to the Grand Portage Indians within the United States Inventory, August 1844."

The Cleveland Company's trading license for Grand Portage in 1843 threatened, if not broke, the exclusive trading privileges of the HBC. The next year, the Cleveland Company began a smaller fishing operation on Isle Royale during the summer of 1844. These events must have cheered the Grand Portage Band, as it gave them some trading options. Fort William Post Returns, April 25, 1844, microfilm M19, MHS.

76. 28th Cong., 2nd sess., Exec. Doc., Cong. serial no. 469, 1844.

77. The Indian [Land] Claims Commission opinion was that the 1842 treaty had been duly ratified, including Isle Royale. However, the opinion did not consider whether the Isle Royale question and subsequent compact without ratification affected the legal title. *The Minnesota Chippewa Tribe et al. v. The United State of America*, docket no. 18-S, January 14, 1976, for Royce Area 261 of the 1842 Treaty, p. 147.

78. There is written documentation of Grand Portage Ojibwe protests about Isle Royale in 1849, 1851, 1864, 1889, 1947, 1971, and 2006. John S. Livermore letter to Ordland Brown, Commissioner of Indian Affairs, 31st Cong., 1st sess., House Doc. no. 5, serial no. 570, 1849, p. 1157; H. H. McCullough letter to J. Watrous, February 26, 1851, to Sandy Lake Subagency, Office of Indian Affairs, microfilm M234, roll 767, National Archives; John D. Nichols, ed., "Statement Made by the Indians," The Centre for Research and Teaching of Canadian Native Languages, University of Western Ontario, 1988; "A Communication from the Secretary of the Interior Relative to the Chippewa Indians in the State of Minnesota, March 6, 1890," in 51st Cong., 1st sess., House Exec. Doc. no. 247, serial no. 2747; E. A. Allen, Consolidated Chippewa Agency, "United States Relations to Grand Portage Indians," 1930, MHS; "Indians Seek Payment for Isle Royale," *Daily [Houghton, Michigan] Mining Gazette*, April 29, 1947; "Chippewa May Own Isle Royale," *Duluth News Tribune*, August 21, 1971; and Wally Deschampe, Campaign Letter for Grand Portage Tribal Council, 2006.

At this time, an unratified treaty was not considered a treaty. It is quite possible that the Grand Portage Band title to Isle Royale was not extinguished in 1842 or 1844 and was only purchased when the U.S. Indian [Land] Claims Commission Opinion extinguished the title when issued on January 14, 1976. The same commission determined that the treaty price for the area was too low. Its fair market value in timber and copper in 1842 was determined to be $8.862 million, instead of the total treaty money paid of $875,000. Using these figures from the commission report, the value of Isle Royale was $112,377—much closer to Joseph Peau de Chat's original request. My computation goes like this: 10,538,000 treaty acres divided by $8,862,818 equals 84 cents per acre. This figure should be multiplied by the 133,782 acres that make up Isle Royale. This determination of Ojibwe being unfairly compensated was made by John T. Vance, Commissioner of the Indian [Land] Claims Commission, *The Minnesota Chippewa Tribe et al. v. The United States of America*, 1976.

79. General Cunningham to Lieut. Col. G. Talcott, August 14, 1844, in Fadner, *Fort Wilkins 1844*, 174.

80. William Ives, Survey Notes, General Land Office Survey of Isle Royale, 1847. Copy of the notes are found at Isle Royale National Park Archives, Houghton, Michigan. Lt. Col. G. Talcott to John Stockton, Superintendent Mineral Lands, February 6, 1845, and May 28, 1846, in Fadner, *Fort Wilkins 1844*, 183 and 217; Attorney General J. Y. Mason, "Leases of Mineral Lands on Isle Royale," 4 U.S. Op. Atty. Gen. 480, April, 1846; Charles K. Hyde, "From 'Subterranean Lotteries' to Orderly Investment: Michigan Copper and Eastern Dollars, 1841–1865," *Mid-America: An Historical Review* 66, no. 1 (January 1984): 6–7.

81. William Benjamin Robinson was named to complete the treaty after preliminary discussions had taken place with some of the tribal leaders the year before. Robinson was a member of a powerful family. His brother was the attorney general of Ontario at the time. His brother-in-law was the superintendent of Indian Affairs. Robinson, himself, was superintendent of works of the Mica Bay [Lake Superior] mining operation that had been shut down by an Ojibwe raid prior to the treaty making.

82. Peau de Chat complained of being cold. In response, Robinson had clothing—the only gift he had to offer—given to Peau de Chat. And Robinson had the treaty

location changed from Garden River (further to the east) to the Sault Ste. Marie to reduce the travel strain on Peau de Chat.

83. Jesuit Father Nicholas Fremiot report to his Superior, October 18, 1849, in L. Cadieux, ed., *Lettres des Nouvelles Missions du Canada, 1843–1852* (Montreal: Les Editions Bellarmin, 1973), 448–53. At one time in 1847, Joseph Peau de Chat was "not expected to live." HBCA Fort William Post Returns records, January 10, 1844, and November 14 and 17, 1847, microfilm M19, MHS.

84. Mission of Immaculate Conception Diary, Fort William, August 25, 1849, and August 1, 1851. A month and half before his death, he was suffering, as his legs would not function and he could not see. Mission of Immaculate Conception Diary, June 14, 1851. A copy of the diary is held at Grand Portage National Monument and Lakehead University, Northern Studies Collection, Thunder Bay, Ontario.

85. A full text of the Robinson-Superior Treaty of 1850 can be found in many references. Perhaps the most accessible reference is in Alexander Morris, *The Treaties of Canada with the Indians of Manitoba and the North-West Territories* (1862; Toronto: Coles, 1979), 302–4. The original is found at the Public Archives of Canada, record group 10, vol. 1844, "Treaty no. 60," Robinson-Superior Treaty.

86. Lise C. Hansen, "Research Report: The Anishinabek Land Claim and the Participation of the Indian People Living on North Shore of Lake Superior in the Robinson Superior Treaty, 1850," Ontario Native Affairs Secretariat, Toronto, 1985, 23ff.; and Robert J. Surtees, "Treaty Research Report: The Robinson Treaties (1850)," Indian and Northern Affairs Canada, Ottawa, 1986, no pagination.

87. Chute, *The Legacy of Shingwaukonse*, 130–36.

88. W. B. Robinson, "Report," to the Superintendent-General of Indian Affairs, September 24, 1850, in Morris, *The Treaties*, 17.

89. Mission of Immaculate Conception Diary, July 31 and August 11, 1851.

90. The Fort William Reserve was six miles by five miles in size. Morris, *The Treaties*, 304. Shortly after the treaty making, there arose a question of whether the bounds of the reserve was negotiated in miles or leagues. Peau de Chat asserted the boundaries should be in leagues, making the reserve larger. Only a few years after the treaty, other government actions reduced the land area of the reserve considerably. The Fort William Ojibwe also asserted that the "Islands at the mouth of the [Kaministiquia] River, on the ground of their having been used as a burying

ground, and being necessary to them for a Fishing Station" were theirs. "Report of the Special Commissioners to Investigate Indian Affairs in Canada," appendix 21 (Toronto: Derbishire & Desbarats, 1858), 6.

91. Mission of Immaculate Conception Diary, September 22 and 26, 1849.

92. Hansen, "The Anishinabek Land Claim," 53. Where payments were provided was important because of the distances, effort to travel, and interference with the harvesting of food for home consumption and storage. For example, for the 1850 Treaty negotiations in the third week of August, the Fort William delegation left on July 22, roughly a month early. Mission of Immaculate Conception Diary, July 22, 1850.

93. Morris, *The Treaties*, 302; and Hansen, "The Anishinabek Land Claim," 82. The first payment was made at Fort William and not at the Sault. Each Fort William Band member received the equivalent of $6 on September 30, 1850. Mission of Immaculate Conception Diary, September 30, 1850.

94. "Chief Peau de Chat's Report," A-16-1, Archives of the Société de Jesus du Canada Français, St. Jerome, Quebec. An English translation of this can be found in Elizabeth Arthur, ed., *Thunder Bay District, 1821–1892* (Toronto: The Champlain Society, 1973), 17. Mission of Immaculate Conception Diary, September 9, 1849.

95. Ibid. Peau de Chat's interest in being recognized as the original owner of lands on both sides of the border, and paid for both, is not as far-fetched as it might first appear. In one early treaty, the State of New York paid the "Seven [Indian] Nations of Canada," to cede lands in upstate New York. See Charles J. Kappler, ed. and comp., *Indian Affairs: Laws and Treaties* (Washington, D.C.: Government Printing Office, 1904), 2:45–46.

96. Mission of Immaculate Conception Diary, Mayard Copy, St. Jerome, Quebec, August 4, 1854, and August 1854 (no day given).

97. Mission of Immaculate Conception Diary, August 18, 1854.

98. Attikons, or Little Caribou, was likely born in 1789. He frequented an area from Grand Portage along the border country as far west as Rainy Lake. He was likely a member of the Fish clan. As early as 1831, he identified himself as an American Indian. Richard F. Morse, "IV.—Atte-Konse, Little Carriboo, etc.," in *Collections of the State Historical Society of Wisconsin*, edited by Lyman Copeland Draper, 3:354–55 (Madison: State Historical Society of Wisconsin, 109); personal communication

with Gilbert Caribou, Secretary-Treasurer, Grand Portage Tribal Council, July 19, 2000, Grand Portage, Minnesota; HBCA, B.105/a/15, *Lac la Pluie Post Journal*, May 20 and 23, 1831.

99. Mission of Immaculate Conception Diary, St. Jerome, Quebec, October 7, 1854.

100. Morse, "Atte-Konse," 354–55.

101. Kappler, ed., "Treaty with the Chippewa, 1854," *Indian Affairs, Laws and Treaties*, 2:648–52. The Grand Portage Ojibwe did not understand or have access to the written provisions of the treaty, so that almost a year after the signing, the principal negotiator, Attikons, requested Father du Ranquet to translate its terms. Mission of Immaculate Conception Diary, July 25, 1855.

102. Mission of Immaculate Conception Diary, October 7 and 27, 1854

103. Mission of Immaculate Conception Diary, July 19–August 16, 1855. The Jesuits disproved of lacrosse because of the minimal clothing worn by the men. At one point, a lacrosse ball rolled in the chapel door. Jesuit Father vehemently disapproved of traditional activities such as a dog feast and the Midewiwin ceremony. The first year, the treaty provisions arrived September 27, 1855, long after wild rice was harvested. During the first treaty payments for the Robinson-Superior treaty, Joseph Peau de Chat's brother arrived from the western border lake country; this appears to have emboldened Peau de Chat to defy the nearby Jesuit fathers.

104. Ellen Olson, interviewed by Carolyn Gilman, November 1, 1989, copy held by Grand Portage National Monument.

105. Commissioner of Indian Affairs, Annual Reports for 1859, p. 73; 1860, p. 52; 1878, p. 147; 1881, p. 182; 1887, p. 230; and 1901, p. 404.

106. Commissioner of Indian Affairs, Annual Report for 1855, p. 52.

107. Commissioner of Indian Affairs, Annual Reports for 1857, p. 32; 1870, p. 311; and 1880, p. 173.

108. Mission of Immaculate Conception Diary, September 28, 1855.

109. Mission of Immaculate Conception Diary, July 15, 1849; February 24 and 27, 1851; and August 11, 1851.

110. HBCA, B.231/e/1, 1824 Report; B.231/e/6, "Report for Fort William District, 1828/29"; and B.231/e/9, "Report, 1833/34."

111. Fort William Band petition to Lord Elgin, Governor of Canada, January 3, 1852,

National Archives of Canada, Ottawa.

112. HBCA, B.231/e/1, "Report on the State of the Country & Indians in Lake Superior Department, 1824."

113. Ibid. See also Edward S. Rogers, "Northern Algonquians and the Hudson's Bay Company, 1821–1890," in *Aboriginal Ontario: Historical Perspectives on the First Nations*, edited by Edward S. Rogers and Donald B. Smith (Toronto: Dundern Press, 1994), 317.

114. Henry Sibley, "Report no. 13," Commissioner of Indian Affairs, Annual Report for 1850, 31st Cong., 2nd sess., House Exec. Doc., serial no. 595, p. 59.

115. "Arrival from Fort William, Perilous Journey on Snow Shoes, Starvation among the Indians, Delay of the United States Mails," *St. Paul Daily Press*, February 28, 1870, p. 4.

116. Mission of Immaculate Conception Diary, August 17, 1855.

117. Frederic Baraga, *Short History of the North American Indians*, translated and edited by Graham MacDonald (Calgary: University of Calgary Press, 2004), 88–89. The original book was published in German and French in 1837.

118. Hurlbert to James Evans, December 17, 1838, in John McLean, *James Evans: Inventor of the Syllabic System of the Cree Language* (Toronto: Methodist Mission Rooms, 1890), 133–35; Fred Landon, "Letters of Rev. James Evans, Methodist Missionary, Written during his Journey to and Residence in the Lake Superior Region, 1838–1839," *Ontario Historical Society's "Papers and Records"* 28 (1932): 56; and F. Franz Pierz Papers, MHS.

119. HBCA, B.105/e/9, J. D. Cameron, "Lac la Pluie Report for 1829–1830," May 26, 1830. For help in interpreting this windigo event, I am indebted to elder Ellen Olson, personal communication, September 31, 2001. It is not my goal here to discuss the complicated and controversial windigo phenomena, only to point out that someone who would stand up to a windigo was deemed to be a person with great courage and spiritual power.

120. Christopher Vecsey, *Traditional Ojibwa Religion and Its Historical Changes* (Philadelphia: American Philosophical Society, 1983), 54.

121. Joseph Specht letter, September 5, 1879, *Woodstock Letters* 9, no. 1 (1880): 29. Savanne River is seventy-two miles west of Fort William.

122. Mission of Immaculate Conception Diary, July 7, 1857.

123. Polygamy was an accepted practice among the Ojibwe, especially for leaders and skilled providers who could support multiple wives and their collective children.

124. Mission of Immaculate Conception Diary, February 2, March 9, and December 24, 1850, and January 26, 28, 29 and July 22, 26, 1851. Clearly the Jesuit fathers were trying to make a very public example out of Joseph Peau de Chat, including standing aside during charges that he misused his leadership role for private gain. At one point, a Métis man stood up in a church service and asked that the mistreatment of Peau de Chat stop because the last few days had been full of incriminations. He was told by Father Chone to leave if he was not happy. Mission of Immaculate Conception Diary, January 26, 1851.

125. Mission of Immaculate Conception Diary, September 9, 1849.

126. McLean, *James Evans*, 134–41; Charles E. Cleland, *Rites of Conquest: The History and Culture of Michigan's Native Americans* (Ann Arbor: University of Michigan Press, 1992), 241; and Patricia A. Shifferd, "A Study of Economic Change: The Chippewa of Northern Wisconsin, 1854–1900," *Western Canadian Journal of Anthropology* 6, no. 4 (1976): 20.

127. Mission of Immaculate Conception Diary, June 1853.

128. Caven Clark, "A Dog Burial from Isle Royale, Lake Superior: An Example of Household Ritual Sacrifice in the Terminal Woodland Period," *Midcontinental Journal of Archaeology* 15, no. 2 (1990): 265–78; and Mission of Immaculate Conception Diary, August 25, 1854.

129. Sister Aquinas, "Catholic Activity," 60–61.

130. Father Pierz to Shopee, September 20, 1838, *Central Blatt* 27: 250.

131. Father Fremiot letter, September 27, 1850, *Letters from the New Canada Mission*, 188; and Mission of Immaculate Conception Diary, October 1, 1854.

132. HBCA, John Mackenzie to Sir George Simpson, December 27, 1850; Father Fremiot letter, January 1850, *Letters from the New Canada Mission*, 140; and an unnamed Ojibwa in Jennifer S. H. Brown, "'I Wish to Be as I See You': An Ojibwa Methodist Encounter in Fur Trade Country, Rainy Lake, 1854–1855," *Arctic Anthropology* 24, no. 1 (1987): 24.

133. Father Fremiot letter, December 3, 1851, *Letters from the New Canada Mission*, 348–56 and 267–68. The fathers reasoned that if the American policy was to "drive

Sauteaux beyond the Mississippi then why not [have them] on English territory."
Father P. Chonet [*sic*] letter, June 6, 1858, in "Report of the Special Commissioners
to Investigate Indian Affairs in Canada" (Toronto: Derbishire & Desbarats, 1858),
appendix 28, no pagination.

134. Communication with Ellen Olson, January 30, 2003, Grand Portage.

135. *Cook County Herald*, September 28, 1901; and Frances Densmore, "An Ojibway
Prayer Ceremony," *American Anthropologist* 9, no. 2 (1907): 443–44.

136. Personal communication with Gilbert Caribou, July 2, 2004, Grand Portage.
Gilbert called this "Bringing Life" ceremony. Personal communication with Kalvin
Ottertail, May 17, 2005, Grand Portage; Mission of Immaculate Conception Diary,
September 17, 1858.

137. Vecsey, *Traditional Ojibwa Religion*, 50; and Billy Blackwell et al., *A History of
Kitchi Onimgaming: Grand Portage and Its People* (Cass Lake: Minnesota Chippewa
Tribe, 1982), 62 and 63.

138. James W. Taylor, "The Sioux War: What Shall We Do with It?" and "The Sioux
Indians: What Shall We Do with Them?" St. Paul: Press Printing Company, 1862. A
copy of this pamphlet can be found in the collections of the Minnesota Historical
Society, St. Paul, Minnesota.

139. Bruce White, "Give Us a Little Milk: The Social and Cultural Meanings of Gift
Giving in the Lake Superior Fur Trade," *Minnesota History* 48 (Summer 1982):
60–71.

140. Roderick McKenzie reminiscences, appendix 1 in Bruce White, "Grand Portage
as a Trading Post: Patterns of Trade at 'the Great Carrying Place,'" Grand Portage
National Monument, Grand Marais, Minnesota, September 2005, 189. The original
manuscript is in the Masson Collection, MG 19, vol. 32, National Archives of
Canada, Ottawa.

141. Mission of Immaculate Conception Diary, October 12, 1848; March 17, 1849;
February 9, 1852; July 15, 1854.

142. There is a local legend of a deadly pitched battle between Cornish and Irish miners
on Isle Royale. The Jesuit diary notes one such fight provoked by heavy drinking;
Mission of Immaculate Conception Diary, September 28–29, 1854.

143. Father Fremiot letter, December 3, 1851, in *Letters from the New Canada Mission*,
pt. 2, p. 275; and Mission of Immaculate Conception Diary, October 29, 1851.

144. HBCA, B.231/a/11, Fort William Post Returns, November 16, 1831.

145. Mission of Immaculate Conception Diary, February 9, 1852; and Baraga, *Short History of the North American Indians*, 68.

146. Commissioner of Indian Affairs, Annual Reports for 1858, p. 47; 1859, p. 76; and 1862, p. 90.

147. *Cook County Herald*, May 2, 1896.

148. Commission of Indian Affairs, Annual Report for 1875, p. 371.

149. Personal communication with Ellen Olson, November 1, 1989, Grand Marais, Minnesota; Prucha, *Great White Father*, 224–28; and Commissioner of Indian Affairs, Annual Report for 1898, p. 319.

150. Mr. Vankoughnet to Sir John A. Macdonald, December 13, 1882, in Arthur, *Thunder Bay District, 1821–1892*, 186.

151. Commissioner of Indian Affairs, Annual Report for 1901, p. 72; and Billy Blackwell, *A History of Kitchi Onigaming: Grand Portage and Its People* (Cass Lake, Minn.: Minnesota Chippewa Tribe, 1983), 54.

152. William Raff, *Pioneers in the Wilderness: Minnesota's Cook County, Grand Marais and the Gunflint in the Nineteenth Century* (Grand Marais: Cook County Historical Society, 1981), 188.

153. Franz Pierz, "Report of the Catholic Mission School of Grand Portage, commenced 1st August, 1838," Annual Report of the Commissioner of Indian Affairs, 1839–40," MHS, microfilm 1599; and Commissioner of Indian Affairs, Annual Reports for 1857, p. 32; 1858, p. 48; and 1859, p. 75.

154. As the population of Grand Portage rose in the second half of the nineteenth century, fewer students attended school. In 1838–39, there were 44 students out of a population of 135. By 1894, there were 317 Portagers counted in the census—94 of school age, but only 20 attending school. Annual Reports, Commissioner of Indian Affairs, for 1839–40, pp. 201 and 168; 1868, pp. 376–78; 1887, pp. 228 and 230; and 1901, pp. 401–2.

155. Ellen Olson, November 1, 1989; and Commissioner of Indian Affairs, Annual Report for 1883, p. 160.

156. Keith Denis Papers, "Parkerville," Thunder Bay Historical Museum Society, Thunder Bay, Ontario.

157. Thomas W. Dunk, "Indian Participation in the Industrial Economy on the North

Shore of Lake Superior, 1869 to 1940," *Thunder Bay Historical Museum Society Papers and Records* 15 (1987): 7; and Raff, *Cook County*, 136.

158. Arthur, *Thunder Bay District*, 121, 128, and 230. The first railroad trip from Port Arthur to Winnipeg would occur the next year, 1883.

159. Raff, *Cook County*, 149.

160. United States Engineer Department, 1884 Annual Report, "Upon the Improvement of the Harbor at Duluth, Minnesota and of the Entrance to Superior Bay, Lake Superior, and the Harbor at Grand Marais, Minnesota" (Washington, D.C.: General Printing Office, 1884); Commissioner of Indian Affairs, Annual Reports for 1882, p. 176, and 1896, p. 332.

161. Work Projects Administration, *The Minnesota Arrowhead Country* (Chicago: Whitman, 1941): 205–9.

162. Commissioner of Indian Affairs, Annual Report for 1878, p. 147.

163. Keith Denis, "Oliver Daunais, the Silver King," *Thunder Bay Historical Museum Society Papers and Records* (1979): 13.

164. *Portage Lake [Houghton, Michigan] Mining Gazette*, November 16, 1876; 1880 Federal Census for Isle Royale County, Michigan; Raff, *Cook County*, 39; Commission of Indian Affairs, Annual Report for 1874, p. 190.

165. Commissioner of Indian Affairs, Annual Report for 1898, p. 320; personal communication with Roy Oberg, October 16, 1988, Grand Marais, Minnesota; personal communication with A. A., March 1, 2007, Grand Portage; and Julius F. Wolff Jr., "Hot Fur," in *Rendezvous: Selected Papers of the Fourth North American Fur Trade Conference, 1981*, edited by Thomas C. Buckley (St. Paul: Minnesota Historical Society Press, 1984), 227. Many Indians were not permitted to vote until 1924 when the Indian Citizenship Act was passed. It permitted those Indian males who did not own lands to vote.

166. Ellen Olson interview by Carolyn Gilman, November 1, 1989.

167. Matti Kaups, "Norwegian Immigrants and the Development of Commercial Fisheries along the North Shore of Lake Superior: 1870–1895," in *Norwegian Influence on the Upper Midwest* (Duluth: University of Minnesota Duluth, 1976), 270.

168. William Gibbard, "Report on the Fisheries of Lakes Huron and Superior," 7th Parliament, 1st sess., Province of Canada, Sessional Papers, 1862, vol. 3: 11, no

pag.

169. Father Fremiot letter to Rev. Micard, February 2, 1851, in Cadieux, *Letters from the New Canada Mission*, 277.

170. Bruce White, "The Regional Context of the Removal Order of 1850," in *Fish in the Lakes, Wild Rice, and Game in Abundance: Testimony on Behalf of Mille Lacs Ojibwe Hunting and Fishing Rights*, compiled by James McClurken (East Lansing: Michigan State University Press, 2000), 187–98.

171. HBCA, John Mackenzie letter to Sir George Simpson, July 17, 1851; and Arthur, *Thunder Bay District*, 74.

172. Chute, *The Legacy of Shingwaukonse*, 68. Shingwaukonse appears to have first advocated American Ojibwe moving to English territory to escape stifling treaty agreements beginning in 1836.

173. National Archives of Canada, record group 10, vol. 198, pt. 1, 116288–89.

174. Chute, *The Legacy of Shingwaukonse*, 153.

175. Commissioner of Indian Affairs, Annual Reports for 1871, p. 600, and 1887, p. 228.

176. Isle Royale Lighthouse Log, Menagerie Island, May 21, 1886. A copy of the log is held at the Isle Royale National Park Archives. The *Algoma* tragically sunk November 7, 1885.

    Occasionally lands purchased were announced in the Cook County newspaper—such as two dozen islands purchased by Alfred Merritt and other St. Paul, Minneapolis, and Michigan men. *Cook County Herald*, October 6, 1906, and April 20, 1907.

177. Blyden Hawver's Diary, Isle Royale National Park Archives, 1912. The Grand Portage Ojibwe trappers took young Blyden Hawver under their wing and taught him how to use a toboggan and tumpline; they may also have provided his moose-hide moccasins.

178. Interview with Violet Johnson Miller, October 12, 1988, by Tim Cochrane, MHS, St. Paul. The anonymity of Adam Roach—the last Ojibwe to die on Isle Royale—is symbolic of the waning Ojibwe use of Minong. He does not appear in any official death notices in Michigan or Minnesota. The grandson of a proud boat builder, Paul LaPlante, who made boats for Isle Royale fishermen, he is remembered by few.

179. Interview with Richard Anderson, October 16, 1988, by Tim Cochrane, Grand Marais, Minnesota, MHS, St. Paul; Raff, *Cook County*, 28; "Cove Township" record book, April 7, 1879, Keweenaw County Courthouse, Eagle River, Michigan.

180. Mentioned as early as July 18, 1867, the "Great Indian Head" remained a staple for tourist visitation into the twentieth century. Sometime during the 1970s, a large portion of the rock formation broke off and fell into Lake Superior. "Journal of Lieut. Green," July 18, 1867, Cheynoweth Papers, Michigan Technological University.

181. Linklater has had a biography and a fictional novel written about him. He is also notable in that conservationist Sigurd Olson considered him somewhat of a role model. Sister Noemi Weygant, *John (Jack) Linklater: Legendary Indian Game Warden* (Duluth, Minn.: Priory Books, 1987); Darragh Aldrich, *Earth Never Tires* (New York: Little & Ives, 1936); Sigurd Olson, *The Singing Wilderness* (New York: Knopf, 1956), 198–99; and Record of Deeds, Robert F. Francis and Sarah Francis to William A. Hansen, December 3, 1926, Keweenaw County Courthouse, "Isle Royal [*sic*]," Eagle River, Michigan.

182. George A. West, "Copper: Its Mining and Use by the Aborigines of Lake Superior Region, Report of the McDonald-Massee Isle Royale Expedition, 1928," *Bulletin of the Public Museum of the City of Milwaukee* 10, no. 1.

183. Reuben Hill letter to Carol Maass, February 16, 1984, Isle Royale National Park Archives; and "Centennial Notes," *Michigan History Magazine* 19 (1935): 455.

184. Frank Warren letter to Superintendent George Baggley, December 9, 1941, Isle Royale National Park Archives.

185. O. R. Tripp, "Hunting Moose with a Camera," *Minneapolis Journal Magazine* (June 1930), 6.

186. *Ely [Minnesota] Miner*, July 21, 1933, and November 23, 1934; Joe Brickner, "Jack Linklater: As I Knew Him," *Minnesota Conservation Volunteer* 6, no. 34 (July 1943): 36–40; and Arnold Aslakson, "Jack Linklater: Son of Nature Whose 'Day' Came at 67," *Minneapolis Tribune*, August 13, 1933.

187. Benjamin Cheynoweth to John Smith, August 4, 1966, Cheynoweth Collection, Michigan Technological University.

## Conclusion. The Good Place Today

1. Personal communication with Grand Portage tribal chairman Norman Deschampe, May 3, 2007, Grand Portage; and Erwin F. Mittelholtz, "A Historical Review of the Grand Portage Indian Reservation with Special Emphasis on Indian Education," master's thesis, University of North Dakota, 1953, 44. Mittelholtz wrote: "Economically, the reservation is too poor to support any growing population."

2. *Cook County News Herald*, January 9 and 30, 1918, February 6, 1918; Interview of Willy Droulliard, by Nancy Leinke, 1961, Grand Portage. The author has a copy of this tape. Ben East, "Winter Sky Roads to Isle Royal [*sic*]," *National Geographic* 60, no. 6 (December 1931): 769 and 772; *Cook County News Herald*, July 15, 1948; personal communication with Dick Anderson, May 5, 2004, Grand Marais; personal communication with Norman Deschampe and Grand Portage tribal councilman Ken Sherer, May 3, 2007, Grand Portage, and "Summary of Review of Lake Desor Fire," August 2, 1948, "Fire," Isle Royale National Park, National Archives, Record Group 79.

3. Grand Portage Reservation Council, Resolution #1, February 7, 1945, Ranger Karl T. Gilbert Memorandum to Isle Royale Superintendent, February 15, 1946, Acting Director, U.S. Fish and Wildlife Service to Director, National Park Service, December 13, 1945, and Assistant Director Hillory A. Tolson to Regional Director, Region Two, January 26, 1949, "Beaver," Isle Royale National Park, National Archives, Record Group 79. Interestingly, four years after the decision was made to not trap beaver and transplant them to Grand Portage, the Assistant Director of the National Park Service somewhat reversed the NPS decision and now "left the [decision] to the superintendent." However, by this time there is no record of any communications made to the Grand Portage tribal council.

4. *Cook County News Herald*, September 19, 1946. The band was seeking a loan from the Bureau of Indian Affairs for the vessels and a lodge building and fifteen cabins to respond to the growing tourist trade.

   The Sivertson ferry business has a long-standing tradition of providing free rides to Isle Royale for reservation residents. Many Grand Portage "kids" have ridden the *Wenonah* or *Voyageur II* to Isle Royale, and indeed this has been the sole means of going there for a number of Grand Portage residents.

5.  Francis E. Andrews letter to George F. Baggley, Superintendent and Newston B. Drury, Director, National Park Service, March 6, 1945 and George F. Baggley, Isle Royale Superintendent, "Memorandum for the Director," March 9, 1945, "Fishing," Isle Royale, National Park Service, Record Group 79, National Archives, College Park, Maryland.

6.  Tim Cochrane, "Isle Royale Leisure," in *Borealis: An Isle Royale Potpourri*, ed. David Harmon (Houghton: Isle Royale Natural History Association, 1992), 97; and personal communication with Ken Sherer, May 3, 2007, Grand Portage. Ken was on the tribal council when this activity occurred.

7.  "Reservation Development Program, Grand Portage Reservation, Minnesota," March 31, 1971; endorsed by the Reservation Tribal Council, a copy is held by Grand Portage National Monument. *Moccasin [Grand Portage] Telegraph*, May 21, 1971; and personal communication with Norman Deschampe, May 3, 2007, Grand Portage.

8.  Ron Cockrell, "Grand Portage National Monument: An Administrative History," Midwest Region, National Park Service, October 1983, 62–63.

9.  "Memorandum of Agreement between the Department of the Interior, the Minnesota Chippewa Tribe and the Grand Portage Band of Indians Relating to the Establishment of Grand Portage National Historic Site," August 1951, p. 2. A copy of the agreement is held at Grand Portage National Monument.

10. Mary Ann King, "Co-Management or Contracting? Agreements between Native American Tribes and the U.S. National Park Service Pursuant to the 1994 Tribal Self-Governance Act," *Harvard Environmental Law Review* 31, no. 2 (2007): 508–23.

11. *Moccasin Telegraph*, June 2000, 9; and Ray DePerry, Executive Administrator, Great Lakes Indian Fish and Wildlife Commission, to Superintendent Thomas Hobbs, September 30, 1995, Isle Royale National Park Archives, Houghton, Michigan.

12. "Grand Portage Forest Management Plan and Environmental Assessment," Bureau of Indian Affairs, Minneapolis Office, 1986, 9.

13. Andrew M. Small to Superintendent Douglas Barnard, May 5, 2000, Isle Royale National Park Archives. A copy of the letter was sent to fourteen neighboring Ojibwe bands. The subject line of the letter was "Preservation of Fishing Resources around Isle Royale." The letter was written, in part, to address rumors about some South

Shore Ojibwe fishermen interested in fishing Isle Royale waters. Superintendent Douglas Barnard to Andrew M. Small, May 18, 2000, Minneapolis, Minnesota. Copies are held at Grand Portage National Monument.

14. For example, the Grand Portage Band and the four national park units on Lake Superior jointly completed a plan that seeks to halt the potentially disastrous introduction of the fish virus into the Big Lake. "VHS Prevention and Response Plan," March, 2008, NPS and Grand Portage Band, a copy of which is held at Grand Portage National Monument.

15. For more on "mackinaw boats"—the equivalent of "pickup trucks" on Lake Superior in the 1800s—see my and Hawk Tolson's *"A Good Boat Speaks for Itself:" Isle Royale Fishermen and Their Boats* (Minneapolis: University of Minnesota Press, 2002), 69–80.

16. Personal communication with Ellen Olson, August 23, 2003, Grand Portage.

17. Sigurd Olson, *The Singing Wilderness* (New York: Knopf, 1956), 198–99; and personal communication with Warner Wirta, August 10, 2007, Grand Portage.

18. There were native centralization forces in addition to those brought by the whites. For example, North Shore Ojibwe gathered in large groups for fall fishing, for the Midewiwin ceremony, and along important water routes or portages. However, centralization forces appear to have overwhelmed the more common decentralization of Ojibwe "camps" by the 1830s and '40s. The long tradition of fur trading and advantages of being by a fur trade post began the centralization process earlier, but treaties, priests, and schools radically quickened the pace of centralization.

19. "Fort William First Nation Boundary Claim, Frequently Asked Questions, November 2006," Indian and Northern Affairs, Canada and Fort William First Nation, and "Fort William First Nation Boundary Claim Negotiations," Ministry of Aboriginal Affairs, Ontario, Canada, November 7, 2007.

20. "Fakelore" means false folklore appearing in print, as compared to folklore, which is most commonly transmitted verbally. Fakelore often manipulates or makes up wholesale folklore, such as stories about Paul Bunyan and Pecos Bill. Richard Dorson describes fakelore as a "synthetic product claiming oral tradition but actually tailored for mass edification." Richard Dorson, *Folklore and Fakelore* (Cambridge, Mass.: Harvard University Press, 1976), 5. Peter Nabokov and Lawrence Loendorf also note the play of fakelore in their study of Yellowstone and American Indian

relationships, *Restoring a Presence: American Indians and Yellowstone National Park* (Norman: University of Oklahoma Press, 2004), 21–26.

21. Writers and critics of the National Park Service sometimes speak of "creation myths," reusing an anthropological term to talk about the public story that is often circulated to explain how a particular park was created. In the case of Yellowstone National Park, the first national park, the "creation myth" is about how the idea of a national park was supposedly the product of a campfire conversation among explorers and promoters. Paul Schullery and Lee Whittlesey, *Myth and History in the Creation of Yellowstone National Park* (Lincoln: University of Nebraska Press, 2003); and Schullery and Whittlesey, "Yellowstone's Creation Myth: Can We Live with Our Own Legends?" *Montana: The Magazine of Western History* 53 (Spring 2003): 2–27.

22. Multiple personal communications with Dr. Ted Birkedal, 1992–1997, Alaska Region Office, Anchorage, Alaska; and Dale Vinson, "Bears, Fish, Prehistory, and Deferred Maintenance at Brooks Camp, Katmai National Park and Preserve," April 19, 2007, George Wright Society Meeting, St. Paul, Minnesota.

23. "Trust responsibilities are the duties and obligations of the federal government (and its employees) to protect the interests of recognized tribes." At Isle Royale this would mean that Grand Portage has an interest in how the NPS manages or impacts resources of special significance such as animals—fish in particular—plants, water, and areas such as McCargoe Cove. "Draft Director's Order # 71: Relationships with American Indians and Alaska Natives," National Park Service, Washington, D.C., 1999.

24. Patricia L. Parker and Thomas F. King, "Guidelines for Evaluating and Documenting Traditional Cultural Properties," *National Register Bulletin* 38, National Park Service (1990): 1.

25. John O. Anfinson, "Oral Interviews: The Significance of Grand Portage Bay to the Grand Portage Chippewa Band," January 1994, U.S. Army Corps of Engineers. A copy of this assessment is held at Grand Portage National Monument.

26. Thomas F. King, *Places That Count: Traditional Cultural Properties in Cultural Resource Management* (Walnut Creek, Calif.: Altamira Press, 2003), 169–74.

# BIBLIOGRAPHY

## Unpublished Sources

### ARCHIVES

American Philosophical Society, Philadelphia, Pennsylvania
William Jones Papers
Archives de la Compagnie de Jesus, St. Jerome, Quebec
Francois Maynard Transcription, Mission of Immaculate Conception Diaries
Bayliss Public Library, Sault Ste. Marie, Michigan
American Fur Company Collection
Bentley Historical Library, University of Michigan, Ann Arbor
Minong Mining Company
Isle Royale Collection
Douglas Houghton Papers
Cornelius G. Shaw Diary
Buffalo and Erie Historical Society, Buffalo, New York
Peter B. Porter Papers

Creighton University Archives, Omaha, Nebraska
>   The Woodstock Letters Collection
General Land Office Records, Sault Ste. Marie Office, Michigan
>   www.glorecords.blm.gov/patentsearch
Grand Portage National Monument, Grand Portage, Minnesota
>   John Flatte Diary
>   Nancy Lienke Notes (fragment)
>   Jean Morrison unpublished papers
>   "Memorandum of Agreement between the Department of the Interior, the Minnesota Chippewa Tribe and the Grand Portage Band of Indians Relating to the Establishment of Grand Portage National Historic Site," August 1951
>   J. Wesley White, unpublished "historical sketches"
Hudson's Bay Company Archives, Winnipeg, Manitoba
>   Fort William Post Returns
>   Fort William District Reports
>   Rainy Lake Post Returns
>   Rainy Lake District Reports
>   Moose Factory Reports
>   Pic District Reports
Historical Society of Pennsylvania, Philadelphia, Pennsylvania
>   A. Myers Papers
Isle Royale National Park Archives, Houghton, Michigan
>   Blyden Hawver Diary
>   William Ives survey notes
>   Menagerie Island Lighthouse Log
>   Mining and Fishing vertical files
>   Lawrence Rakestraw, "Post-Columbian History of Isle Royale: Part I, Mining"
Library of Congress, Washington, D.C.
>   Henry Rowe Schoolcraft Papers
Michigan Technological University Archives, Houghton, Michigan
>   Ben Cheynoweth Collection

Minnesota Historical Society, St. Paul, Minnesota
  American Board of Commissioners of Foreign Missions
  U.S. Commissioner of Indian Affairs Microfilm and Annual Reports, 1838–1943
  Dewey Albinson Collection
  Gabriel Franchere Papers
  Father Francis Pierz Papers
  James W. Taylor, The Sioux War Pamphlets
  Henry Sibley Papers
  Map Collection
  North West Company Microfilm Collection
National Archives of Canada, Ottawa, Ontario
  Record Group 10, Superior-Robinson Treaty, Lake Nipigon Census
  Masson Collection
  North West Company Letterbook
  MG11, Indian Affairs, S. J. Dawson
New York Historical Society, New York, New York
  American Fur Company Papers
Princeton University Library, Princeton, New Jersey
  Delafield Family Papers
Public Archives of Ontario, Toronto, Ontario
  W. B. Robinson Papers
  Father Specht Papers
  David Thompson Journals
Regis College Archives, Toronto, Ontario
  Mission of Immaculate Conception Diaries and Letters
St. Anne's Church, Thunder Bay, Ontario
  Father William Maurice Genealogical Records
  Father Francis Nelligan, S.J. unpublished history
St. Louis County Historical Society, Duluth, Minnesota
  Edmund F. Ely Journal
State of Michigan, East Lansing, Michigan
  Michigan Department of Community Health, Death Notices

Thunder Bay Historical Museum Society, Thunder Bay, Ontario

    Fort William Post Returns for 1824

    Keith Denis Papers

Toronto Public Library, Toronto, Ontario

    North West Company Inventory, 1797

U.S. National Archives, College Park, Maryland

    Record Group 76, map series

    Record Group 79, National Park Service, Isle Royale

U.S. National Archives, Washington, D.C.

    Record Group 26, Light House Board Letters

Office of Indian Affairs, LaPointe Agency and Sandy Lake Subagency

Wisconsin Historical Society, Madison, Wisconsin

    Articles of Association of the Isle Royale and Ohio Mining Company

**INTERVIEWS** (ALL INTERVIEWS BY AUTHOR, UNLESS NOTED)

A. A., Grand Portage and Grand Marais, Minnesota

    November 20, 1988, and December 30, 1998

Richard Anderson, Grand Portage, Minnesota

    October 16, 1988, copy held at Minnesota Historical Society; May 5, 2004

Rick Anderson, Grand Portage, Minnesota

    February 23, 2006

Norman Deschampe, Grand Portage, Minnesota

    June 20, 2002; March 2, 2006; and May 3, 2007

Willie Droulliard, Grand Portage, Minnesota

    Tape-recorded by Nancy Lienke, 1961.

Ed and Ingeborg Holte, Isle Royale, Michigan

    Tape-recorded by Lawrence Rakestraw, September 10, 1965

Ellen Olson, Grand Portage and Grand Marais, Minnesota

    Interviews by Carolyn Gilman: October 16, 1988; August 23, 2002; January 30, 2003; April 10, 2003; February 17, 2006; and March 14, 2007

Gilbert Caribou, Grand Portage, Minnesota

    August 19, 2002; July 2, 2004; and March 1, 2007

Ellen Hanson, Floodwood, Minnesota
November 11, 1988
Tony LeSage, Grand Portage, Minnesota
October 16, 1988
Nancy Lienke, Grand Portage, Minnesota
June 2002
Violet Johnson Miller, Ahmeek, Michigan
October 12, 1988
Roy Oberg, Grand Marais, Minnesota
October 15, 1988
Kalvin Ottertail, Grand Portage, Minnesota
June 23, 2004; March 7, 2005; and July 20, 2005
Stan Sivertson, Duluth, Minnesota
April 4, 1980; and October 14, 1988

## Published Sources

Adams, Arthur T., ed. *The Explorations of Pierre Esprit Radisson*. Minneapolis: Ross and Haines, 1961.

Albright, Horace M. National Park Service Director. *Congressional Record*, February 25, 1931; *Congressional Record*, Senate, March 3, 1931.

Aldrich, Darragh. *Earth Never Tires*. New York: Little & Ives, 1936.

Allen, Durward L. *Wolves of Minong*. Boston: Houghton Mifflin Company, 1979.

Angel, Michael. *Preserving the Sacred: Historical Perspectives on the Ojibwa Midewiwin*. Winnipeg: University of Manitoba Press, 2002.

Arthur, Elizabeth. *Thunder Bay District, 1821–1892*. Toronto: Champlain Society, 1973.

Arthurs, David. "An "IHS": Finger Ring from Lake Nipigon." *Arch Notes: Newsletter of the Ontario Archaeological Society* (May–June 1983): 17–22.

———. "Lake Superior Surveys, 1978–1989." North Central Region Conservation Archaeology Report, Ontario Ministry of Citizenship, Culture and Recreation, Thunder Bay.

Baraga, Iraneus Frederic. "Baptismal Records, 1835–1887, Kept at LaPointe and Bayfield Indian Missions." Transcribed by John L. Schade. *Lost in Canada? Canadian-American Journal of History & Genealogy* 17, no. 3 (Summer 1994): 111–18 and 18, no 2 (Fall 1995): 67–80.

———. *Short History of the North American Indians.* Translated and edited by Graham MacDonald. Calgary: University of Calgary Press, 2004.

Barnouw, Victor. *Wisconsin Chippewa Myths and Tales and Their Relation to Chippewa Life.* Madison: University of Wisconsin Press, 1977.

Bastian, Tyler J. "Archeological Survey of Isle Royale National Park, Michigan, 1960–1962." Ann Arbor, Mich.: University of Michigan Museum of Anthropology, 1963.

Bird, William. "Reminiscences of the Boundary Survey." *Publications of the Buffalo Historical Society* 4 (1896): 1–14.

Bishop, Charles A. "Northern Algonquins, 1760–1821." In *Aboriginal Ontario: Historical Perspectives on the First Nations*, edited by Edward S. Rogers and Donald B. Smith, 289–306. Toronto: Dundern Press, 1994.

———. "The Question of Ojibwa Clans." In *Actes du vingtième congrés des Algonquinistes*, 43–61, edited by William Cowan. Ottawa: Carlton University, 1989.

Blackwell, Billy, et al. *A History of Kitchi Onimgaming: Grand Portage and Its People.* Cass Lake: Minnesota Chippewa Tribe, 1982.

Boatman, John. *My Elders Taught Me: Aspects of Western Great Lakes American Indian Philosophy.* New York: University Press of America, 1992.

Bohnak, Karl. *So Cold a Sky: Upper Michigan Weather Stories.* Nagaunee, Mich.: Cold Sky Publisher, 2006.

Bourgeois, Arthur P., ed. *Ojibwa Narratives of Charles and Charlotte Kawbawgam and Jacques LePique, 1893–1895.* Detroit: Wayne State University Press, 1994.

Brightman, Robert. "The Windigo in the Material World." *Ethnohistory* 35, no. 4 (Fall 1988): 337–79.

Brito, Silvester John. "The Witch Tree Complex." *Wisconsin Academy of Sciences, Arts, and Letters* 70 (1982): 61–67.

Bronte, Charles R. "Evidence of Spring Spawning Lake Trout in Lake Superior." *Journal of Great Lakes Research* 19 (1993): 625–29.

————, and Shawn P. Sitar. "Harvest and Relative Abundance of Siscowet Lake Trout in Michigan Waters of Lake Superior, 1929–61." In press, 2008.

Brown, Jennifer S. H. "'I Wish to Be As I See You': An Ojibwa Methodist Encounter in Fur Trade Country, Rainy Lake, 1854–1855." *Arctic Anthropology* 24, no. 1 (1987): 19–31.

————, and Robert Brightman. *"The Orders of the Dreamed": George Nelson on Cree and Northern Ojibwa Religion and Myth, 1823*. St. Paul: Minnesota Historical Society Press, 1988.

Burnham, Philip. *Indian Country, God's Country: Native Americans and the National Parks*. Washington, D.C.: Island Press, 2000.

Burpee, Lawrence J., ed. *Journals and Letters of Pierre Gaultier de Varennes De La Verendrye and His Sons*. Toronto: The Champlain Society, 1927.

Cadieux, Lorenzo, ed. *Lettres des nouvelles missions du Canada, 1843–1852*. Montreal: Les Editions Bellarmin, 1973.

————, ed. *Letters from the New Canada Mission, 1843–1852*. Part 2. Translated by William Lonc and George Topp. Privately published, 2001.

Cameron, M. Duncan. "A Sketch of the Customs, Manners and Way of Living of the Natives in the Barren Country about Nipigon, 1804–1805." In *Les bourgeois de la Compagnie du Nord-Ouest*, edited by L. R. Masson, 239–300. New York: Antiquarian Press, 1960.

Catton, Theodore. *Inhabited Wilderness: Indians, Eskimos, and National Parks*. Albuquerque: University of New Mexico Press, 1997.

"Centennial Notes." *Michigan History Magazine* 19 (1935): 449–56.

"Charlie and Angelique Mott." In *Borealis: An Isle Royale Potpourri*, edited by David Harmon, 79–84. Houghton, Mich.: Isle Royale Natural History Association, 1992.

Christian, Sarah Barr. *Winter on Isle Royale: A Narrative of Life on Isle Royale during the Years 1874 and 1875*. Privately printed, 1932.

Chute, Janet. *The Legacy of Shingwaukonse: A Century of Native Leadership*. Toronto: University of Toronto Press, 1998.

Clark, Caven. "Archeological Survey and Testing, Isle Royale National Park, 1987–1990 Seasons." Edited by F. A. Calabrese. Midwest Archeological Center Occasional Studies in Anthropology no. 32, 1995.

————. "A Dog Burial from Isle Royale, Lake Superior: An Example of Household Ritual Sacrifice in the Terminal Woodland Period." *Midcontinental Journal of Archaeology* 15, no. 2 (1990): 265–78.

————. "Group Composition and the Role of Unique Raw Materials in the Terminal Woodland Substage of the Lake Superior Basin." Ph.D. dissertation, Michigan State University, 1991.

————. "Late Prehistoric Cultural Affiliation Study, Grand Portage National Monument." Cultural Resources Report No. 111, Archeological Consulting Services, November 1999.

————, and Timothy Cochrane. "Haytown: A Nineteenth Century Copper Mining Site on Isle Royale's North Shore." *Michigan Archaeologist* 44, no. 2 (June 1998): 55–88.

Clark, Thomas, "The Physical Geography, Meteorology, and Botany of the Northeastern District of Minnesota." *Report of the State Geologist.* St. Paul: Frederick Driscoll, 1865.

Cleland, Charles E. "Analysis of the Fauna of the Indian Point Site on Isle Royale in Lake Superior." *Michigan Archaeologist* 14, no. 3–4 (1968): 143–46.

————. *Rites of Conquest: The History and Culture of Michigan's Native Americans.* Ann Arbor: University of Michigan Press, 1992.

Cochrane, Jean. "Woodland Caribou Restoration at Isle Royale National Park: A Feasibility Study." Isle Royale National Park, 1996.

Cochrane, Tim. Introduction to "Charlie and Angelique Mott," and "Isle Royale Leisure." In *Borealis: An Isle Royale Potpourri*, edited by David Harmon. Houghton, Mich.: Isle Royale Natural History Association, 1992.

————. "Isle Royale: 'A Good Place to Live.'" *Michigan History* 74, no. 3 (May–June 1990): 16–18.

————, and Hawk Tolson. *A Good Boat Speaks for Itself: Isle Royale Fishermen and Their Boats.* Minneapolis: University of Minnesota Press, 2002.

Cockrell, Ron. "Grand Portage National Monument: An Administrative History." Midwest Region, National Park Service, October 1983.

Coleman, Sister Bernard, Ellen Frogner, Estelle Eich. *Ojibwa Myths and Legends.* Minneapolis: Ross and Haines, 1962.

Cooper, Dennis Glen. "The Tragedy of Mott Island." *Inland Seas* 3, no. 1 (January 1947): 17–20.

Copway, George, or Kah-ge-gah-bowh. *The Traditional History and Characteristic Sketches of the Ojibway Nation.* Toronto: Coles, 1972.

Costain, Thomas B. *The White and the Gold: The French Regime in Canada.* Toronto: Doubleday Canada, 1954.

Croil, James. *Steam Navigation and Its Relation to the Commerce of Canada and the United States.* Toronto: William Briggs, 1898.

Cude, Daniel G. "Identifying the Ojibway of North Lake Superior and the Boundary Water Region, 1650–1750." In *Papers of the Algonquian Conference, 32nd Conference,* edited by John D. Nichols, 74–99. Winnipeg: University of Manitoba, 2001.

Cuthbertson, G. A. "Fur Traders on Fresh Water: An Account of the Northwest Company's Sailing Ships on the Great Lakes." *The Beaver* (December 1934): 26–30 and 41.

Delafield, Major Joseph. *An Unfortified Boundary.* New York: privately printed, 1943.

Denis, Keith. "Oliver Daunais—The 'Silver King.'" *Thunder Bay Historical Museum Society Papers and Records* 2 (1979): 12–21.

———. "The Winter Mail to Pigeon River." *Thunder Bay Historical Museum Society* 1 (1973): 13–17.

Densmore, Frances. "An Ojibway Prayer Ceremony." *American Anthropologist* 9, no. 2 (1907): 443–44.

———. *Chippewa Customs.* Minneapolis: Ross and Haines, 1970.

———. *How Indians Use Wild Plants.* New York: Dover, 1974.

Dickenson, George. "Report on the Geological and Mineralogical Survey of the Mineral Lands of the United States in the State of Michigan." Edited by Charles T. Jackson. 503–506. 31st Cong., 1st sess., Senate Executive Document no. 1, serial no. 551, 1849.

"Discussion." *The Canadian Agriculturist and Journal of the Board of Agriculture of Upper Canada* 9, no. 5 (May 1858): 116–17.

Dorson, Richard. *Bloodstoppers and Bearwalkers: Folk Tales of Immigrants, Lumberjacks, and Indians.* Cambridge, Mass.: Harvard University Press, 1952.

———. *Folklore and Fakelore.* Cambridge, Mass.: Harvard University Press, 1976.

Drier, Roy W., and Octave Josephy De Temple. *Prehistoric Copper Mining in the Lake Superior Region.* Calumet, Mich.: privately printed, 1961.

Dunk, Thomas W. "Indian Participation in the Industrial Economy on the North Shore of Lake Superior, 1869–1940." *Thunder Bay Historical Museum Society Papers and Records* 15 (1987): 1–13.

Dunning, R. W. *Social and Economic Change among the Northern Ojibwa.* Toronto: University of Toronto Press, 1959.

Dustin, Fred. "A Summary of the Archaeology of Isle Royale, Michigan." *Papers of the Michigan Academy of Science, Arts and Letters* 16 (1931): 1–16.

———. "An Archaeological Reconnaissance of Isle Royale." *Michigan History* 41, no. 1 (March 1957): 1–34.

East, Ben. "Winter Sky Roads to Isle Royale." *National Geographic* 60, no. 3 (December 1931): 759–74.

"Enumeration of the Indian Tribes Connected with the Government of Canada; the Warriors and Armorial Bearings of Each Nation, 1736." *Documents Relative to the Colonial History of the State of New York.* Paris Documents, vol. 8. Albany: Weed, Parson & Co., 1853–1887.

Fadner, Lawrence Trever, ed. *Fort Wilkins 1844 and the U.S. Mineral Land Agency 1843.* New York: Vantage Press, 1966.

Ferguson, William P. F. "The Franklin Isle Royale Expedition." *Michigan History* 8 (1924): 450–68.

Foster, F. W., and J. D. Whitney. "Report on the Geology and Topography of a Portion of Lake Superior Land District in the State of Michigan." 31st Cong., 1st sess., House of Representatives, Executive Document no. 69, serial no. 578.

Fox, G. R. "The Ancient Copper Workings of Isle Royale." *Wisconsin Archeologist* 10, no. 2 (1911): 73–100.

Gibbard, William. "Report on the Fisheries of Lakes Huron and Superior." December 31, 1861, *Sessional Papers*, vol. 3, 1st Session of the Seventh Parliament, Province of Canada, 1962.

Gidmark, David. *Building a Birchbark Canoe.* Mechanicsburg, Penn.: Stackpole Books, 1994.

Gillman, Henry. "Ancient Works at Isle Royale, Michigan." *Appleton's Journal* 10 (August 9, 1873): 173–75.

Gilman, Carolyn. "Grand Portage Ojibway Indians Give British Medals to Historical Society." *Minnesota History* 43 (Spring 1980): 26–32.

————. *Grand Portage Story.* St. Paul, Minnesota Historical Society Press, 1992.

Goodier, J. L. "The Nineteenth-Century Fisheries of the Hudson's Bay Company Trading Posts on Lake Superior: A Biogeographical Study." *Canadian Geographer* 28, no. 4 (1984): 341–57.

Graham, Loren R. *A Face in the Rock: The Tale of a Grand Island Chippewa.* Washington, D.C.: Island Press, 1995.

Hallowell, A. Irving. *The Ojibwa of Berens River, Manitoba.* Edited by Jennifer S. H. Brown. New York: Harcourt Brace, 1992.

Hansen, Lise. "The Anishinabek Land Claim and the Participation of the Indian People Living on the North Shore of Lake Superior in the Robinson Superior Treaty, 1850." Ontario Ministry of Natural Resources, November 22, 1985.

Hartley, Alan H. "The Expansion of Ojibway and French Place-Names into the Lake Superior Region in the Seventeenth Century." *Names* 28, no. 1 (March 1980): 43–68.

Hauser, Judith Ann. "Jesuit Rings from Fort Michilimackinac and Other European Contact Sites." Mackinac Island State Park Commission, Archeological Report no. 5 (1982).

Heidenreich, Conrad E. "The Fictitious Islands of Lake Superior." *Inland Seas* 43, no. 3 (Fall 1987): 168–77.

Henry, Alexander, the elder. *Travels and Adventures in Canada and the Indian Territories between the Years 1760 and 1776.* New York: I. Riley, 1809.

Hickerson, Harold. "The Southwestern Chippewa: An Ethnohistorical Study." *American Anthropological Association* 64, no. 3, pt. 2 (June 1962).

Hilger, Sister M. Inez. "Chippewa Hunting and Fishing Customs." *Minnesota Conservationist* 35 (1936): 2–3 and 17–19.

Hoffman, Walter J. "The Midewiwin or 'Grand Medicine Society' of the Ojibwa." *Bureau of Ethnology, Seventh Annual Report, 1885–1886.* Washington, D.C.: General Printing Office, 1891.

Houghton, Douglas. "Dr. Houghton's Remarks at the Canal Meeting." 28th Cong., 1st sess., Senate Executive Documents, 1843, serial no. 434.

Hyde, Charles K. "From 'Subterranean Lotteries' to Orderly Investment: Michigan Copper and Eastern Dollars, 1841–1865." *Mid-America: An Historical Review* 66, no. 1 (January 1984): 3–20.

———. *The Northern Lights: Lighthouses of the Upper Great Lakes.* Lansing, Mich.: Two Peninsula Press, 1986.

Jackson, Charles T. "Mirage on Lake Superior." In *The Annual of Scientific Discovery, Or, Year-book of Facts in Science and Art*, edited by David Ames Wells et al., 151–53. New York: Gould and Lincoln, 1850.

———. "Report on the Geological and Mineralogical Survey of the Mineral Lands of the United States in the State of Michigan." 31st Cong., 1st sess., Senate Executive Document no. 1, serial no. 551, 1849.

Jaenen, Cornelius J., ed. *The French Regime in the Upper Country of Canada in the Seventeenth Century.* Toronto: Champlain Society, 1996.

James, E., ed. *A Narrative of the Captivity and Adventures of John Tanner during Thirty Years Residence among the Indians.* Minneapolis: Ross and Haines, 1956.

Johnson, Nancy A. "Suzie Island: Minnesota's Arctic Outpost." *Minnesota Monthly* (June 1984): 20 and 23.

Johnston, Basil. *The Manitous: The Spiritual World of the Ojibway.* New York: Harper Collins, 1995.

Johnston, John. "An Account of Lake Superior: 1792–1807." In *Les bourgeois de la Compagnie du Nord-Ouest*, edited by L. R. Masson, 146–74 (New York: Antiquarian Press, 1960).

"Joint Report upon the Survey and Demarcation of the Boundary between the United States and Canada from the Northwestern most Point of Lake of the Woods to Lake Superior." Washington, D.C.: U.S. Printing Office, 1931.

Jones, William. "Ojibwa Tales from the North Shore of Lake Superior." *Journal of American Folklore* 29 (1916): 368–91.

———. "Ojibwa Texts." Edited by Truman Michelson. *Publications of the American Ethnological Society*, vol. 7, pt. 1 (1917) and pt. 2 (1919).

Kappler, Charles J., ed. and comp. *Indian Affairs: Law and Treaties.* Vol. 2. Washington, D.C.: Government Printing Office, 1904.

Karpinski, Louis C. "Michigan and the Great Lakes upon the Map, 1636–1802. *Michigan History Magazine* 29, no. 3 (July–September 1945): 292–312.

Karrow, Robert W. "Lake Superior's Mythic Isles: A Cautionary Tale for Users of Old Maps." *Michigan History* 69, no. 1 (January–February 1985): 24–31.

Kaups, Matti. "North Shore Commercial Fishing, 1849–1870." *Minnesota History* 46 (Summer 1978): 43–58.

———. "Norwegian Immigrants and the Development of Commercial Fisheries along the North Shore of Lake Superior: 1870–1895." In *Norwegian Influence on the Upper Midwest*, edited by Harold Naess, 21–34. Duluth: University of Minnesota Duluth, 1976.

Kegg, Maude. *What My Grandmother Told Me*. Translated by John D. Nichols. St. Paul: Minnesota Historical Society Press, 1983.

Keller, Robert H., and Michael F. Turek. *American Indians and National Parks*. Tucson: University of Arizona Press, 1998.

Kerfoot, Justine. *Gunflint: Reflections on the Trail*. Duluth, Minn.: Pfeifer-Hamilton, 1991.

King, Huber N. "Glacial and Postglacial History of Isle Royale National Park, Michigan." U.S. Geological Survey, Professional Paper 754-A, 1973.

King, Mary Ann. "Co-Management or Contracting? Agreements between Native American Tribes and the U.S. National Park Service Pursuant to the 1994 Tribal Self-Governance Act." *Harvard Environmental Law Review* 31, no. 2 (2007): 475–530.

King, Thomas F. *Places That Count: Traditional Cultural Properties in Cultural Resource Management*. Walnut Creek, Calif.: Altamira, 2003.

Kinietz, W. Vernon, ed. *The Indians of the Western Great Lakes, 1615–1760*. Ann Arbor: University of Michigan Press, 1940.

Kohl, Johann Georg. *Kitchi-Gami: Life among the Lake Superior Ojibway*. St. Paul: Minnesota Historical Society Press, 1985.

Koziol, Ann M. "Dynamics of Lightly Exploited Populations of the Lake Whitefish, Isle Royale Vicinity, Lake Superior." Fisheries Research Report No. 1911, Michigan Department of Natural Resources, 1982.

Krause, David J. *The Making of a Mining District: Keweenaw Native Copper, 1500–1870*. Detroit: Wayne State University Press, 1992.

Krefting, Laurits W. "Beaver of Isle Royale." *Naturalist* 14, no. 2 (Summer 1963): 2–11.

Lamb, W. Kaye, ed. *The Journals and Letters of Sir Alexander Mackenzie*. Cambridge: Cambridge University Press, 1970.

———, ed. *Sixteen Years in the Indian Country: The Journal of Daniel Williams Harmon*. Toronto: Macmillan, 1957.

Landes, Ruth. *Ojibwa Sociology*. New York: AMS Press, 1969.

Landon, Fred. "Letters of Rev. James Evans, Methodist Missionary, Written during his Journey to and Residence in the Lake Superior Region, 1838–1839." *Ontario Historical Society's "Papers and Records"* 28 (1932): 47–70.

Lane, Alfred C. "Geological Report on Isle Royale Michigan." *Geological Survey of Michigan VI*. Lansing: Robert Smith Printing, 1900.

Lanman, Charles. *A Summer in the Wilderness*. New York: Appleton, 1847.

Lass, William. *Minnesota's Boundary with Canada*. St. Paul: Minnesota Historical Society Press, 1980.

Law, W. H. *Among the Lighthouses of the Great Lakes*. Detroit: privately printed, 1908.

Leighton, Louise. *The Great Carrying Place*. New York: Harbinger House, 1944.

Lewis, G. Malcolm. "First Nations Mapmaking in the Great Lakes Region in Intercultural Contexts: A Historical Review." In *Mapping in Michigan and the Great Lakes Region*, edited by David I. Macleod, 39–61. East Lansing: Michigan State University Press, 2007.

———. "Metrics, Geometries, Signs, and Language: Sources of Cartographic Miscommunication between Native and Euro-American Cultures in North America." *Cartographica* 30 (1993): 98–106.

Longstreth, Morris T. *The Lake Superior Country*. New York: Century, 1924.

Lyford, Carrie A. *Ojibwa Crafts*. Washington, D.C.: Bureau of Indian Affairs, 1953.

McKinney, Thomas L., and J. Hall. *The Indian Tribes of North America*. Edinburgh: John Grant Co., 1933.

Martin, Susan. *Wonderful Power: The Story of Ancient Copper Working in the Lake Superior Basin*. Detroit: Wayne State University Press, 1999.

Martin, Terrance J., "Prehistoric Animal Exploitation on Isle Royale." In Caven Clark, *Archeological Survey and Testing Isle Royale National Park, 1987–1990 Seasons*, edited by F. A. Calabrese, 205–16. Midwest Archeological Center Occasional Studies in Anthropology no. 32 (1995).

"McCulloch, Hugh." *American National Biography.* New York: Oxford University Press, 1999.

McLean, John. *James Evans: Inventor of the Syllabic System of the Cree Language.* Toronto: Methodist Mission Rooms, 1890.

Margry, Pierre, ed. *Découvertes et établissements des Français dans l'ouest et le sud de l'Amérique Septentrionale, 1615–1754.* Paris: D. Jouast, 1876–86.

Martinson, David, ed. *"A Long Time Ago is Just Like Today.* Duluth, Minn.: Duluth Indian Education Advisory Committee, 1976.

Mason, Philip P., ed. *Schoolcraft's Ojibwe Lodge Stories.* East Lansing: Michigan State University Press, 1997.

Meeker, James, Joan E. Elias, and John A. Heim. *Plants Used by the Great Lakes Ojibwa.* Odanah, Wisc.: Great Lakes Fish and Wildlife Commission, 1993.

Mills, James Cooke. *Our Inland Seas: Their Shipping and Commerce for Three Centuries.* Chicago: A. C. McClurg, 1910.

Mittelholtz, Erwin F. "A Historical Review of the Grand Portage Indian Reservation with Special Emphasis on Indian Education." Master's thesis, University of North Dakota, 1953.

Moen, Sharon. "Ice Cover Lacking on Lake." *Seiche* (April 2006): 2.

Moore, Seth A., and Charles R. Bronte. "Delineation of Sympatric Morphotypes of Lake Trout in Lake Superior." *Transactions of the American Fisheries Society* 130 (2001): 1233–40.

Morris, Alexander. *The Treaties of Canada with the Indians of Manitoba and the North-West Territories.* Toronto: Coles, 1979.

Morriseau, Norval. *Legends of My People, the Great Ojibway.* Toronto: McGraw-Hill, 1965.

Morrison, Jean. *Fort William in the Canadian Fur Trade.* Toronto: Natural Heritage/ Natural History, 2001.

———. *Superior Rendezvous Place.* Toronto: Natural Heritage, 2001.

Morse, Richard F. "Atte-Konse, Little Carriboo, etc." In *Collections of the State Historical Society of Wisconsin,* 3:354–55, edited by Lyman Copeland Draper. Madison: State Historical Society of Wisconsin, 1904.

Mushkat, Jerome. "Mineral and Timber Prospects in Upper Michigan: The Diary of John V. L. Pruyn." *Inland Seas* 30, no. 2 (Summer 1974): 84–93.

N., R. "A Summer's Ramble on the North-West Shore of Lake Superior." *Anglo-American Magazine* 6, no. 3 (March 1855): 278–81.

Nabokov, Peter, and Lawrence Loendorf. *Restoring a Presence: American Indians and Yellowstone National Park.* Norman: University of Oklahoma Press, 2004.

Neill, Edward D. "The Development of Trade on Lake Superior and Its Tributaries during the French Regime." *Macalester College Contributions* 4 (1890).

Nichols, John D., ed. "Statement Made by the Indians [1864]." London, Ont.: Centre for Research and Teaching of Canadian Native Languages, 1988.

———, and Earl Nyholm. *A Concise Dictionary of Minnesota Ojibwe.* Minneapolis: University of Minnesota Press, 1995.

North Central Caribou Corporation. "Report of the North Central Caribou Corporation, 1988–1994." Duluth, Minn.: privately printed, 1994.

Norton, Sister Mary Aquinas. *Catholic Missionary Activities in the Northwest, 1818–1864.* Washington, D.C.: Catholic University of America, 1930.

Nute, Grace Lee. "The American Fur Company's Fishing Enterprises on Lake Superior." *Mississippi Valley Historical Review* 12, no. 4 (March 1926): 483–502.

———. "Calendar of the American Fur Company's Papers." *Annual Report of the American Historical Association*, vols. 1 and 2. Washington, D.C.: U.S. Government Printing Office, 1945.

———. *Lake Superior.* Indianapolis: Bobbs-Merrill, 1944.

Olson, Sigurd. *The Singing Wilderness.* New York: Knopf, 1956.

Page, Gay. "Legendary Lore of Lake Superior." *Thunder Bay Historical Museum Report* 7 (1916): 25.

Parker, John, ed. *The Journals of Jonathan Carver and Related Documents, 1766–1770.* St. Paul: Minnesota Historical Society Press, 1976.

Parker, Patricia L., and Thomas F. King. "Guidelines for Evaluating and Documenting Traditional Cultural Properties." *National Register Bulletin 38*, National Park Service, 1990.

Parkman, Francis. *La Salle and the Discovery of the Great West, Part Third.* Boston: Little, Brown and Company, 1869.

Peers, Lara. *The Ojibwa of Western Canada, 1780 to 1870.* St. Paul: Minnesota Historical Society Press, 1994.

———, and Theresa Schenk, eds. *My First Years in the Fur Trade: The Journals of 1802–1803 [of] George Nelson*. St. Paul: Minnesota Historical Society Press, 2002.

Piper, W. S. *The Eagle of Thunder Cape*. Thunder Bay, Ont.: Thunder Bay Historical Museum Society, 2001.

Prucha, Frances Paul. *American Indian Treaties*. Berkeley: University of California Press, 1994.

Raff, William. *Pioneers in the Wilderness: Minnesota's Cook County, Grand Marais, and the Gunflint in the Nineteenth Century*. Grand Marais, Minn.: Cook County Historical Society, 1981.

Rajnovich, Grace. *Reading Rock Art*. Toronto: Natural Heritage, 1994.

Ratigan, William. *The Adventures of Captain McCargo*. New York: Random, 1956.

"Readers Want to Know." *Seiche* (May 2007): 5.

Reagan, Albert. "Plants Used by the Bois Fort Chippewa (Ojibwa) Indians of Minnesota." *Wisconsin Archeologist* 7, no. 4 (July 1925): 230–48.

Reid, Dorothy M. *Tales of Nanabozho*. Toronto: Oxford University Press, 1963.

Rich, E. E., ed. *Colin Robertson's Correspondence Book, September 1817 to September 1822*. London: Champlain Society, 1939.

Rideout, Henry Milner. *William Jones: Indian, Cowboy, American Scholar, and Anthropologist in the Field*. New York: Stokes Co., 1912.

Rogers, Edward S. "Northern Algonquians and the Hudson's Bay Company, 1821–1890." In *Aboriginal Ontario: Historical Perspectives on the First Nations*, edited by Edward S. Rogers and Donald B. Smith, 307–43. Toronto: Dundern Press, 1994.

Roland, Walpole. *Algoma West: Its Mines, Scenery and Industrial Resources*. Toronto: Warwick & Sons, 1887.

Romig, Walter. *Michigan Place Names: The History of the Founding and the Naming of More Than Five Thousand Past and Present Michigan Communities*. Grosse Pointe, Mich.: privately printed, 1973.

Root, Robert, Jr. *Time by Moments Slips Away: The 1848 Journal of Ruth Douglas*. Detroit: Wayne State University Press, 1998.

Rostlund, Erhard. "Freshwater Fish and Fishing in Native North America." *University of California Publications in Geography* 9 (1952).

Rowe, William Hutchinson. *The Maritime History of Maine*. New York: Norton, 1948.

Satz, Ronald N. "Chippewa Treaty Rights: The Reserved Rights of Wisconsin's Chippewa Indians in Historical Perspective." *Wisconsin Academy of Sciences, Arts and Letters* 79, no. 1 (1991).

Scadding, Rev Henry. "Canadian Local History." *Canadian Journal of Science, Literature, and History* 14, no. 5 (July 1875): 658–67.

"Scenery of Lake Superior—Isle Royale," *Canadian Agriculturist* 3, no. 4 (April 1851): 94.

Schoolcraft, Henry R. *Algic Researches: Indian Tales and Legends.* Baltimore: Clarfield Co., 1992.

———. *Personal Memories of a Residence of Thirty Years with the Indian Tribes of the American Frontier: With Brief Notices of Passing Events, Facts, and Opinions, A.D. 1812 to A.D. 1842.* Philadelphia: Lippincott, Grambo and Co., 1851.

Schullery, Paul, and Lee Whittlesey. *Myth and History in the Creation of Yellowstone National Park.* Lincoln: University of Nebraska Press, 2003.

———. "Yellowstone's Creation Myth: Can We Live with Our Own Legends?" *Montana: The Magazine of Western History* 53 (Spring 2003): 2–27.

Scott, William P. "Reminiscences of Isle Royale." *Michigan History Magazine* 9, no. 3 (1925): 398–412.

Shelton, Napier. *The Life of Isle Royale.* Washington, D.C.: National Park Service, 1975.

Shifferd, Patricia A. "A Study of Economic Change: The Chippewa of Northern Wisconsin, 1854–1900." *Western Canadian Journal of Anthropology* 6, no. 4 (1976): 16–41.

Simpson, George. *Narrative of a Journey Round the World during the Years 1841 and 1842.* London: Henry Colburn, 1847.

Slavick, Allison D., and Robert A. Janke. *The Flora of Isle Royale National Park, Michigan.* Houghton: Michigan Technological University, 1985.

Smith, James G. E. "Leadership among the Southwestern Ojibwa." *Publications in Ethnology*, no. 7. Ottawa, Ont.: National Museum of Man, 1973.

Smith, Theresa S. *The Island of the Anishnaabeg: Thunderers and Water Monsters in the Traditional Ojibwe Life-World.* Moscow, Idaho: University of Idaho Press, 1995.

Spence, Mark David. *Dispossessing the Wilderness: Indian Removal and the Making of the National Parks.* New York: Oxford University Press, 1999.

Stansby, Maurice E. "Development of Fish Oil Industry in the United States." *Journal of the American Oil Chemists' Society* 55 (February 1978): 238–43.

Sundet, Paula. "Anishinabe Mat and Bag Weaving." Master's thesis, Vermont College, 2002.

Surtees, Robert J. "Treaty Research Report: The Robinson Treaties (1850)." Indian and Northern Affairs Canada, Ottawa, 1986.

Swineford, A. P. *History and Review of the Mineral Resources of Lake Superior.* Marquette, Mich.: The Mining Journal, 1876.

Tanner, John. *The Falcon: A Narrative of the Captivity & Adventures of John Tanner.* Introduction by Louise Erdrich. New York: Penguin Books, 1994.

"Through an Icy Hell." *The Magazine of Michigan* (May 1929): 6, 7, 22, and 24.

Thwaites, Reuben Gold, ed. *Jesuit Relations and Allied Documents.* Vols. 50, 54, and 55. Cleveland, Ohio: Burrows, 1899 and 1900.

U. S. Engineer Department. "Upon the Improvement of the Harbor at Duluth, Minnesota and of the Entrance to Superior Bay, Lake Superior, and the Harbor at Grand Marais, Minnesota." Washington, D.C.: General Printing Office, 1884.

U.S. Environmental Protection Agency. "Lake Superior Lakewide Management Plan 2000."

U. S. National Oceanic and Atmospheric Administration. "Great Lakes Ice Cover, 2003" and "Average Ice Duration, 2004." Great Lakes Environmental Research Laboratory, Ann Arbor, Michigan.

Vecsey, Christopher. *Traditional Ojibwa Religion: And Its Historical Changes.* Philadelphia: The American Philosophical Society, 1983.

Verwyst, Chrysostom. "Geographic Names in Wisconsin, Minnesota, and Michigan, Having a Chippewa Origin." In *Collections of the State Historical Society of Wisconsin*, edited by Reuben Gold Thwaites, 12:390–98. Madison: Democrat Printing Co., 1892.

———. "A Glossary of Chippewa Indian Names of Rivers, Lakes and Villages," *Acta et Dicta* 4, no 2 (1916): 253–274.

Vizenor, Gerald. *Anishinabe Aadizookaan.* Minneapolis: Nodin Press, 1970.

Vogel, Virgil J. *Indian Names in Michigan.* Ann Arbor: University of Michigan Press, 1986.

———. *Indian Names on Wisconsin's Map.* Madison: University of Wisconsin Press, 1991.

Waisberg, Leo G., and Tim E. Holzkammn. "'A Tendency to Discourage Them from Cultivating': Ojibwe Agriculture and Indian Administration in Northwestern Ontario." *Ethnohistory* 40, no. 2 (1993): 175–211.

Warren, William W. *History of the Ojibway People.* St. Paul: Minnesota Historical Society Press, 1984.

Webster, A. A., "Minong—the Floating Island." *American Forests* (August 1932): 439–41.

Weygant, Sister Noemi. *John (Jack) Linklater: Legendary Indian Game Warden.* Duluth, Minn.: Priory Books, 1987.

White, Bruce M. "Give Us a Little Milk: The Social and Cultural Meanings of Gift Giving in the Lake Superior Fur Trade." *Minnesota History* 48 (Summer 1982): 60–71.

———. "Grand Portage as a Trading Post: Patterns of Trade at 'the Great Carrying Place.'" Grand Marais, Minn.: Grand Portage National Monument, September 2005.

———. "The Regional Context of the Removal Order of 1850." In *Fish in the Lakes, Wild Rice, and Game in Abundance: Testimony on Behalf of Mille Lacs Ojibwe Hunting and Fishing Rights,* compiled by James McClurken, 141–328. East Lansing: Michigan State University Press, 2000.

———. "A Skilled Game of Exchange: Ojibway Fur Trade Protocol." *Minnesota History* 50 (Summer 1987): 229–40.

Whittlesey, Lee H., "Native Americans, the Earliest Interpreters: What Is Known about Their Legends and Stories of Yellowstone National Park and the Complexities of Interpreting Them." *George Wright Forum* 19, no. 3 (2002): 40–51.

Wilberg, Michael J., Michael J. Hansen, and Charles R. Bronte. "Historic and Modern Abundance of Wild Lean Lake Trout in Michigan Waters of Lake Superior: Implications for Restoration Goals." *North American Journal of Fisheries Management* 23 (2003): 100–108.

William, Ralph D. *The Honorable Peter White.* Cleveland, Ohio: Penton, 1907.

Woelker, Donald W. "Robert Stuart: A Man Who Meant Business." *Michigan History Magazine* (September–October 1990): 12–18.

Wolff, Julius F., Jr. "Hot Fur." In *Rendezvous: Selected Papers of the Fourth North American Fur Trade Conference, 1981,* edited by Thomas C. Buckley," 215–31. St. Paul: Minnesota Historical Society Press, 1984.

Woolworth, Nancy. "The Grand Portage Mission: 1731–1965." *Minnesota History* 39, no. 8 (Winter 1965): 301–10.

Works Projects Administration. *The Minnesota Arrowhead Country.* Chicago: Whitman, 1941.


## Government Documents


Canada. Census of Canada, 1856–1871. Vol. 4, Ottawa, 1876.

Canada. Census, Province of Ontario, 1871 and 1881.

Canada. Indian and Northern Affairs. "Fort William First Nation Boundary Claim." November 2006.

Canada. "Sketch of the Current River Route to the Great Dog Lake" and "Report of the Special Commissioners to Investigate Indian Affairs in Canada." Appendix 3. Toronto: Derbishire & Desbarats, 1858.

"Chippewa Indians in Minnesota." 51st Cong., 1st sess., House Executive Documents no. 247, serial no. 2747, 1889.

Cunningham, General Walter, to James Madison Porter, Secretary of War, October 2, 1843. 28th Cong., 1st sess., Executive Documents, serial no. 438, 1843.

McGillivrary, William, to Honorable John Hale, September 4, 1824. 25th Cong., 2nd sess., House of Representatives Executive Document no. 451, "Boundary between the United States and Great Britain."

Mason, Attorney General J. Y. "Leases of Mineral Lands on Isle Royale." 4 U.S. Op. Atty. Gen. 480, April, 1846.

*The Minnesota Chippewa Tribe et al. v. The United States of America.* Docket no. 18-S, January 14, 1976, for Royce Area 261 of the 1842 Treaty.

Province of Ontario, *Sixth Report of the Bureau of Mines, 1896.* Toronto: Legislative Assembly of Ontario, 1897.

Province of Ontario, Ministry of Aboriginal Affairs. "Fort William First Nation Boundary Claim." November 7, 2007.

"Scientists Conduct First Large-Scale Study of Lake Superior." Press release, National Science Foundation, October 24, 1997.

Stockton, John. "Map of the Part of the Mineral Lands Adjacent to Lake Superior Ceded to the United States by the Treaty of 1842." U.S. 29th Cong., spec. sess., Senate 175, no. 461.

U.S. Census, 1880, Isle Royale County, State of Michigan.

22nd Cong, 2nd sess, Senate Documents no. 90, serial no. 213, 1832.

26th Cong., 1st sess., Senate Documents no. 1, serial no. 354, 1840.

Vance, John T. Commissioner of the Indian [Land] Claims Commission, *The Minnesota Chippewa Tribe et al. v. The United States of America*, 1976.


## Newspapers

*Cook County [Grand Marais, Minnesota] News Herald.* Grand Marais, Minnesota.

*Daily [Houghton, Michigan] Mining Gazette.* Microfilm. Michigan Technological University Archives, Houghton, Michigan.

*Daily Times [Fort William] Journal.* Thunder Bay Historical Museum Society, Thunder Bay, Ontario.

*Detroit Tribune.* Bentley Historical Library, Ann Arbor, Michigan.

*Duluth Minnesotan.* Microfilm. Duluth Public Library, Duluth, Minnesota.

*Duluth News Tribune.* Microfilm. Duluth Public Library, Duluth, Minnesota.

*Duluth Weekly Tribune.* Microfilm. Duluth Public Library, Duluth, Minnesota.

*Lake Superior [Sault Ste. Marie] News and Miners' Journal.* Microfilm. Bentley Historical Library, Ann Arbor.

*Marquette Mining Journal.* Microfilm. Peter White Library, Marquette, Michigan.

*Minneapolis Star Tribune.* Microfilm. Minnesota Historical Society, St. Paul, Minnesota.

*Moccasin [Grand Portage] Telegraph.* Grand Portage National Monument, Grand Portage, Minnesota.

*St. Paul Daily Press.* Microfilm. Minnesota Historical Society, St. Paul, Minnesota.

*Thunder Bay Sentinel.* Microfilm. Thunder Bay Historical Museum Society, Thunder Bay, Ontario.

# INDEX

beaver, 62, 83, 96, 114, 140, 153, 160, 193
(n. 16), 210 (n. 71), 210 (n. 72), 248
(n. 3); as food, 87; in storytelling,
48–49
Beaver Bay, 10, 96
Belle Isle, 98, 102, 156
Bellin, Jacques Nicolas, 36–37
berries, 10, 30–31, 83, 86–87
Birch Island (McCargoe Cove), 157
Bois Forte Band. *See* Ojibwe, Nett Lake;
Ojibwe, Rainy Lake
British government, 39, 120, 132–34
Brunson, Alfred, 74, 123–27, 229 (n. 32)
Bullhead clan, 13, 35, 47, 94, 96, 188
(n. 55)

### C

Canadian government, 167, 225 (n. 3)
canoe, birch bark, 22, 23, 27, 157, 165
caribou (woodland), 7, 49, 62, 81–83,
87, 96, 140–41, 144, 154, 209 (n. 61),
209 (n. 66)
Caribou, Gilbert, xii, 30, 172
Caribou clan, 13, 94, 96, 178 (n. 19)
Caribou family, 105
Carver, Jonathan, 29, 37
Catholicism, 5, 66, 105–106, 134,
142–44. *See also* Jesuits
Checker Point (Siskiwit Bay), 79, 98
Chippewa Harbor, 3, 39, 41
clans (*dodems*), 12, 13, 16, 17, 94–96, 107,
108, 121, 165, 180 (n. 26)
Clark, Caven, 73

Cleveland Company, 131, 236 (n. 75)
Collin, Michel, 85, 95
Collin family, 105
Cook County, Minnesota, 152
copper, 2, 8, 35, 36, 45–47, 58, 62, 64,
66, 71, 100, 116, 119, 125, 157, 169,
237 (n. 78); fear of, 8, 46, 64, 99,
197 (n. 51); mining, 26, 35, 73–75,
84, 92, 93, 99, 100, 102, 124, 152,
187 (n. 47); in Ojibwe culture,
8, 47, 56, 61, 63, 65, 69, 107, 171;
respect for, 65, 171, 196 (n. 48), 198
(n. 67); rush, 19, 32, 40, 117, 119,
124
Copper Harbor, Michigan, 132
copper miners, 101
Corcoran, Jim, vii
Cotte, Pierre, 98, 129, 145, 234 (n. 70)
Crane clan, 13
Crawford, T. Hartley, 121, 131
Cree, 30, 34, 35, 71, 74
cultural change, 112, 142, 171; and cash
economy, 102, 116, 151; and centralization, 16, 112–13, 167, 250 (n.
18); and language loss, 171–72; and
Sedentism, 139, 146, 155
cultural persistence, 110, 112, 138, 146,
150, 166, 173; "roving" habits of
Ojibwe, xiii, 7, 139, 141, 150
Cunningham, Walter, 126–27, 132, 167,
231 (n. 54)

124–27, 131, 164, 169, 173, 229 (n. 32), 249 (n. 13)

Isle Royale Compact, 108, 130–32, 167, 172, 230 (n. 38), 235 (n. 74). *See also* treaties, 1842

Isle Royale County, 152

Isle Royale National Park, xi, 19, 159, 160; creation myths about, 168–69, 251 (n. 21)

Ives, William, 61, 78, 84

## J

*Jesuit Relations,* 30, 32, 62

Jesuits, 22, 35, 46, 135, 145, 148, 154; baptisms by, 105, 106; diaries of, 6; proselytizing by, 27, 141, 142, 142, 145–46, 226 (n. 14); rings of, 72; and traditional Ojibwe religion, 66, 67, 88, 144. *See also* Catholicism

Jones, William, 48, 50, 180 (n. 2), 190 (n. 4), 192 (n. 14), 192 (n. 16)

## K

Kaministiquia River, 9–12, 77, 80, 142, 238 (n. 90); as canoe route to the west, 9, 11

Kohl, Johann Georg, 53, 63, 195 (n. 37)

## L

La Bete, 7, 82, 96

Lac La Croix, 13

L'homme du Sault, 92, 93, 96, 164, 210 (n. 224), 217 (n. 119)

Lake Nipigon, 34

Lake Superior, 9, 10, 11, 25, 34–36, 171; currents, 23, 108; crossing, 3, 7, 10, 20, 22, 23, 24, 27, 54, 70, 107, 157, 181 (n. 4); ice, 6, 26, 82, 110; fictitious islands in, 36–37

lake trout, 10, 24, 76–78, 153, 170. *See also* siscowet

LaPlante, Adam Roach, 156, 246 (n. 178)

La Pointe, 58, 106, 117, 119, 121, 123, 131, 135. *See also* Madeline Island, Apostle Islands; treaties

LeSage, Alex, 153

Linklater, Helen (Tchi-ki-wis), 26, 68, 111, 157–58, 165

Linklater, John (Jack), 26, 61, 68, 111, 157–58, 165–66, 247 (n. 181)

Little Englishman (Shawgawnaw-sheence), 108, 117, 125, 131, 136–37, 139, 154

Little Spirit Cedar Tree (Manido Gee-zhi-gance) 24, 25, 146, 166, 171, 182 (n. 15)

Loon's Foot, 107, 108, 123

## M

McCargo, Capt. Robert, 40, 89–90, 189 (n. 70), 200 (n. 8)

McCargoe Cove, 23, 27, 39, 68, 72, 73, 80, 89–91, 152, 156–57, 165, 171, 173, 200 (n. 8), 224 (n. 184), 251 (n. 23)

McKay, Nancy, 90, 214 (n. 109)

MacKenzie, Alexander, 37

McCullough, Hugh H., 19, 78–80, 83, 102–103, 105–106, 110, 115, 116, 135, 205 (n. 41), 206 (n. 46), 207 (n. 48), 220 (n. 162), 221 (n. 163)

McLoughlin, John, 90

Madeline Island, Apostle Islands, 20, 22, 107

mail delivery to Isle Royale, 26, 102, 151, 152, 156

Manitoulan Island, Lake Huron, 20, 120

maps of Isle Royale/Minong, 29, 32–40, 172, 187 (n. 53), 188 (n. 62), 222 (n. 174)

Maurice, William, 5

Medishean, 82, 96, 179 (n. 21), 209 (n. 64)

Memashkawash, Alexis (Alex Posey; Maymaushkewash), 31, 149

Memashkawash (May-mosh-caw-wosh), Joseph, 88, 137, 144

Memashkawash, Paul, 105

Memashkawash, Susan, 222 (n. 171)

Memashkawash family, 109

Mendenhall, Cyrus, 58, 129

Metis, 40, 90, 97, 99, 100, 133; "half-breed," 74, 99

Mica Bay Copper Mine, 133

Michipicoten Island, 46, 48

Midewiwin ceremonies, 57, 88, 89, 143, 146, 183 (n. 17), 214 (n. 106). *See also* religion

mining, 26, 35, 73–75, 84, 92, 93, 99, 100, 102, 124, 152, 187 (n. 47)

Minong: as floating island, 31, 45, 52, 53, 68, 69, 168, 172–73, 194 (n. 24), 194 (n. 26); meaning of name of, 5, 28, 29, 30, 31, 32, 54, 122, 184 (n. 32), 186 (n. 42), 187 (n. 47); misconceptions about, 21, 31, 68

Minong Ridge Trail, 29, 32

mirages, 53–54

Mishipizheu, 25, 45–47, 51, 54, 55, 62, 66, 69, 171, 191 (n. 13)

Mishosha (magician of the lake), 56, 190 (n. 2)

Mission of Immaculate Conception, Fort William, 5, 27, 30, 139, 142, 145, 148, 151, 175 (n. 4), 176 (n. 5), 226 (n. 14)

Mitchell, John, 36

Mongazoid (Mong o zet), 107, 108, 123

moose, viii, 140, 159, 209 (n. 60), 209 (n. 61)

Mott, Angelique, 57–61

Mott, Charlie, 57–61

Mt. McKay, 51, 171, 215 (n. 109)

Muskegoes, 29, 37

**N**

Nanabushu, 42–44, 47–50, 52, 54–56, 62, 168, 171, 190 (n. 4), 192 (n. 16), 203 (n. 23)

National Park Service, xi, xii, 8, 9, 156, 160–62, 173, 248 (n. 3), 249 (n. 5), 251 (n. 21)

National Parks, 7–9